PRODUCTION RELATIONS, CLASS AND BLACK LIBERATION

PHILOSOPHICAL CURRENTS

Volume 24

David H. DeGrood

Editor

B. R. Grüner Publishing Co., Amsterdam
1978

PRODUCTION RELATIONS, CLASS AND BLACK LIBERATION

A Marxist Perspective in Afro-American Studies

by

Clarence J. Munford
University of Guelph

B.R. Grüner Publishing Co., Amsterdam
1978

ISBN 90 6032 107 3
© Clarence J. Munford, 1978
Printed in The Netherlands

To Helmi: whose encouragement, support and assistance made this book possible.

CONTENTS

PART I

BLACK AMERICA: THE ODYSSEY FROM SLAVES TO PROLETARIANS

Chapter 1 Antiquity, Black Slavery, and the "Rosy Dawn" 3

Chapter 2 Service Strata, Proletarians and Lumpenproletarians: Explorations in the History of Black Social Structure, 1865-1970 49

Chapter 3 The Lumpenproletariat Revisited 66

Chapter 4 The Function of Racism in Contemporary America 89

Chapter 5 Manchild in the Land of Lenin: Or, the Alternative to Capitalism 115

PART II

REVOLUTION IN AFRICA AND U.S. IMPERIALISM PROBLEMS OF THE NATIONAL LIBERATION MOVEMENT

Chapter 6 The Anatomy of Imperialism. .135

Chapter 7 Africa and the Political Economy of Underdevelopment. . .161

Chapter 8 Classes and Class Struggle in Africa. 179

Chapter 9 Racism – The Ideology of Imperialism: From Gobineau to Shockley 194

Bibliography. 225

Part I

BLACK AMERICA: THE ODYSSEY FROM
SLAVES TO PROLETARIANS

Chapter 1

ANTIQUITY, BLACK SLAVERY, AND THE "ROSY DAWN"

Once again slavery has become a burning issue in American academic circles, and the "peculiar institution" has won back its pride of place in the review articles of the monopoly press. Smeltered in the racist crucible of imperialist ideology, the "seminal influence" of U.B. Philips[1], after a period of "neglect", has resurged to prominence, defended, refurbished, "revised", and restated with more or less "elegance" by a band of reactionary historians and sociologists active on the campuses of America's universities. Their rehabilitation of slavery has proceeded to the fanfare of the media, and has been encouraged by the publishing largesse of "prestigious" university presses. A good part of the campaign is being carried out under the panoply of quantification and data analysis.

From the "traditional", "humanistic" interpretations[2] to the quantified mystifications of the Cliometricians[3], to the jargon of

1. *American Negro Slavery: A Survey of the Supply, Employment and Control of Negro Labor as Determined by the Plantation Regime*, New York, 1918; and *Life and Labor in the Old South*, Boston, 1929.
2. The range is so great it is hard to decide what constitutes a "traditional" interpretation. However, a fair idea of this trend's recent concerns can be gleaned from the writings of John W. Blassingame, *The Slave Community: Plantation Life in the Antebellum South*, New York, 1972; Stanley M. Elkins, *Slavery, A Problem in American Institutional and Intellectual Life*, Chicago, 1959; George M. Frederickson, *The Black Image in the White Mind*, New York, 1971; Winthrop D. Jordan, *White Over Black: American Attitudes Toward the Negro, 1550-1812*, Chapel Hill, N.C., 1968, and perhaps C. Van Woodward, *The Strange Career of Jim Crow*, 2nd rev. ed., New York, 1966.
3. Here the most notorious work is R.W. Fogel and S.L. Engerman, *Time on the Cross: The Economics of American Negro Slavery*, Boston, 1974, and *Time on the Cross: Evidence and Methods - A Supplement*, Boston, 1974. Not nearly so publicized, but equally devoted to showing that the slave trade and Black slavery were not so bad are P.D. Curtin, *The Atlantic Slave Trade: A Census*, Madison, Wis., 1969; S.L. Engerman and E.D. Genovese, eds., *Race and Slavery in the Western Hemisphere: Quantitative Studies*, Princeton, 1975; and Claudia D. Goldin, *Urban Slavery in the American South, 1820-1860: A Quantitative History*, Chicago, 1976. These works share a false and

self-styled "Marxians",[4] a long-drawn-out "controversy" has probed the profitability and viability of slavery,[5] its effects on economic progress, the "civilizations" "made" by slaves and slaveholders. Nor have the alleged benefits of slavery for the slaves been overlooked. The purpose of this flurry of research and debate is to glorify slavery, gloss over the fierce centuries-long resistance of Black people to enslavement, and update•the racist doctrines of the monopoly bourgoisie in regard to the history of slavery in the U.S. The fury of the latest defence of slavery has even elicited an *anti-slavery counterattack* by petty bourgeois radical scholars.[6] To this point, however, the debate has remained on the whole strictly within the parameters set by bourgeois and petty bourgeois ideology. The contribution even of those opposed to the glorification of

phony quantitative approach designed to absolve chattel slavery of its crimes against Blacks. For an excellent and caustic criticism of Fogel's and Engerman's defense of slavery see Herbert Aptheker, "Heavenly Days in Dixie: Or, the Time of their Lives", in *Political Affairs: Journal of Marxist Thought and Analysis*, Vol. LIII, No. 6, June 1974, pp. 40-54, and Vol. LIII, No. 7, July 1974, pp. 44-57.

4. The leading proponent is Eugene D. Genovese, a bourgeois historian who conjures with Marxist categories and terms in order to oppose historical materialism. His "Marxian" sleight-of-hand enables him to snipe at Marx and Engels, portray Blacks as dignified and docile slaves who "accommodated" their masters, and denigrate the real Marxist historians of U.S. slavery. The list of his works in this vein is now quite substantial including, *The Political Economy of Slavery: Studies in the Economy and Society of the Slave South*, New York, 1965; *In Red and Black: Marxian Explorations in Southern and Afro-American History*, New York, 1968 (for a gem of hypocritical self-justification by a racist see the "By Way of a Dedication ..." with which Genovese begins his book); *Ulrich B. Phillips: The Slave Economy of the Old South*, Baton Rouge, 1968; *The World the Slaveholders Made: Two Essays in Interpretation*, New York, 1969; and *Roll, Jordan, Roll: The World the Slaves Made*, New York, 1974.

5. See e.g., Hugh G.J. Aitken, ed., *Did Slavery Pay? Readings in the Economics of Black Slavery in the United States*, Boston, 1971.

6. See P.A. David, H.G. Gutman, R. Sutch, P. Temin, and G. Wright, *Reckoning with Slavery: A Critical Study in the Quantitatve History of American Negro Slavery*, New York, 1976; H.G. Gutman, *Slavery and the Numbers Game: A Critique of Time on the Cross*, Urbana, 1975; K.M. Stampp, *The Peculiar Institution: Slavery in the Ante-Bellum South*, New York, 1956; and R. Starobin, *Industrial Slavery in the Old South*, New York, 1970.

slavery and the distortion of the history of Blacks, is unenlighten-
ed by Marxism-Leninism, the scientific sociology of our epoch.

The purpose of this essay is to help in a small way to remedy
this failing by subjecting the general features of slavery and the
problem of the relation between modern slavery and pre-capitalist
socio-economic forms to a Marxist analysis.[7]

*

Let us begin by seeking to define what is meant by *slave* and *slavery* in general. Thereafter we shall attempt to understand and get
at the differences and similarities between the slave mode of production which existed in ancient times and the exploitation of
Black slave labour in the United States under the capitalist mode
of production. We will examine these and all related terms and issues strictly in the light of *Marxist-Leninist political economy*, my
conviction being, as a Marxist, that bourgeois historiography and
economics − no matter how "good willed" − have done little but
obscure and confuse matters, or expound irrelevancies.

When we speak of a *slave* we mean a human being reduced to
the status of a commodity over whom an owner − another human
being − has an absolute right of property. A commodity is a thing

7. Scientific study of the slave trade and U.S. slavery in general has a solid
foundation in the following Marxist-Leninist works: 1) Herbert Aptheker,
*And Why Not Every Man?: The Story of the Fight Against Slavery Assembled
and Edited*, Berlin, 1961; *American Negro Slave Revolts*, New York, new
edition 1969 (*a classic*); *A Documentary History of the Negro People in the
United States, Vol. I, From Colonial Times through the Civil War*, New York,
1951; *Essays in the History of the American Negro*, New York, 1945; *To Be
Free: Studies in Negro History*, New York, 1948; and *Toward Negro Freedom*, New York, 1956. 2) Maurice Dobb, *Studies in the Development of
Capitalism*, London, 1947. 3) William Z. Foster, *The Negro People in American History*, New York, 1954. Also indispensable are W.E.B. DuBois, *John
Brown*, New York, 1962; *Suppression of the African Slave Trade to the
United States of America, 1638-1870*, New York, 1969; and *Black Reconstruction*, New York, 1935. Philip S. Foner has edited 5 volumes of the *Life
and Writings of Frederick Douglass*, New York, 1950-1975. Oliver C. Cox,
Caste, Class and Race, New York, 1948, and Walter Rodney, *A History of
the Upper Guinea Coast, 1545 to 1800*, Oxford, 1970, offer interesting in-
sights. While not a Marxist analysis, Eric Williams, *Capitalism and Slavery*,
Chapel Hill, N.C., 1944, contains useful information.

produced for sale, and not for immediate consumption, which satisfies some human want or need. The slave, incorporating his labour power, i.e. his ability to work purposefully, can be bought and sold. In extreme cases the master even has the right to do a-way with his slave. History draws a distinction between the private slave, who was the property of a single person, family or corporate individual, and the public slave, owned by a public establishment, a city or a state. Regarded as being outside civil society, the slave, being the property of another person or persons, was thus *forcibly* subjected to exploitation. To be exploited is to be obliged, in one manner or another, to work free of charge for the benefit of others, to produce a surplus product over and above one's own maintenance, which is seized by others who own the means of production. A slave is compelled to work by brute force, not by economic means. The slave owns no means of production himself, but, depending upon the circumstances, may be in the possession (in the sense of usufruct) of means of production not his property.

A *slave society* is a society where the antagonism between a class of slaveholders, who also own other means of production, and the slaves is the dominating feature. A class, in the socio-economic sense, is a large group of people united by an identical relation to property in the means of production and hence by similar economic and socio-political interests, and opposed to other such groups. The term slave society does not necessarily imply that production in such a society is *exclusively* the result of slave labour, or that there does not exist a mass of free or semi-dependent producers.

Karl Marx said that in the course of history the slave economy passed through a metamorphosis from the patriarchal system mainly for home use to the plantation system for the world market.[8] Slavery as an economic system allows the slaveowner to appropriate the *entire* surplus product of his slave's labour. The master's total ownership of both the means of production and servile labour is the foundation of what is known as *slave relations of production.*

Relations of production mirror objective circumstances existing

8. *Capital. A Critique of Political Economy*, Volume III, Moscow, 1959, p. 784.

in any society independently of what anyone may think. Relations of production are formed between people in the process of social production, exchange, and distribution of material wealth, and thus cannot fail to exist. In fact, there is a sense in which it can be argued that slavery owes its emergence to the operation of the general economic laws which make social development a single logical natural historical process. These laws are four in number: 1) the law of the correspondence of the relations of production to the nature of productive forces; 2) the law of rising productivity of labour; 3) the law of the saving of labour time, and 4) the law of the proportional distribution of the means of production and labour among various branches of production. The operation of the second law fostered the development of slavery. Originally it was the gradual increase in the *productivity of a man's labour* which made it possible to own a human being, the direct producer of material goods. At the dawn of history before human society divided into classes, when each individual could produce no more than was strictly necessary to keep from starving, the exploitation of man by man was impossible. The rise in the productivity of labour made it possible to produce more than the vital requirements of each producer. From then on a group of men forced others to work for them, depriving these producers of their own surplus product.

Cooperation is the simplest and most rudimentary method for the increase of the productivity of social labour. The characteristic feature of *simple cooperation* is that the workers do the same kind of work simultaneously. Simple cooperation was the basic work procedure used in slavery during both its ancient history and its modern version, and was the key to the increased productivity of labour effected by the introduction of slavery. Society henceforth came to include a category of labourers deprived of rights and kept alive only so long as they created surplus product which was appropriated by the masters of the slaves. Slave labour became a source of wealth, and in some cases the basis of social existence. The government of a slave state was by definition an antagonistic, exploiter formation which could *never* represent the slaves.

For those who like to think in legal terms and prefer to express themselves in binding injunctions, labour power under the slave system is a capability which is purchased by buying the labourer himself, or otherwise acquiring legally recognized title of ownership. But Marxism views things differently. It establishes that the relations of production prevailing where slave labour is allowed create the title, or right of ownership, of slaves, and not any specific deed, purchase, contractual agreement, legal sentence, or even kidnapping or war capitivity. Yet since relations based on exploitation are mystifying, a typical illusion arises in the minds of slave owners (and even in the minds of some slaves) — the slaveholder considers a bondsman, whom he has bought, as his property, *not* because the institution of slavery as such entitles him to that bondsman, as it actually does in reality, but because he has acquired him like clothing, wine, a horse, or any other commodity, through purchase. But, as Marx teaches us,

> the title itself is simply transferred, and not created by the sale. The title must exist before it can be sold, and a series of sales can no more create this title through continued repetition than a single sale can. What created it in the first place were the production relations.[9]

Production relations entailing ownership of one human being by another must therefore include *extra-economic* coercion — crude physical compulsion — as an essential and inherent component. It is a base lie that any form of slavery can be benign.

Yet another of the general features of slavery is that the labourer himself belongs to the objective conditions of production.[10] In this setup the process of consuming labour power and creating means of production and articles of personal use necessary for the existence and development of society cannot begin until slaves are acquired. In a slave economy, landed property, "ownership of certain portions of our planet by certain individuals", is merely incidental to the ownership of slaves, the immediate producers themselves, by some individual or collective body.[11] The main productive force in any society are the producers, working people who, unless something in the society prevents them, constantly improve the instruments of labour and raise the productivity of labour. In societies divided into exploited and exploiters, an acute conflict and contradiction arises between new productive forces

9. *Ibid.*, p. 757.

10. Karl Marx, *Theories of Surplus Value* (Volume IV of *Capital*), Part III, Moscow, 1971, p. 422.

11. K. Marx, *Capital*, Vol. III, p. 619.

and old relations of production, leading inevitably to social revolution of some kind. We credit this eventuality to the operation of the first general economic law — the basic law of the economic development of any society. Every new and higher mode of production signifies a new and higher level in the history of man's development. The capitalist mode of production, for instance, is incomparably higher than the slave mode of production which prevailed during antiquity.

Slavery thus emerged and developed under specific historical conditions. Following a phase of decline and almost complete regression, it sprang up anew for a limited, but long, period in North and Latin America. This rebirth was based on rudimentary technology and simple cooperation of labour under the *capitalist* mode of production, and on the availability of new slaves provided by the Atlantic slave trade in Africans and by slave breeding.

The capitalist mode of production differs from the ancient mode of production based on slavery, and, in principle, from slavery *per se* by the fact that in capitalism the value, accordingly the price, of labour power appears as the value, or price, of labour itself, or as wages paid to free wage earners who sell their labour power.[12] This fact made slavery an *anomaly* under the capitalist mode of production. An anomaly is an irregularity, something that seems to be in the wrong place, something that surprises us when we encounter it in an unexpected situation. One suspects that it is this anomaly which has created the great practical and theoretical problem regarding slavery in relation to capitalism. Both the slave and the free wage worker are direct producers, but the slave is sold once and for all and is most typically the property of one master. The wage worker sells his labour power, his capacity to work, not himself, and he must sell his labour power over and over again. While the wage labourer is the "property", so to speak, of the entire capitalist class, the slave is accounted a *thing*, not a person, and is not a member of civil society. The product of capitalism, the modern wage worker is, from the standpoint of political economy, the phenomenon of a higher stage of development than the slave. And politically, as F. Engels put it,

12. *Ibid.*, p. 30.

the slave frees himself by *becoming a proletarian*, abolishing from the totality of property relationships *only* the relationship of *slavery*. The proletarian can free himself only by abolishing *property in general*.[13]

In Marx's famous words,

the discovery of gold and silver in America, the extirpation, enslavement and entombment in mines of the aboriginal population, the beginning of the conquest and looting of the East Indies, the turning of Africa into a warren for the commercial hunting of black-skins, signalised the rosy dawn of the era of capitalist production. These idyllic proceedings are the chief momenta of primitive accumulation.[14]

I will try to show that *primitive accumulation* is the key to the relation between American slavery and capitalism.

*

But let us first turn our attention to the slave mode of production which, in ancient times, prevailed over large areas of the globe. *Antiquity* is taken to mean the long centuries from about 4000 B.C. to 476 A.D. We cannot know how the slave mode of production proper differs from slavery under the capitalist mode of production unless we first have some idea of the former. When guided by historical materialism, analysis of familiar and widely-accepted data of ancient history reveals the laws of development of the ancient slave mode of production. A brief survey will suffice and no specialist expertise in ancient history is required beyond the general knowledge of a university-trained historian. Four ancient societies have been selected for typicalness — or classicality of historical development —, Egypt, Babylonia, Greece and Rome.[15]

13. F. Engels, "Draft of a Communist Confession of Faith" (1847) in Karl Marx and Frederick Engels, *Collected Works*, Volume 6, New York, 1976, p. 100.

14. *Capital: A Critical Analysis of Capitalist Production*, Volume I, Moscow, 1959, p. 751.

15. For those readers who seek a more precise scientific and in-depth analysis of primitive communalism and the ancient slave mode of production, and of antiquity in general, I suggest the magnificent Soviet literature in this field, especially the following works which have been translated into Western languages: W.I. Awdijew, *Geschichte des Alten Orients*, Berlin, GDR, 1953; W.N. Djakow and S.I. Kowaljow, eds., *Geschichte des Alten Griechenlands*,

Paradoxically it was a good thing — rising productivity of labour — which opened the way for the tragedy of the ownership of one human being by another. The increased productivity of labour in turn was caused by improved productive forces, signalized by better fishermen's nets, peasants' hoes and miners' picks, and so forth. Labour had to be able to produce more than the bare necessities to enable exploitation. At the dawn of history, enemies were usually killed outright and not taken prisoner. By way of exception, a primitive clan, in order to increase its labour force or fighting capacity, would adopt and assimilate a prisoner of war. With the new productivity, however, the time came when the forced labour of a captive would regularly yield more than was needed just to keep him alive. Now the captive was made to work to support himself and create a surplus product. The forced labourer was never allowed an equal share of the social surplus product, which meant that he was being exploited by a privileged group who appropriated the goods he created. Captives were no longer killed,

Berlin, GDR, 1960; V. Diakov and S. Kovalev, eds., *Histoire de L'Antiquité*, Moscow, n.d.; I.M. Diakonoff, ed., *Ancient Mesopotamia. Socio-Economic History: A Collection of Studies by Soviet Scholars*, Moscow, 1969; M.O. Koswen, *Abriss der Geschichte und Kultur der Urgesellschaft*, Berlin, GDR, 1957; A.Z. Manfred, ed., *A Short History of the World in Two Volumes*, Volume I, Moscow, 1974; and N.A. Muschkin, *Römische Geschichte*, Berlin, GDR, 1953. Not so long ago the Paris Centre for Marxist Study and Research (*Centre d'Etudes et de Recherches Marxistes*), which is closely connected with the French Communist Party, published a three-volume collection treating the controversy surrounding aspects of pre-capitalist social formations: 1) *Premières Sociétés de Classes et Mode de Production Asiatique*, Paris 1967; 2) *Sur le "Mode de Production Asiatique"*, Paris, 1969; and 3) *Sur les Sociétés Précapitalistes, Textes Choisis de Marx, Engels, Lénine*, Paris, 1970. See also E.J. Hobsbawm, ed., *Karl Marx: Pre-Capitalist Economic Formations*, London, 1964; and E. Medvedev, *Le Régime Socio-Economique de l'Inde Ancienne*, C.E.R.M., Paris, 1969. On the debate among Marxists concerning the place of the slave mode of production in West African history see Amady Aly Dieng, *Classes Sociales et Mode de Production Esclavagiste en Afrique de l'Ouest*, C.E.R.M., Paris, 1974; Majhemout Diop, *Histoire des Classes Sociales dans l'Afrique de l'Ouest*, Vol. I: *Le Mali*; Vol. II: *Le Sénégal*, Paris, 1971-72; J.J. Goblot and A. Pelletier, *Matérialisme Historique et Histoire des Civilisations*, Paris, 1969; and J. Suret-Canale, "Contexte et conséquences sociales de la traite africaine" in *Présence Africaine*, no. 50, 2ème trimestre, Paris, 1964; and *Afrique Noire Occidentale et Centrale*, Volume I: *Géographie, Civilisations, Histoire*, 2nd ed., Paris, 1961.

they became slaves, valuable only so long as they were capable of creating surplus products. The threat of sudden death, or some other calamity, hung over any producing slave whose labour ceased to yield surplus product.

Slaveowning had an early history and a later history. The first stage was *communal slaveowning* which evolved within the primitive communal system and encompassed only a small minority of society. Slaves were the common property of the clan, extended family or kinship line as a whole. *Patriarchal slavery* came somewhat later and was similar. Poorer members of the community or lineage line became the virtual slaves of wealthy chieftains or sorcerers (proto-priests) in return for a meagre subsistence and patronage.

However, it soon became clear that the exploitation of slaves was not only the first form of exploitation but the most vicious. Slave labour had only one purpose — to create surplus product for others. Satisfaction of their own needs was secondary for slaves. Slave labour became a source of wealth gained at the expense of the moral and physical exhaustion of those who actually produced the wealth. The emergence of slavery marked a new stage in social development.

Society split into three groups respectively: slaves, slaveholders, who also owned instruments and other means of production, and, lastly, ordinary freemen who managed to hold on to their own means of work and subsistence. As the centuries passed, many of the latter were ruined and transformed into slaves. Warfare, the slave trade, and the enslavement of people who fell into debt became the principal sources of slaves in ancient times. Later in the epoch slaves became the *main* productive force. As more and more slaves were worked to death, the bitterer grew the basic contradiction between them and their owners. The result was fierce class struggle between the slaves and the slaveholders, including full scale slave revolts. After several thousands of years it was these mighty popular insurrections, combined with external factors, which finally caused the collapse of the slave regime, and its replacement by feudalism.

The rise of slaveholders' governments, of *slave states*, sealed the victory of the slave mode of production. Egypt and the valley of the Tigris and Euphrates in Mesopotamia (Babylonia) were the sites of history's first slave states. Governments representing slaveholders appeared in India and China in the 4th — 2nd millenia B.C.

The slave states of ancient Greece came into being in the 8th – 6th centuries B.C. The 6th century B.C. witnessed the birth of the Roman slave state. Sub-Saharan African states in which slaveholding played a significant role – although it is doubtful whether they were full-fledged slave economies – date from the Middle Ages. The slave states of Central and South America were formed approximately 150 to 200 years before the advent of the Spanish *conquistadores*, but this does not hold true for the Mayan city-states in the Yucatan peninsula which apparently sprang up much earlier, and where the enslavement of "criminals", debtor's slavery, warfare and the slave trade seem to have been the main catalysts.

An issue of controversy is whether or not all these states were fully developed slaveholding empires. The question is whether material production was performed to a *decisive and characteristic extent* by forced labour for the benefit of a ruling class of slaveowners. Everything depends on the definition of a slave. If we stick to the doctrinaire legal description of the Greek and Roman slave as a "tool with a soul", as an *object* which belonged exclusively to the slaveholder, then such slavery as the basis of production was prevalent only in a few countries. In all the class societies of antiquity there were independent.producers – free peasants and small craftsmen. But the picture changes if we recognize that forced labour was subject to endless variation caused by non-economic compulsion based on war captivity, kidnapping, unfree birth, national oppression, female tribute etc. Forced labour took the forms of house, field and handicraft slavery. Slavery could be collective, as in the cases of the Indian pariahs, Sparta and Syria, or individual as in Athens and Rome. In some instances only strangers were enslaved, in others members of the same tribe or people. Thus ancient slavery took many different forms. There were gradations between the classic model of slavery and the less well-defined degrees of economic, political and legal bondage and dependence. For example, in many respects the status of the ancient Egyptian peasants reminds one of serfdom with actual slavery occupying only a secondary position. In the West African states – Ghana, Mali, Gobir, Kanem, *et al* – the holding and exploitation of slaves played as great a role as it did in old Mwanamutapa, Ethiopia, Nubia, and later in the Hima-Tussi states of the Great Lakes region, yet there is debate as to whether these constituted real slave economies.[16]

Whatever the case, because it depended on unfree labour, the ancient slaveholding system was doomed to stagnate technologically. Given the low level of productive forces, there were only two ways to meet the growing social demand for articles of production. Any working day can be divided into two parts, the first part during which the worker creates the wherewithal required to maintain himself, and the rest of the working day during which he creates a surplus over and above the minimum needed for his consumption if he is to stay alive. The first part is known as the necessary labour time, the second part as surplus labour time. It was usual for the slaveholder to appropriate the entire product of slave labour, returning to his slave the smallest possible amount of means of existence, just enough to keep him slaving for the master. The slaveholder appropriated not only surplus product, but also the *necessary* product of the labour of slaves. Where slavery forms the broad foundation of social production, as in antiquity, wrote Marx in *Capital*, "the domination of the producers by the conditions of production is concealed by the relations of dominion and servitude, which appear and are evident as the direct motive power of the process of production."[17] In this situation production was enlarged, first, by intensifying exploitation through grinding, brute force, meaning that the slave was either forced to work faster, or that his working day was prolonged, thereby increasing surplus labour time in the working day. The other recognized way to raise production to fill demand was to increase the number of slaves in proportion to the enlarged social demand. So steady growth of the army of slaves became indispensable for the growth of production during antiquity. Furthermore, under the ancient slave system the means of production used in one branch of production could be shifted to another sphere of production only with the greatest difficulty.[18]

Records show that the difference between a slave and a free hired worker employed on the same estate in Babylonia lay mainly in the different portions of the product of their own labour they received. The slave got a ration amounting to one-and-a-half liters

16. See preceding note.
17. *Capital*, Vol. III, p. 810.
18. *Ibid.*, p. 174.

of barley a day. The hired labourer's wages were three and some-times four times as much.[19] Now even though it may seem that the slave toiled the entire day for nothing, as though even that portion of labour which replaces the outlay for the maintenance of the slave was unpaid labour for the master, that was not so. The subsistence the slave received in order to keep him alive was pay-ment for at least a portion of his necessary labour. But even as ear-ly as 2140—2030 B.C. Babylonian owners were appropriating part of the slave's necessary labour time, in addition to his whole sur-plus labour time, thereby depressing the value of slave labour power near to, or even below, the physical minimum. For the val-ue of any labour power is determined by the value of the means of subsistence the labourer requires for himself. Quite naturally high death rates among slaves were common.

Slaveowners were not concerned with perfecting production technology. They felt that even without special aids and applian-ces slaves could be forced to accomplish any task. So slavery was bound to hinder the development of technology, culture and sci-ence. The slave had no personal interest in the results of his labour. The strident claims to the contrary of some modern American white historians like Genovese and Fogel and Engerman would have astonished the slave in antiquity. He worked under the club, very unwillingly, and his labour had a very low yield. On the farms slave labour exhausted the soil and diminished fertility. So long as slavery existed, no complicated labour devices, refined instruments or machines could be introduced, at least the risk of breakage was very high. Slaves treated tools roughly, smashed and ruined them. The slave mode of exploitation oppresses producers to the extreme, leaving them no opportunity to develop themselves or their labour skills. But ordinarily people with their skills are the most dynamic element of the productive forces. Weaving, spinning, woodworking and mining were thus carried out with very rudimentary tools, often by slaves working in large gangs applying the principles of simple cooperation of labour (although slaves could also be found in trading houses, in minor government positions, tax-farming, in urban public works, domestic service, etc.). The Greeks employed

19. V.V. Struve, "The Problem of the Genesis, Development and Dis-integration of the Slave Societies in the Ancient Orient" in I.M. Diakonoff, ed., *Ancient Mesopotamia*, p. 50.

the primitive weaver's loom, the potter's wheel and the hammer, spade and pickaxe in mining — very rudimentary tools. The technology of metallurgical handicraft was only marginally higher. The Greeks used slaves in agriculture mostly to raise vegetables in the vicinity of towns, and on large plantations to cultivate olives, grapes and other fruits. In Phoenicia, which was located along the coast of what is now Lebanon, slaves were used primarily as oarsmen to row galley ships. This was the heaviest, most onerous of tasks. Fearing mutiny, Phoenician merchants kept the slaves chained to their oars at sea.

In ancient Egypt and Babylonia it was *fishing* which originally fostered the growth of slavery. This occurred when communities began to lead a sedentary existence. First, as compared to hunting and food gathering, fishing ensured a more stable supply and greater amount of food. Second, slave labour was relatively efficient in making nets and catching fish. Fishing alone yielded enough both to feed the slaves and leave a surplus for their masters to take. Next came *hoe agriculture* on marshy soils and *primitive stock-breeding*. Wars brought a lot of captives. Prosperous families began to expand farm lands by means of crude small scale drainage. Slave labour was very effective in digging the ditches and moving earth. Expansion of the arable land in the marshy valleys resulted in a very tangible increase in the harvest. The enlarged yield provided the means to feed the slaves engaged in this work. For these reasons labour power very early acquired exchange value in the societies of the Nile and Euphrates valleys, which meant that slaves, the human repositories of labour power, were valuable objects.

The free Egyptian or Babylonian peasant was thus both an exploiter and an immediate producer. In the former capacity, he tilled land made fertile only by an *irrigation system* constructed and maintained with the help of slave labour. In the latter capacity he worked for himself as a husbandman in the fields. "Since the land which he cultivated owed its fertility to the irrigation system, he was in possession of an instrument of production which could not be entrusted to a slave, namely the land itself."[20] It was only later, at a higher level of the development of the productive forces, that slaves were allowed to till land. *Large scale* farming based on irrigation — the next stage — laid the foundation for the *collective*

20. *Ibid.*, p. 33.

ownership of slaves by the territorial communitites of early Egypt and Babylonia.

During the millenium from 4000 to 3000 B.C. the Egyptian economy achieved a stable surplus product. This was accomplished by a further rise in the productivity of labour combined with the appropriation of the product of slave labour. The social nucleus, the traditional farming commune, grew more differentiated socially. The slaveowners in the community exploited the commune viciously, pillaging the common lands. Gradually, huge temple lands, controlled by a priestly caste, took shape. Society was stratified hierarchically with slaveholders, big landowners, priests, usurers and officials holding sway. Slaves were the majority of workers on estates belonging to the Pharaoh, the temples and secular bigwigs. The Pharaohs, heads of the slaveholding class and supreme rulers, waged endless wars to seize booty, cattle and slaves. The great pyramids of Egypt were constructed as everlasting tribute to the bloody Pharaohs and the slaveholding class as a whole. Eugene Genovese's glorification of the Southern U.S. slaveholders notwithstanding, not even 5,000 years ago was there anything "ambivalent" about slavery!

The 6th Dynasty (2423-2263 B.C.) — following the epoch of pyramid construction (2700-2400 B.C.) — still saw much patriaarchal house slavery, the early form of slavery. But already the priesthood, with its gangs of slaves, held great power in Egypt. Around 1789-1786 B.C. slavery in the Middle Kingdom underwent a boom. 1200 to 1086 B.C. were years when the exploitation of slave labour intensified as the overall economic situation worsened. Finally, under the Ptolemaic Dynasty (323-30 B.C.), slavery ran riot through Egypt with slaves being acquired through piracy, war, trade, debt, and the breeding of slaves. They were set to toil in households, in handicrafts, industry, mining, stone-pits, in farming and on the many temple estates. This raised Egypt from the traditional, and now economically outdated, patriarchal form of slavery to the classical, mass form of ancient slavery, especially in urban centers like Alexandria. However, mass slavery is most properly connected with the Roman economy.

In Babylonia *private* ownership of land and slaves occurred relatively early. As in Egypt, the rich seized the collective patrimony — crop and pasture lands, cattle, and above all, slaves. Territorial communities became antagonistic slaveholders' states whose main function was the subjugation of slaves to freemen. Male slave labour proved to be more efficient in irrigation works than female slave labour. But male slaves were more likely to raise insurrections than females, especially when concentrated in large groups as they had to be for irrigation works. So the freemen of different Babylonian communities united under single governments in order to establish armed forces powerful enough to police the slaves. In some Babylonian city-states real slave latifundia evolved on royal estates managed by governors.

Hammurabi's Code (ca. 1800 B.C.) throws light on ancient production relations and relations between masters and slaves. There was no restriction on the sale of slaves, they could be given away as gifts, inherited, or exchanged for other slaves and chattels. The slave's family status was of no account. His family, if he had one, was not a recognized institution and thus had no safeguards. Since slaves were the most valuable form of property, theft of a slave or harbouring a runaway was punished by death.

Thus the evidence shows that the *slaveholder's complete ownership not only of the means of production, but of the workers themselves, of the slave, comprised the essence of the slave system's production relations*. The *basic economic law of slaveholding society* is the production of surplus product for the slaveholder through rapacious and unrelenting exploitation of slaves who are mere chattels of their masters. The very *goal of production* in slaveholding society is the surplus product created by the labour of slaves and appropriated by the slaveholder. Since slaves are unwilling workers, *only the cooperative labour of large masses of slaves is profitable in the long run*. Babylonia, in its later development, had big handicraft workshops and big landed estates staffed with female slaves herded together in droves of 30 to 40, and male slaves in gangs of 20 to 30.

The first millenium B.C., which saw the emergence of an international market embracing all the ancient societies of North Africa, the Middle East and the eastern Mediterranean, also witnessed the gradual attachment of some slaves to means of production, a phenomenon which was to recur in Athens in the late 5th century B.C., and in Rome during the imperial period. This represented a considerable change in favour of economic independence. These slaves were often settled in independent handicraft and paid their masters quitrent. Slaves with a household and family held a *peculium.* The *peculium* might include even a slave, so slaves in late Babylonian society, like those in the late Roman Empire many centuries after, sometimes owned their own slaves. Such slaves were certainly only nominally slaves, and in fact were already members of the exploiting class. Slaves who worked as quitrent-paying craftsmen, or tenanted small plots of ground, represent emergent elements of a new mode of production, feudalism, within the framework of the old Babylonian slave society. But these were a minority. Most slaves were still branded with the hot iron and went on as before toiling away on irrigation, on landed estates, or in artisan workshops. They were exploited mercilessly, as no other class had ever been exploited.

*

More so than in the ancient African and Asian states, slavery peaked in classical Greece and Rome. The Greeks and Romans were able to borrow from and build upon the achievements of Egyptian, Chinese, Babylonian and Indian tillers and craftsmen in raising the level of productive forces and corresponding production relations. Influenced by all the institutions of the slave systems of Africa and Asia, the Greeks and Romans accomplished in a few centuries what it had taken those before them several thousands of years.

In a characteristic acceleration of history, in just 350 or so years the *advanced* form of the slaveholding economy already held sway in the Greek city-states. By the 5th and 4th centuries B.C. slaves were the main producers. As in every slaveholding society, the labour power of the slave was not a commodity which the slave himself could sell for a period of time to an employer, as in the case of a free wage earner. Not labour power, but *labour itself* in the person of the slave was appropriated, and not by hiring, but rather by extra-economic means, by force and violence. The human being rather than labour power was the commodity, and in the advanced slave mode of production, purchase and sale of the "human commodity" was a profitable branch of Greek, and later Roman, commerce. Slave labour was widely used in agriculture, mainly in truck farming and on plantations. Both big landowners and prosperous "yeomen" small-holders worked their fields with slaves. Many slaves were house servants which in prosperous Greek families could number as many as five or six. Those who could not afford that many made do with one slave — male or female. Rich households — 50 slaves were accounted a large property in Greek slave society — were closed, diminutive economic worlds with their own mills, bakeries, weaving setups, and workshops, all staffed with slaves.

In ancient Greece slaveholding was backed by the city-state, the *polis*. For the Greeks the concept of community was synonymous with the concept of the *polis*. However, this was not the same thing as the Egyptian or Babylonian community of toilers. The Greek *polis* was a community of slaveowners. Its members were the privileged minority, and only they enjoyed full civil rights. Slaves and several categories of "inferior" freemen were excluded from the *polis* proper. The *polis* was the basic form of slave system and state in Greek and early Roman history (*civitas*). The *poleis* (city-states) had two distinct forms. In one, known as *slaveowning democracy*, the rule of the entire class of slaveholders was established. In the other, government was monopolized by a few super-rich aristocrats who had to possess land as well as slaves. This was the so-called *oligarchy*. Athens is a classical example of a slave-owning democracy, while Sparta typifies an oligarchy.

Following the Greco-Persian Wars (499-479 B.C.), a steadily growing number of *slave factories* began to operate in competition with the traditional small artisan workshops — especially in the 4th century B.C. These huge handicraft establishments, applying the advantages of large scale simple cooperation and division of labour, were set up mostly by resident aliens, that is, "metics", who were not citizens of the *polis*. The rise of large enterprises run by slaveholders was triggered by a boom in Mediterranean export commodity trade (wine, olive oil, grain, pottery, dyes, etc.). While finishing industry remained the sphere of free labour, *basic industry* was entirely handed over to slaves, mining in particular, where a notorious example was the Athenian state-owned Laurion mines in southern Attica, which were leased to private entrepreneurs who, in turn, employed slaves in the diggings.

The crisis of the Greek *polis* began as the land was monopolized more and more by the slaveholders. Impoverished peasants either fell into debt and were enslaved, or swelled the ranks of the urban lower classes. The declassed stratum grew, the so-called lumpen-proletariat. Here again slave labour blocked the way to technical advancement and social progress. Internecine warfare ripped Hellas apart. The Greeks fell victim to Macedonian and Roman conquest.

Slaves became the basic producers of material values also in the *Roman* slave system. Only here in the West, in Italy, Sicily and North Africa, the slave economy underwent a *hypertrophic growth*. The history of Rome was tortured by the most antagonistic class struggle between the slaves and the slaveholders, and it was in Rome that the most typical economic, social and political processes unfolded within the ancient slave mode of production.

From about 326 B.C. onwards, slaves began to become the chief producers in Roman society. This resulted in the extension of the Roman Republic's aggression beyond the boundaries of Italy. Conquest of foreign territory enriched the ruling class of Roman slaveholders. There was a crying demand for slaves, for, as Marx pointed out, in Roman Italy, "the slaves died out again and again, and had constantly to be replaced by new ones."[21] Yet slavery became the basis of the entire production process. Military victories provided an influx of cheap slaves. The accretions in turn increased the weight of slave labour in the economy. Economic life became more and more dependent on slaves. Mass employment of slave labour in farming led to the rise of latifundia (great estates). Latifundian produce was intended chiefly for sale. The latifundia were the scene of *large scale commodity production*.

This process was more or less completed by 129 B.C. which thus marked a turning point in the evolution of slavery on a mass scale. By that year Rome had conquered most of the Mediterranean area. Its victory caused a tremendous, almost overnight growth of slavery, for at times the victors sold the vanquished peoples or tribes in their entirety into slavery, flooding the market with cheap slaves. Simultaneously a new system of slaveholding developed — *mass slavery* entailing intense exploitation. Mass slavery was brought into being by the great expansion of the latifundia and forced labour in mines and workshops.

From then on slaves were the basic producers of the Roman slave-holding system. A ramified network of slave trading arose with slave markets flourishing in Rome and elsewhere. The slave market was stocked by war, debt, and mass kidnappings by pirate

21. Karl Marx and Frederick Engels, *The German Ideology*, in *Collected Works*, Volume 5, New York, 1976, p. 85.

vessels which swooped suddenly from the sea to attack coastal habitations. Roman imports always remained greater than exports. However, the lack of exports was compensated for by outright pillage of conquered lands and by the influx into Rome of large sums of money.

Streams of money flooded Rome in the form of war booty, tribute, taxes and interest payments. The outcome was the growth of merchant and usurer's capital which sprang up alongside the large agricultural estates. This early capital was concentrated mainly in the hands of the class known as the Knights estate which was transformed into a money aristocracy. "In all the forms in which slave economy (not the patriarchal kind, but that of later Grecian and Roman times) serves as a means of amassing wealth, where money therefore is a means of appropriating the labour of others through the purchase of slaves, land, etc., money can be expanded as capital, i.e. bear interest, for the very reason that it can be so invested," noted Marx.[22] Marx called merchant capital, and money-dealing capital, and usurer's capital the antidiluvian form of interest-bearing capital. But this early form of capital was always subordinate, existing only on the basis of the slave mode of production, and operating only under conditions set by the Roman slaveholders.

On the whole, the ancients never thought of transforming the surplus product into capital, i.e. value, which enables the holder to obtain *surplus* value by directly or indirectly exploiting producers. Where they did transform surplus product into capital, they did so only to a limited extent. The slaveholders, principal owners of the surplus product, were the chief consumers of wealth and luxury.[23] Treasure was hoarded in the narrow sense of storing gold away in coffers. Hence much surplus product lay idle. Ancient slaveholders devoted a large part of the surplus product to unproductive expenditure on art, religious and public works. Their enterprise was not directed to the release and development of the division of labour, or machinery, nor to the application of the powers of nature and science to private production. By and large, they were content not to go beyond handicraft labour. The ruling class was

22. K. Marx, *Capital*, Vol. III, pp. 580-581.
23. *Ibid.*, p. 325.

quite satisfied to enforce the simple cooperation of gang slave labour.

> The wealth which they produced for private consumption was therefore relatively small and only appears great because it was amassed in the hands of a few persons, who, incidentally, did not know what to do with it. Although, therefore, there was no *over-production* among the ancients, there was *over-consumption* by the rich, which in the final periods of Rome and Greece turned into mad extravagance. The few trading peoples among them lived partly at the expense of all these essentially poor nations.[24]

Roman slaves belonged either to the state or to private persons. Slaves owned by the government did public works, constructed aqueducts and public buildings, paved roads, etc. They were fewer in number than their privately-owned compeers, and on the whole better off. Some were even appointed as low-level officials, i.e. temple servants, messengers, prison guards or executioners. Among the private slaves the gladiators formed a special group. So in a different way did slaves who worked the mines. Mining and stone quarrying were tasks reserved for slaves exclusively. Mines and quarries were the property of the state, but were leased to wealthy tenants who exploited them with slaves who were either their own property or rented from other slaveholders. 40,000 of these unfortunates worked the silver mines of Cartagena in Spain. The remaining bondsmen were divided into town and plantation slaves. A rich owner could have hundreds of town slaves. Included were bodyguards, cooks, hairdressers and barbers, weavers, shoemakers, dyers, masons, architects, scribes, teachers, musicians, actors, writers, in a word, every occupation needed to service the lavish mansions of the wealthy. The plantation slaves tilled the latifundia. Their number depended on the size of the estate. During the olive and grape harvests free small or landless peasants were hired to assists slaves. Worst off were slaves who worked under the eyes of strict overseers. Without their masters' permission slaves could found no families and hold no property, personal or otherwise. On the plantations recalcitrants were locked in dungeons at night and made to work in shackles.

---

24. Karl Marx, *Theories of Surplus Value* (Volume IV of *Capital*), Part II, Moscow, 1968, p. 528.

About the time of Julius Caesar (102- 44 B.C.) the Roman Republic fell, to be replaced by the Empire, a new form of the Roman slave state. It differed from the Republic in that it represented a broader spectrum of slaveholders than just those of the city of Rome. The Empire was the state of the slaveholding class not only of the narrow Roman *polis* but of Italy as a whole and all the territories conquered by Rome. But the cities of this far flung Empire went bankrupt as urban real estate was taken over by private individuals, and townsmen were impoverished by ruinous taxation. Socio-economic and political crises merged as great popular uprisings undermined the supremacy of the slaveholders. The slaveholding mode of production began its long drawn-out disintegration. The change was already noticeable by the 1st century A.D. Over huge areas slave labour had almost completely ousted free producers. This placed heavy fetters on the further development of productive forces and technology. The time came when the Roman Empire was no longer strong enough to conquer other lands. However, *with the cessation of major wars of conquest, the supply of slaves steadily declined.* Natality was never high enough to reproduce the slave population. The provinces became serious competitors of Rome as the economic center of gravity shifted away from Italy. With fewer and fewer commodities to sell, Italy's unfavourable balance of trade and payments grew. Roman slaveholders persisted in importing Eastern spices and luxury goods which had to be paid for, so in lieu of export commodities, the current of gold and other precious metals now reversed and flowed to the East. The currency was devaluated by reducing the metal content of coins, but this failed to alter the unfavourable trade balance. The price of slaves rose in the 3rd century A.D. as their procurement became more difficult. Laws were now proclaimed requiring careful treatment of slaves, a phenomenon that would recur many centuries later in the Antebellum South after the curtailment of the external slave trade.

The outcome was an important social change — the emergence of the *colonus* relation. Slaves and propertiless workers were granted parcels of land and thus became personally motivated to increase production. The *colonus* relation did not infringe upon the continued growth of the latifundia, but it did change the method of production thereby relieving the symptoms of crisis somewhat. Undeniably, slaves of the Roman Empire were objectively interested in liquidating the slave mode of production and the political system it supported. They were, therefore, objectively a *revolutionary class*, and the armed uprisings of the slaves was the most striking form of class struggle in antiquity. But their revolutionary character was limited, chiefly by the fact that nearly all rebellious slaves merely hoped to free *themselves*, not do away with the institution of slavery *per se*. Slave resistance in ancient times thus could not raise itself to the level of the American Abolitionist movement against slavery under the capitalist mode of production.

*

The history of "classical" pre-monopoly capitalism is best understood when broken down into three stages: 1) simple cooperation; 2) manufactory; and 3) machinery and large scale industry. Coincidental in time with the first and second stages are the *momenta* of the *primitive accumulation of capital*, among which the most portentous for the Americas were the extermination of the Amerindians and the Atlantic slave trade in Africans. Usually primitive accumulation of capital is restricted to the foregoing crimes (plus similar goings-on in the Far East). The history of slave labour in the New World usually is treated in a *separate chapter* following upon, and disconnected from the chapter on primitive accumulaton. I think this is wrong. A correction should be made from the standpoint of the theory of Marxist political economy. Not only is it wrong to view U.S. slavery in particular as a phenomenon separate from the primitive accumulation of capital, I believe that the *only* way to unravel the history of U.S. slavery is to regard it as a phase of the pre-history of capitalism proper, as *an integral feature, as perhaps the most long-lasting momentum of primitive accumulation*! Rather than viewing it in the old way as part of the developmental history of post-accumulation capitalism, I suggest that we continue to regard the slave economy under capitalism as a stubborn *"remnant"* or *"survival"*, but *not* as the remnant of any pre-capitalist social formation, as Genovese and others have done, for that is incorrect. We should view the "peculiar institution", rather, as the survival of that "rosy dawn" of the primitive accumulation of capital, as the continuation of that transitional epoch from feudalism to capitalism when Indians were being

25

slaughtered, Africans were being dragged off to slave ships, and white "mercantilists" were getting rich,[25] a period that is traditionally too rigidly dated from ca. 1485 - 1776/1789.

The colonization of North and South America is inseparable from the primitive accumulation of capital. Primitive accumulation proceeded by various methods, each bloody and repressive, one of the most lasting being slavery. But before the introduction of African slaves the Caribbean and South America witnessed the depradations of the Spanish and Portuguese *conquistadores* who slaughtered the native American tribes and looted their wealth (so much gold and silver was stolen and mined in the Spanish colonies that it caused a "prices revolution" in 16th century Europe, i.e. a long drawn-out spiral of inflation). From early on, unequal trade also became a permanent mode of capital formation for the colonial powers. However, the capitalists of the 17th and 18th centuries, facing changed circumstances, had to proceed more systematically than their 16th century predecessors. They continued to rob, levy tribute, and engage in nonequivalent exchange. But in order to up the rate of profit, they had to *organize regular production* in the New World according to the requirements of the capitalist world market. Now the appetites of the colonists were no longer confined to the extraction of *existing* natural resources or confiscation of wealth created by the native Amerindians. The Caribbean islands and the southern part of the United States, along with Brazil and parts of Central and South America were transformed into plantation staple economies — sources of sugar, tobacco, indigo, rice and cotton. By means of African slave labour, France and England officially continued — more efficiently — the "work" of the Spaniards, Portuguese and Dutch in meeting the demand of the capitalist world market for colonial merchandise. Soaring demand for colonial staples improved the market situation. A bigger, more dynamic market attracted larger capital investment. America's forests were felled, new settlements founded, and masses of new slaves were imported from Africa to do the heavy work.[26]

25. See the careful probe of the problem of transition in Maurice Dobb, *Studies in the Development of Capitalism.*
26. "The transformation of necessaries into luxuries by means of foreign trade, ... is important in itself: ... because it determines the whole social

I am suggesting that to get started, to accumulate "take-off" capital, the "rosy dawn's" budding capitalists would literally do anything, try anything, including some strange things that were characteristically *uncapitalist*!

Undeniably, capitalism entails the exploitation of free wage labourers, of proletarians despoiled of means of production. Nevertheless, the bourgeois relations transferred from England and Holland to the *real* world of the Thirteen Colonies in the early 17th century were significantly mixed or combined with pre-capitalist forms of exploitation. This peculiar mixture was the indispensable agent for the primitive accumulation of capital in and from America. The outcome, however, was some very complex and anomalous social and economic relations during the early history of capitalist society in America. In short, the rise of capitalism brought the slave economy to America, the tiger gave birth to the snake. "To steal a slave is to steal the instrument of production directly", observed Marx. "But then the production of the country for which the slave is stolen must be structured to allow of slave labour, or (as South America, etc.) a mode of production corresponding to the slave must be created."[27]

Thus the colonization of North America is part and parcel of the process of the primitive accumulation of capital. The bourgeoisie in the colonies did not lag behind their European counterparts.[28] On the contrary, they exceeded them in applying every

pattern of backward nations — for example, the slave-holding states in the United States of North America ... which are associated with a world market based on capitalist production. No matter how large the surplus product they extract from the surplus labour of their slaves in the simple form of cotton or corn, they can adhere to this simple, undifferentiated labour because foreign trade enables them [to convert] these simple products into any kind of use-value", K. Marx, *Theories of Surplus Value*, Part III, p. 243.

27. Karl Marx, *Grundrisse der Kritik der politischen Ökonomie*, Berlin, GDR, 1953, p. 19.

28. The best general works on early American history are by Herbert Aptheker: *The Colonial Era: A History of the American People*, 2nd ed., New York, 1966; and *The American Revolution, 1763-1783; A History of the American People: An Interpretation*, New York, 1969. Another fine study of the American Revolution is David H. DeGrood, *The New Era*, Special Issue, *Revolutionary World: An International Journal of Philosophy*, Volume 16, Amsterdam, 1976. Outstanding as a seminal work regarding the relation of manufactory capitalism to American slavery is R. Ivanov, *American History and the Black Question*, Moscow, 1976, pp. 79-129.

possible method of accumulation based on brutality and raw force. The only extraordinary feature is that due to conditions specific to America, not only the slave trade in Africans, but the slave mode of production itself also figured prominently in this process and among these methods. But it was not any pre-capitalist mode of production that was coming into being, it was capitalism that was hoisting itself up by the bootstraps of slave labour. This modern slave economy was never to have an independent identity as a mode of production; it existed only on the basis of the conditions set for it, and as an agent of capitalism.

Primitive accumulation, which in Europe featured ruination of small commodity producers, and peasants driven from the land and reduced to begging, thus took a different path in America.

Marx said that where a land is conquered and man himself is captured as an organic accessory of the land, and as one of the conditions of production, this is the origin of slavery. Under the ancient slave mode of production this was undeniably so. In the case of modern American slavery, some of the terms were reversed. The land was conquered through the physical extermination of its original appropriators or owners — the Amerindians. These tribes had either roamed over delimited hunting grounds reproducing themselves and their production relations by means of more or less domesticated herds, or practiced sedentary agriculture or fishing. Once the Native American had been removed, the "organic accessory" of the land was then *imported* in the person of the African slave whose forced labour was the condition of production in the colonial plantation economy.

Under normal capitalist circumstances the worker himself is the seller of his labour as a commodity. In as much as he does not sell himself as a slave, he places his labour power at the disposal of the capitalist only for a certain number of hours. But the very person of the Black slave himself was sold as a commodity whose use-value was to be the repository of labour power. In other words, although his labour power remained a commodity for others — for his sellers and buyers — the Afro-American himself had no freedom to dispose of it as a commodity. His labour power, along with his person, were placed on the market by someone else, by slavers who thus dehumanized him, who transformed him into a walking means of production, saleable like all other means of production under capitalism. The captive African thus became for slave

28

traders and planters the most valuable, the ideal commodity — a source of additional wealth. The proverbial goose who lays golden eggs. Enslavement of the African was crucial for the historical development of the world capitalist system because means of production become capital *only* when used to pump surplus value from living labour. Africans were slaves of *capitalism*, unlike the slaves of antiquity who were bondsmen of an entirely different, *pre-capitalist* mode of production — the ancient slave mode of production. Forced African labour created the *original* stock of capital which made possible the subsequent squeezing of more capital (surplus value or profit) from free wage labour, and which oiled the wheels of enlarged capitalist reproduction.

Under capitalism the worker, as a human being, does not constitute a condition of production, only his *labour* is a condition of production. Marx saw this as a universal principle of capitalism. But New World plantation capitalism was exceptional in that the labour of the Black slave could not be exacted apart from his appropriation as a man, as the epitome of labour embodied in the human creature, thus once again making the *worker himself*, the human being, and not merely his labour power, a condition of production. Marx, in one passage on the circuit of money-capital in Vol. II of *Capital,* [29] quite in passing defines a slave as one who is himself a *means of production*, belonging to the general category of means of production along with land, farm implements, seed, beasts of burden, etc. The prerequisite for capitalism in its classical European form, in which it exploited free wage labour, was the appearance in America of a denatured, bastardized form of capital, so to speak, that functioned on the renewed, anachronistic unity of worker and labour as the *sine qua non* of production. This is why plantation owners, while being plain capitalists, were nevertheless *anomalies* within the capitalist world market. This economic system was confined to the Americas; chattel slavery was not a major economic factor in any European country from the 17th century on.

Having lasted about 250 years, the first stage of capitalism — the simple cooperation stage — drew to a close around 1550. Colonial America dates from 1607 to 1776 and thus coincides with the

29. Karl Marx, *Capital. A Critique of Political Economy*, Volume II, Moscow, 1957, p. 31.

second stage, the *manufactory* stage of capitalist development. During the colonial period the North developed on the basis of manufactory capitalism, while the South, by contrast, was dominated by the planter system of slave economy which represented *a cross between slavery and capitalism*. In the simple cooperation of labour characteristic of the first stage of capitalism and also characteristic of gang slave labour, all workers perform the same tasks. In manufactory, however, the worker specializes in carrying out just one single operation. *Obviously manufactory was merely capitalist cooperation based now on division of labour and handicraft technology*. It is important that we note that the method of production used by the capitalist North in its manufactory stage and the simple cooperation of labour which prevailed in the slave-holding South as the method best adapted to slavery, did not differ all that much. The level of productive forces of the manufactory stage of capitalism corresponds roughly to simple cooperation. At this stage there was no great gap in the level of development of productive forces between the North and the South. It was this lack of great disparity that laid the common ground for the marriage between Northern manufactory capitalism and the Southern planter economy, for the cross between slavery and capitalism. As long as Northern capitalism remained at the manufactory stage the partners were compatible; when Northern capitalism progressed beyond manufactory, the marriage ended in divorce.

No one has explained the manufactory stage of capitalism better than Karl Marx. Whatever the starting form of manufactory, "its final form is invariably the same — a productive mechanism whose parts are human beings."[30] Here the productive power of labour is increased and *relative* surplus value extracted, primarily by increasing the intensity of labour by constant labour of one uniform kind,[31] and the "direct dependence of the operations, and therefore of the labourers, on each other", which "compels each one of them to spend on his work no more than the necessary time", and begets "a continuity, uniformity, regularity, order, and even intensity of labour, of quite a different kind, ... than is to be found

30. *Capital*, Vol. I, p. 338.
31. *Ibid.*, p. 341.

in an independent handicraft or even in simple cooperation."[32] Manufactory accomplishes the separation of the labourers into skilled and unskilled. Alongside this distinction develops "a hierarchy of labour power, to which there corresponds a scale of wages" based on different values of labour power which arise from different degrees of training. This corresponds with the stage of narrow craft unions.

The advantage of manufactory over simple cooperation consists thus in the division of labour which saves much labour and increases the productivity of labour. In simple cooperation each labourer, one after another, must perform all the operations required to fabricate the product. In manufactory each worker specializes in accomplishing just one or just a few operations. Performing the same operation over and over again, the worker learns to do this task faster, better and more efficiently than those who do not specialize. At the same time his labour becomes more intensive through specialization. No time is lost making the transition from one task to another. In Western Europe, for centuries the main scene of capitalist development, manufactory, as a form of capitalist production, reigned for more than two hundred years from the mid-16th century to the last third of the 18th century.

What did manufactory accomplish historically? Well, in a nutshell it created the necessary prerequisites for the transition to large scale machine production. It also fostered the development of the domestic market. But in the long run manufactory, based as it was on primitive technique and manual labour, proved unable to satisfy the demand for industrial goods caused by the expanding market it had fostered. In their mad chase after profit, capitalists ran headlong into the barriers raised by manual labour and handicraft techniques. The transition to large scale machine production now became an economic necessity. In the first half of the 19th century, with ever greater momentum after the War of 1812, the northern United States underwent the transition from manufactory to machine production, setting the stage for the "irrepressible conflict". And paradoxically, the planter system of slave economy fuelled the engines of the transition with its raw material — cotton.

32. *Ibid.*, p. 345.

But throughout the manufactory stage of capitalist development which featured a relatively slow development of the means of production, the existence of a large number of Black slaves within the work force in North America was a major source of economic and political strength. From the outset, the slaveholding system of planter economy was closely knit to the dominant capitalist mode of production since the planters produced commodities for the capitalist world market. At the level of basic production relations the planter economy was a slaveholding entity based on the exploitation of Black slaves. Nevertheless, the plantation was united with and subordinate to the capitalist economy. Never at any moment was it a "distinct civilization" with an anti-capitalist "ideology". Never at any moment was it an independent "pre-capitalist mode of production". Marx realized that plantations from the very outset constituted commercial speculations ("*Handelsspekulationen*") conditioned primarily by the capitalist world market. Any claims toward self-sufficiency or autarchy individual planters may have uttered were either clearly relative only to local conditions, or pure illusions. Marx explained that capitalist production took place on these plantations, but he did add that this production was only "*formally*" capitalist, for Black slavery excluded the foundation of capitalist production — free wage labour. This remark confuses those who fail to carry the analysis further. The planters were capitalists, capitalists who carried on their businesses by means of Black slave labour. Marx explained that the mode of production which the planters introduced did *not* spring from the historical slave mode of production, but rather was grafted on to slavery. In this system the capitalist, the landowner, and the slaveholder were one and the same.[33] Frederick Engels also referred to "the bourgeois nature of the planters."[34] This was the reason why Marx felt that *cost-price regulated market-value* throughout the history of the U.S. slave economy.[35]

America provides the most graphic confirmation of the truth emphasized by Marx in *Capital*, Volume III, that capitalism in agriculture does not

33. K. Marx, *Theories of Surplus Value*, Part II, pp. 302-303.
34. F. Engels, "Letter to K. Marx", May 23, 1862, in Karl Marx and Frederick Engels, *The Civil War in the United States*, 3rd edition, New York, 1961, p. 245.
35. K. Marx, *Theories of Surplus Value*, Part II, p. 303.

depend on the *form* of land ownership or land tenure. Capital finds the most diverse types of medieval and patriarchal landed property — feudal, 'peasant allotments' (i.e., the holdings of bonded peasants); clan, communal, state and other forms of land ownership ... Capital takes hold of all these, employing a variety of ways and methods.[36]

Since capitalism can thus sweep into its net and extract profit from all these other pre-capitalist forms, it is not surprising that it revived and subordinated slavery to itself, and then battened on the slave economy.

Lenin regarded the Southern plantations as "unimproved" "latifundia",[37] reminiscent in many ways of ancient Roman slave-holding latifundia. Describing the situation in U.S. agriculture after 1900, he wrote, "America demonstrates clearly that it would be imprudent to confuse the latifundia with large-scale capitalist agriculture, and that latifundia are frequently survivals of pre-capitalist relationships — slave-owning, feudal or patriarchal."[38] Lenin was thus aware that slave relations of production prevailed on Southern plantations and between slaves and slaveholders, yet he also knew that those relations existed solely on the basis of a burgeoning world capitalism which required slavery — a mode in principle antithetical to itself — as a prerequisite for the appropriation of the Americas and the accumulation of capital. Only later did the further accumulation of capital require that capitalism free itself from the hindrance of the Southern slave economy.

According to Marx, we must conceive the price of a slave as *capitalized surplus value*. What does this mean? Well,

the price paid for a slave is nothing but the anticipated and capitalized surplus-value or profit to be wrung out of the slave. But the capital paid for the purchase of a slave does not belong to the capital by means of which profit, surplus-labour, is extracted from him. On the contrary. It is capital which the slave-holder has parted with, it is a deduction from the capital which he has available for actual production. It has ceased to exist for agriculture. The best proof of this is that it does not reappear for the slave-holder or the landowner except when he, in turn, sells his slaves or land. But then the same situation prevails for the buyer. The fact that he has bought the slave does not enable him to exploit the slave without

36. V.I. Lenin, *Collected Works*, Volume 22, Moscow, 1964, p. 22.
37. *Ibid.*, pp. 30 and 28.
38. *Ibid.*, p. 50.

further ado. He is only able to do so when he invests some additional capital in the slave economy itself.[39]

The same capital does not exist twice over, once as money in the hands of the seller, and a second time in the hands of the new slaveowner. It passes from the purchaser to the seller. The capital is the money the seller pockets. The buyer now no longer has the capital, but in its stead he owns a slave. The circumstance that the profit derived from the real investment of an additional capital, *a second sum of money*, in the plantation enterprise is calculated by the new slaveholder as interest on the original capital which he has not invested in the business, but has given away to get the slave, does not alter the economic matter in the least.[40] In fact, the money spent for slaves is merely *potential* capital, "*capital in-itself*", as Marx termed it. It is potential capital because it can be converted into capital, into means to exploit living labour. It depends on the use it is put by the seller whether the money obtained by him in exchange for his slave is actually transformed into capital or not. For the slave buyer, it can never again function as such, no more than any other sum of money which he has paid out. Only by selling the slave he has purchased might he get equivalent potential capital back. But then another new owner simply enters the same relationship maintained by the former.

This is the basic formula for the circuit of capital:

$$M - C \Big\langle {}^{L}_{MP} \quad \dots P \dots C' - M'$$

The slave status of the labourer makes no change in this basic formula when the formula describes the circuit of a planter's capital. Even if in the initial circuit we count the purchase price of the slave as belonging to the productive capital, in subsequent reproductive circuits the labour cost (L) would surely represent a much smaller outlay of the productive capital. Thereafter L should represent only the small cost of the slave's upkeep at a functional subsistence minimum.[41]

39. K. Marx, *Capital*, Vol. III, pp. 788-789.
40. This way of reckoning on the part of the planters leads David and Temin astray. See P.A. David and P. Temin, "Slavery: The Progressive Institution?" in P.A. David, *et al.*, pp. 167-230.

Now labour power, even slave labour power, has a specific value. What determines this value? In order to keep on working, the slave, like any labourer, must satisfy his need for food, clothing, shelter, health care, etc. The satisfaction of these vital necessities replenishes muscle, nerve and brain — it restores the capacity to work. Furthermore, as a capitalist, the planter required a steady influx of labour power. However, after 1808, the influx of fresh slaves into the U.S. was gradually curtailed, which meant that slaves could no longer profitably be kept childless, quickly worked to death, and replaced by a new shipload of cheap fresh slaves from Africa. Henceforth the slave had to be given the opportunity and the wherewithal to maintain not only himself but his children as well. The process of production on the plantation had to allow for the physical reproduction of the slave class. The slave had to raise his substitutes — his children.[42] Furthermore, even the plantation needed not just unskilled field hands, but skilled artisans as well. The acquisition of a special training is tied, however, to the expenditure of a definite amount of labour and costs an equivalent

41. When the circuit of the whole social capital of the Antebellum U.S. economy is described, including both its northern and its southern sectors, the basic formula might be altered thusly:

$$M - C \left\langle \begin{array}{l} \text{L (free wage labour)} \\ \text{SL (slave labour power)} \ \ldots P \ldots C' - M' \\ \text{MP (means of production)} \end{array} \right.$$

However, the alteration is only to differentiate between the two modes of exploitation; it is not a necessary correction.

42. The main reason that the American slave population was in fact able to reproduce itself (400,000 in 1776 to 4,000,000) was simply that, unlike in antiquity and in those places in the Caribbean and South America, where the slave population did not reproduce itself, the sum-total of the forces of production in the U.S. slave system under the capitalist mode of production, even at the manufactory stage, were much superior to those in antiquity, and better developed capitalistically than in Latin America and the Caribbean. After all, the slave South inherited all the achievements of medieval feudal agriculture (plow, stirrup, harness, crop rotation, seed selection, etc.) plus the general mechanical-technological inventions of early capitalist Europe where simple cooperation and early division of labour were being applied. For an excellent analysis of the role of slavery and social structure in colonial Latin America, see Manfred Kossok, "Charakter und historischer Ort der Unabhängigkeitskriege Lateinamerikas" in *Asien, Afrika, Lateinamerika. Zeitschrift des Zentralen Rates für Asien-, Afrika- und Lateinamerikawissenschaften in der DDR*, Berlin, GDR, 1976, pp. 937-960.

in commodities of a greater or lesser amount. From all this emerges the fact that the value of slave labour power was determined by the labour-time necessary to produce and reproduce a whole "basket", so to speak, of items conditioned by the course of early American history. Like other capitalists, the slaveholders sought to press the material and cultural living conditions of their work force down to the lowest possible level. It is hard to conceive how Fogel and Engerman could imagine that a material incentive scheme for bondsmen could function as a basic feature of slavery. In reality, the value of slave labour power tended as a rule to *sink below* its value, that is, the ration and related items left to the slave were sometimes *not* equal to the value of the means of subsistence necessary for his mere physical survival, and certainly not often equal to the historically-evolved value of his labour power.

From the standpoint of the specific production relation between the planter and the slave, *slavery under capitalism was a manner of extracting surplus value mainly by lowering the value of labour power* as near as possible to, or even below, its historico-moral limits, and in hard times even below its physical minimum. In the words of Marx, "under slavery, etc., the false appearance brought about by the previous transformation of the product into money — insofar as it is expended on wages — does not arise; it is therefore obvious that what the slave receives as wages is, in fact, nothing that the slaveowner 'advances' him, but simply the portion of the realized labour of that slave that returns to him in the form of subsistence."[43] Slave labour was a method employed by American capitalism at a stage of its historical development to *increase the rate of exploitation* to a feasible extreme. Slavery should be analyzed therefore mainly from the standpoint of the formula for the *rate of surplus value*:

$$S' = \frac{s}{v} \times 100$$

It can also be looked at from the angle of the organic composition of capital (C : V), i.e. the ratio between the mass of means of production and living labour power, in a situation where due to social relations of production, i.e. slavery, the shares of fixed and variable capital for a long time remained relatively low, while that

43. K. Marx, *Theories of Surplus Value*, Part III, p. 93.

of the circulating capital stood at a relatively high level. The cost of slaves and the price of land should be viewed under the headings of the capitalization of surplus value and the capitalization of rent.

There is conclusive evidence that, when realized, the surplus product appropriated by the owner from an average "prime" American slave, male or female, over a productive lifetime, *definitely yielded the average rate of profit* on a capital outlay equivalent to the purchase price of the slave.[44] Of course it is true that in order to exploit the slave once he has been purchased, it is necessary to invest some additional capital in the enterprise. However, given the growing rate of exploitation, there is no reason to believe that slave labour did not yield the average rate of profit also on the bigger, *total* capital outlay (i.e. on the cost of the slave, plus the accrued annual interest that would have been garnered over the working lifetime of the slave on the sum spent to buy the slave, plus the additional capital required for capitalist production in the given unit) — especially when business was booming. One of the things that has complicated the analysis, and slowed recognition by honest investigators of the private profitability of slavery is the fact that the landlord and the owner of the slaves and other instruments of production are, in this case, one and the same person. Marx wrote:

> Rent and profit likewise coincide then, there occurring no separation of the different forms of surplus-value. The entire surplus-labour of the labourers, which is manifested here in the surplus-product, is extracted from them directly by the owner of all instruments of production, to which belong the land and, under the original form of slavery, the immediate producers themselves. Where the capitalist outlook prevails, as on American plantations, this entire surplus-value is regarded as profit ...[45]

For the plantation economy, *rent* and *profit* were not divorced from one another, for the landlord to whom rent accrued was

---

44. David and Temin put it this way in a recent study: calculations "reveal that purchase prices of prime-age slaves were such that (for either males or females) the flow of net revenues (reckoned as gross earnings less maintenance costs) that could be anticipated over the remainder of the slave's life would represent a normal market rate of yield on the investment in his (or her) purchase," in P.A. David, *et al.*, p. 39.
45. K. Marx, *Capital*, Vol. III, p. 784.

simultaneously a slaveholding capitalist.[46]

A factor which raised the rate of extraction of surplus labour from the class of slaves as a whole, thus ensuring the profitability of slavery, was the large scale participation of Black women in the labour process. At this period in American history most white women were relegated by circumstance, religion and tradition to child-rearing and domestic chores. Generally they did not yet sell their labour power as a commodity, nor did their labour yield marketable commodities in any large scale, organized, independent fashion. Not that they did not work hard, they did, and their living conditions were poor, but the fact that they produced little or no commodities excluded white women from economic activity. This contrasted sharply with Black women who the slaveholders forced to labour alongside male slaves and create material wealth. Even with leeway for Black female slaves involved in non-productive domestic and such-like services, the profit-creating adult Black population was thus nearly *double* a segment of the white population equal in size, assuming the normal male-female proportion in both cases.

Continual expansion of planter territory and slavery beyond their old limits was a law of life for the Southern slaveholders. Production of the main export articles — cotton, tobacco, sugar — was most remunerative on large units with 20 or more slaves, and on wide expanses of naturally fertile soil requiring nothing but simple cooperation of labour. Intensive cultivation which depends less on fertility than on capital investment, skill and interested labour, had a hard row to hoe under slavery.

> Hence the rapid transformation of states like Maryland and Virginia, which formerly employed slaves on the production of export articles, into states which raised slaves in order to export these slaves into the deep South ... As soon as this point is reached, the acquisition of new Territories becomes necessary, in order that one section of the slaveholders may equip new fertile landed estates with slaves, and in order that by this means a new market for slave-raising, therefore for the sale of slaves, may be created for the section left behind it.[47]

46. In the mind of the planter the investment in slaves represented "capitalized rent" for which he "earned" "interest". This is merely a mystification rooted in the economic relation.

47. K. Marx, *The Civil War in the United States*, pp. 66-67.

Thus the development of capitalism in the agriculture of the United States had its own peculiarities. Slavery and the plantation system was simply the unique road capitalism took in Southern agriculture. There was nothing "pre-capitalist" about it. The planter system of slaveholding economy was conducted by predatory methods. The planters used relatively little fertilizer, every few years breaking new ground, abandoning old land, moving relentlessly westward. This system of economy could survive only in vast spaces.

Slaveholding impeded the economic development of the Southern states. It is worth noting that, in the Marxist sense, *growth* and *profitability* are *not* the same thing as *development*. There can be growth without development. The slave South experienced periods of growth in the 19th century, but real development stagnated. The lack of development in turn affected the volume of the internal market for the industry of the North and Northeast. The extensive mode of cultivation reduced soil fertility, for brutal spoliation of the soil was the vogue among American slaveholders. This was contrary to the normal capitalist farmer whose investments "transform the land from mere material into land-capital."[48] Economic law compelled modern slavery to expand in order not to perish.[49] In the 18th century it was sugar which filled the sails of the slave ships, transforming the Caribbean isles into a chain of plantations and providing the raw material for refineries as far away as Bristol in England and Orléans in France. The invention of the cotton gin in 1793 triggered the cotton boom. Despite cyclical dips, on the whole the demand for cotton soared in the first half of the 19th century, buoying the price of cotton, especially during the "prosperous" 1850s. Fertile crop land was abundant in the lower South and Southwest, so it was profitable to invest capital in cotton grown there by Black slaves. Cotton production soared, but the development of factory industry in the South did not keep pace with that in the North. Exploitation of the slaves became more rapacious with the spread of cotton. Some were worked to death in eight to ten years. Slave labour hampered the quick, safe introduction of expensive new farm machinery. Purchase of slaves

48. K. Marx, *Capital*, Vol. III, p. 605.
49. See K. Marx, "The American Question in England" (Sept. 18, 1861) in *The Civil War in the United States*, p. 11.

became more and more costly, the average price of a slave soaring from 150 dollars at the beginning of the 19th century to 2,000 dollars in 1860. To make things worse for the planters, the slaves were in the habit of rebelling or running away from the plantations, or both.

*

Northern capitalism at the manufactory stage and the Southern planter system of slaveholding economy were distinctly different, but they were not isolated from each other. They were obviously cheek-by-jowl geographically. There were thousands of financial bonds, with the planters being generally in hock to the Northern commercial and banking bourgeoisies. Manufactory capitalism gradually created a national market which linked the two systems, although this accomplishment was always limited, and thus a source of growing dissatisfaction and irritation for emerging Yankee industrialists. In fact, since the War of Independence the two systems coexisted within a single administrative apparatus and a single nation state under an arrangement which allowed both overall dominance of the capitalist world market and planter control of the federal government. The "liberty" proclaimed in the U.S. Constitution of 1787 actually consolidated the *joint dictatorship of the slaveholders and the big bourgeoisie.* The constitutional settlement explicitly protected the anomalous but indispensable form of exploitation that was Black slavery. With this joint dictatorship went the hegemony of *bourgeois-slaveholder ideology*, which in colonial America ruled over all the Thirteen Colonies, and following independence continued to hold sway in the pre-Bellum South. It was a compound of contempt for Blacks, Amerindians and poor whites, hatred of the popular masses, *ad hoc* racist practices, sophisticated racist philosophy, rationalizations of slavery borrowed from ancient slaveholder doctrines, and a hypocritical cult of God and greed which justified anything profitable.

Viewed in terms of objective historical development, Black slavery had no future as an economic system, no more than capitalism today. But the marriage was nevertheless long-lived, from 1619 to 1861. Under the reign of King Cotton the 1850s were both the peak years and the crisis years. Throughout the manufactory stage North American capitalists had a big economic stake in the preservation of Black slavery. For that reason alone slavery lasted so long. First the African slave trade, and then cotton production, were important sources of initial capital formation in North America, bringing huge profits to both slaveholders of the South and fractions of the bourgeoisie of the North. "Whilst the cotton industry introduced child-slavery in England, it gave in the United States a stimulus to the transformation of the earlier, more or less patriarchal slavery, into a system of commercial exploitation", wrote Marx.[50] Slaveholding South and manufactory North complemented each other — never perfectly, but enough for mutual profit. The mature slaveholding economy supplied both English and Northern textile industries with cotton. It became the semi-colonial appendage of both the North and the United Kingdom, and in this dual dependence lay the seeds of its final downfall. But not right away. For a long time British and Northern capitalists participated jointly in the exploitation of Black slaves, alongside the Southern planters. If we look closely enough, we can discern *a quasi-tripartite ownership of the class of Black slaves* by planters, Northern bourgeois and British capitalists, with the planters exercizing the direct rule over the slaves.

> No matter whether commodities are the output of production based on slavery, of peasants (Chinese, Indian ryots), of communes (Dutch East Indies), of state enterprise (such as existed in former epochs of Russian history on the basis of serfdom) or of half-savage hunting tribes, etc. — as commodities and money they come face to face with the money and commodities in which the industrial capital presents itself and enter as much into its circuit as into that of the surplus-value borne in the commodity — capital, provided the surplus-value is spent as revenue; hence they enter into both branches of circulation of commodity-capital. The character of the process of production from which they originate is immaterial.[51]

Hence, "in the process C'—M', it is not necessary that M' should represent converted commodity-capital; it may be the realization in money of the commodity labour-power (wages), or of the product of some independent labourer, slave, serf, or community."[52]

50. K. Marx, *Capital*, Vol. I, p. 760.
51. K. Marx, *Capital*, Vol. II, p. 110.
52. *Ibid.*, p. 114.

Lenin reminds us always to refer back to Marx's *Capital*.

> In it you will find references to the extreme variety of forms of land
> ownership, such as feudal, clan, communal (and primitive-squatter), state,
> etc., which capitalism encounters when it makes its appearance on the
> historical scene. Capital subordinates to itself all these varied forms of land
> ownership and remoulds them after its own fashion, ...[53]

Capitalism subordinated to itself especially "the slave-holding
estates in the American South."[54] Lenin recommended that the
theoretical guiding principles of Marx on the relation of capitalism
to agriculture should be applied "to an investigation of the rise of
capitalism *from* the slave-holding economy of the American
South."[55]

1) Following this recommendation it seems wise to regard the
whole grafting of slavery on to capitalism as one manifestation of
the *law of the uneven development of capitalism.*

2) It seems clear that on the basis of the law of uneven development, disparate economic sectors entailing different modes of exploitation were able to coexist within one and the same social
formation. But the upper hand and the commanding heights in the
economy belonged to capitalism, the historically more advanced
mode of exploitation.

3) It is equally certain that history knows no "pure" capitalism, and no "purely" capitalist economy at any stage. Capitalism
never exists without pre-capitalist remnants and survivals and
constant regenerations, any more than without constant generation of petty commodity relations.

Jean Suret-Canale, a French authority on African history, con-
tends that a specific mode of production can only be defined in
terms of the "ensemble" or *totality* of production relations which
correspond to "a type and a determined level of productive
forces".[56] This is a wise suggestion. We should reject any delinea-
tion of a mode of production based primarily on a locally or
regionally prevailing form of exploitation. The level of productive
forces we are dealing with corresponded to manufactory capitalism

53. V.I. Lenin, *Collected Works*, Vol. 22, p. 59.
54. *Ibid.*
55. *Ibid.*
56. "Problèmes théoriques de l'étude des premières sociétés de classes" in
Premières Sociétés de Classes et Mode de Production Asiatique, pp. 7-8.

with a graft of Southern slavery. Letting himself be hypnotized by a regional form is one of Eugene Genovese's basic mistakes, an elementary error that no Marxist would make. We cannot accept the argument that a specific, integral "slave mode of production" existed in the New World in the 17th to the 19th century based on the exploitation of Black slaves. Nor can we accept the reality of any "Southern civilization", or special "world the slaveholders made", given the fact that the real world was dominated by the productive forces of capitalism in its manufactory stage. The enslavement of the African took place in the colonies during the era of primitive accumulation and was a condition for the triumph of the capitalist mode of production in North America and part of Europe. Slavery crept into the interstices of the capitalist world market. It was an underpinning for the dominant capitalist mode of production. Of course it did exist, and its existence lent a distinctly brutal and racist flavour to social organization in the United States.

*

We can safely conclude, therefore, that there are no grounds for confounding the ancient slave mode of production with modern American slavery under the capitalist mode of production. The relationship between capitalism and slavery is clear. I have tried to show that the revival of slavery in the modern era was a phase of the "prehistory" of industrial capitalism, in the same way that all the momenta of primitive accumulation were phases of that "prehistory", and as such it constituted one of the chief devices by which the primitive accumulation of capital was carried out. The slave mode of extracting surplus product from Black labourers remained compatible with, and a definite aid to, capitalism throughout its long manufactory stage. For at least 250 years, capitalism and slavery coexisted in the modern era, and did not conflict. Although the partnership entailed the clear domination of capitalism over slavery, the graft of one upon the other was nevertheless real and very firm. During ancient times the relationship between slavery and capital was the reverse. Explaining the existence of merchant's and usurer's capital in antiquity, Marx noted, "that so long as slavery is predominant, the capital relationship can only be sporadic and subordinate, never dominant."[57]

How different this was from the situation in America — there the planters could exist as planters and exploiters of slave labour only so long as they supplied the capitalist world market with staple commodities produced with the forced labour of African bonds-men. The conceptual "problem" is rooted in the error of equating the ancient slave mode of production with modern slavery under capitalism. Still, as Marx said:

> this error is in no way greater than that of e.g. all philologists who speak of *capital* in antiquity, of Roman, Greek capitalists. This is only another way of expressing that labour in Rome and Greece was *free*, which these gentlemen would hardly wish to assert. The fact that we now not only call the plantation owners in America capitalists, but that they *are* capitalists, is based on their existence as anomalies within a world market based on free labour.[58]

With that understanding, we can safely draw a partial list of the rough analogies and similarities between the ancient slave mode of production and slavery within the U.S. social formation dominated by capitalism. We must be cautioned though that even the crudest comparisons immediately evoke the sharp differences between the two phenomena.

The well-being of the classical Greek *polis* and the mighty Roman empire was based on the merciless exploitation of slaves, whose numbers increased steadily over the centuries. The simple cooperative organization of slaves in workshops and on latifundia raised the productivity of labour. One of the chief features of the Greco-Roman economy was improved social division of labour which brought about the development of commodity production. Having stimulated the development of the productive forces, the slaveholding economy reversed its initial effect and began to act as a drag on the further progress of the productive forces. The slave in ancient times had no interest in the results of his labour, he did not strive to improve his tools or his skills, he could not be en-trusted with costly implements. Slaves were the basic productive force at that time, but the conditions under which they lived and worked were so inhuman that the death rate was staggering. The faster the economy developed, the greater the number of slaves

57. K. Marx, *Theories of Surplus Value*, Part III, p. 419.
58. K. Marx, *Grundrisse*, p. 412.

it employed; the more slaves, the more terrible the conditions under which they suffered. Thus, as the ancient slave system progressed and developed, it proceeded on an ever enlarging scale to destroy its own basic productive force.

Now if we look at a comparable period in the histroy of American slavery, near the end when the modern system of slavery was deep in its géneral crisis, i.e. the great cotton boom decade of the *1850s*, we also discern *deteriorating conditions for American slaves.* As the demand and the price for cotton-producing slaves soared, slaves definitely felt the squeeze. Relatively fewer slaves were allowed to live in the cities, or to work at non-productive urban service jobs. More slaves were driven out to work the fields, to plant, pick and cart cotton under back-breaking conditions. In the 1850s, slaves were given fewer opportunities to learn artisan skills, and in general, as the struggle against slavery mounted, the drive to terrorize the bondsmen swelled to a crescendo.

Ancient and modern slaves were alike in their desire not to break their backs for their masters. In both cases, despite draconic measures and all the devious schemes, the productivity of slave labour remained low. The advanced character of the productive forces under capitalism did assure the modern slave economy of relatively big gross output. But throughout antiquity the level of production as a whole remained very low. The slaveholders of antiquity tried complex systems of control and coercion, all of which raised the cost of production still higher. By the 3rd century A.D., the Roman slave state was in deep trouble. Great changes had taken place in the two basic antagonistic classes, the slaves and the slaveholders, and in the relationship between them. The negligible profits yielded by slave labour prompted owners to free their slaves in increasing numbers. Some masters arranged for their slaves to become *coloni* who worked small plots of the master's land with the master's tools for a share of the harvest. Other owners allowed their slaves to use some of their property on condition that the slaves surrender part of their profits to the master. Late Roman slaveholders were thus forced to abstain from open coercion in order to give the slave some kind of incentive to increase production.

Nothing comparable ever occurred under U.S. slavery with regard to manumission, because slavery was most profitable in the 19th century towards its end. But there was an arrangement whereby some slaveholders in the South allotted slaves patches of land ranging up to a few acres for a family on which they were allowed to raise minor crops of their own, for which the owner paid cash, or which could be exchanged for commodities of personal consumption. This was a scheme to raise the productivity of slave labour. In some cases this was designed as a cheap supplement to meagre slave rations. Some owners used this arrangement as a device to get the slaves to bear part of the cost of their means of subsistence with their own after-hours labour, thus lowering the value of slave labour power even further. This was also a means of tiding over bad times when the master distributed no rations whatsoever.

In one of the most subtle passages on the subject in *Capital*, Marx compares and contrasts ancient and modern slavery:

In the slave system, the money-capital invested in the purchase of labour-power plays the role of the money-form of the fixed capital, which is but gradually replaced as the active period of the slave's life expires. Among the Athenians therefore the gain realized by a slave owner directly through the industrial employment of his slave, or indirectly by hiring him out to other industrial employers (e.g., for mining) was regarded merely as interest (plus depreciation allowance) on the advanced money capital, just as the industrial capitalist under capitalist production places a portion of the surplus-value plus the depreciation of his fixed capital to the account of interest and replacement of his fixed capital. This is also the rule with capitalists offering fixed capital (houses, machinery, etc.) for rent. Mere household slaves, whether they perform necessary services or are kept as luxuries for show, are not considered here. They correspond to the modern servant class. But the slave system too — so long as it is the dominant form of productive labour in agriculture, manufacture, navigation, etc., as it was in the advanced states of Greece and Rome — preserves an element of natural economy. The slave market maintains its supply of the commodity labour-power by war, piracy, etc., and this rapine is not promoted by a process of circulation, but by the actual appropriation of the labour-power of others by direct physical compulsion. Even in the United States, after the conversion of the buffer territory between the wage-labour states of the North and the slavery states of the South into a slave-breeding region for the South, where the slave thrown on the market thus became himself an element of the annual reproduction, this did not suffice for a long time, so that the African slave trade was continued as long as possible to satisfy the market.[59]

59. Vol. II, pp. 478-479.

The ancient slave mode of production also differed from modern slavery under capitalism in knowing no *economic* crises. "Nor have we heard that the ancients with the slave production ever knew crisis, although individual producers among the ancients too, did go bankrupt," observed Marx.[60] I do not mean that the ancient slave mode of production suffered no catastrophes, only that those catastrophes were caused by *non-economic* forces, by social and natural calamities, rather than by economic crises. Upheavals in economic life were frequent in antiquity, but a crisis of overproduction was an impossibility under the ancient slave mode of production. Floods, droughts, bloody wars, earthquakes and epidemics ravaged entire countries condemning the populations to starvation and death. But these disasters differed fundamentally from the perturbations of the world capitalist market, the first major blast of which began in England in 1825, and was felt in the slave South in 1826. The capitalist crisis of 1836 spread to the United States and caused suffering in 1837. Following the hard years of the early and middle 1840s, the crisis of 1848-1849 engulfed the slave system of planter economy, as did the economic crisis of 1857.

Natural calamities aggravated the distress brought on by these *over-production crises* peculiar to capitalism.

As far as the connection between the ideologies secreted by the ancient and modern slave societies is concerned, I have indicated elsewhere[61] that by a kind of historical "natural selection", the ruling class of a more advanced society may select and propagate an ideology first formulated by the rulers of a previous class society which has ceased to exist. A feeling was nourished in ancient slave society that physical labour was degrading, that it was unworthy of a free man. Black slavery in America 1500 years later brought about a resurgence and reinforcement of that prejudice, but now on the basis of *white racist* contempt for "nigger's work", and manual labour in general came to be considered beneath the dignity of a white person — the saying "work like a nigger" had deep meaning in capitalism's slave system.

60. K. Marx, *Theories of Surplus Value*, Part II, pp. 502-503.
61. See C.J. Munford, "Ideology, Racist Mystification and America" in *Revolutionary World: An International Journal of Philosophy*, Vol. 17/18, 1976, pp. 57-85.

*

Conceived in the womb of capitalist society at its simple coop-eration and manufactory stages, modern slavery had no power to alter dominant capitalist social relations of production. On the contrary, insofar as the African slave trade and the exploitation of slave labour created and concentrated wealth in the hands of a few, modern slavery helped increase the number of capitalists and fostered the growth of the capitalist economy and the capitalist spirit. Those bourgeois historians are mistaken who describe slavery in the South as a pre-capitalist system unrelated or diametrically opposed to capitalist relations of production. Capitalism replaced the land-bound serfs of Europe with free wage labour marketable as a commodity. At the same time capitalism did not hesitate to employ slaves on its colonial plantations in America to produce trading goods for the expanding capitalist world market. Nothing is chemically pure in history. But economic laws assert themselves in the long run. Next to the actual mode of production they are the most crucial factor in changing the social structure. In the long run, neither the capitalist factory owner nor the farmer had any use of slaves. The more modern large scale machine production developed, the more it felt tied down by the anachronism of slavery, especially within the national confines of the U.S. From a stimulating agent, slavery was transformed into a factor hindering by forced under-consumption and irrational application of labour power the *sine qua non* of modern capitalist production — the market.

* * *

Chapter 2

SERVICE STRATA, PROLETARIANS AND LUMPEN-PROLETARIANS: EXPLORATIONS IN THE HISTORY OF BLACK SOCIAL STRUCTURE, 1865-1970[1]

There is growing realization among American Blacks that Marxism-Leninism provides humanity with universal principles of social transformation. Marxism-Leninism is a particularly powerful guide in studying the significance of the contemporary social structure of the Black community, as well as in examining the history of its emergence.

Now two sets of phenomena must be seen in relation if we are to comprehend the crisis now confronting Black America: the trend of the U.S. economy, and the Black community's social structure.

In any economy a basic sector is farming, the productive activity which produces the food needed to sustain life and many raw materials for industry. Another basic sector is industry. The "tertiary sector" includes all "service" activities from haircuts to advertising. It is the latter sector that is growing at such a rapid rate in the U.S. economy under the influence of automation and cybernation multiplying non-manual, intellectual or semi-intellectual occupations for white people, and condemning more and more Blacks to permanent unemployment. The technical transformation entailed in automation and cybernation tends to reduce the share of tasks of execution in industry in comparison to jobs of supervision and control. The increasing automation of the mechanisms of manufacture and transformation creates such conditions that some industrial employees are becoming more concerned with conceiving, receiving and transmitting orders than with actually

1. This essay was originally written in 1969-70 and published under the title "Social Structure and Black Revolution" in *The Black Scholar*, Volume 4, Number 3, November-December 1972. It has been revised and corrected.

handling tools and materials. The relative weight of old-type operative jobs is diminishing in certain lines of production. The resulting expansion of the "tertiary sector" fulfills an extremely important social function in the American imperialist system of domination. The constant expansion in the number of "white collar" positions[2] in the tertiary sector is the indispensable condition for the continued lower rate of unemployment among white workers than among Black workers who form the main pool of capitalism's reserve army of labour. This has been so at least since the interruption in the flow of European immigration at the outbreak of the First World War — an event that occurred roughly simultaneously with the rise to hegemony of U.S. imperialism.

*

The social hierarchy in contemporary Black America presents the following spectacle. At the top sits a tiny "service stratum" which can hardly be said to constitute more than 6.2% of the total Black population. The service stratum is composed of persons who have served white America and the Black community in functions traditionally open or reserved to Blacks since the beginning of slavery — clergy, entertainers, sportsmen, professionals, teachers, etc. Existing above, alongside, and often intermingled with the service stratum is the minuscule Black bourgeoisie, the traditional Black "business community" — in both South and North. Its history is old, going back to such eminently bourgeois mutual aid associations as Richard Allen's and Absolom Jones' Free African Society of 1787 which laid the foundations for some of the early Black banks and insurance companies. From the outset its business activities were restricted to marginal segments of the segregated southern economy. This handful of bankers, insurance men, big farmers, publishers, undertakers, etc. were dependent on Jim Crow segregation.

In the course of the last fifty years, however, the southern focus

2. This can be gauged in the twelve million increase in the total number of employed "white-collar" workers, i.e. 81 per cent growth during the years from the outbreak of the Second World War through the second Eisenhower administration, in comparison to a 37 per cent increase in the total employed labour force.

of the Black "business community" has been altered slightly by the fact that in the ghettos a small stratum has sprung up composed of persons who migrated early, arrived in the inner-city first, and were able to acquire small money reserves. Today they appear in the guise of retail traders, proprietors of the ghetto's ubiquitous employment agencies, morticians, beauticians, small bankers, insurance men and manufacturers, and landlords who rent lodgings to other Blacks. Their small weight in the Black community can be gauged from the fact that even in New York City Black merchants constitute no more than 1.2% of all Black residents. There is also a handful of newly-hatched "Black capitalists" who appeared in the 1960s. They are a tiny excrescence on the steadfastly traditional Black bourgeoisie. This group of "entrepreneurs", i.e. stockholding Black vice-presidents and agents of white corporations and white-subsidized Black phantom enterprises, is the class source of accommodationist, conformist, cultural nationalist ideology.[3]

*

Next in rank in the Black community comes a motley group of "employees" and their families that can for the sake of convenience be designated *middle families* until a more descriptive term is found. The heads and other members of Black middle families cling tenaciously to regular, but precarious employment. The very fact of regular employment in a community plagued by joblessness gives them a modicum of prestige. Further prestige is derived from the kind of jobs held by middle families. In the parochial, deprived atmosphere of the ghetto post office jobs, municipal, state and federal positions and civilian and military personnel in the armed services are not only considered the sign of hard work and luck, they command respect.

In the social and political behaviour of this stratum there is an analogy of sorts with the neuroses of the classic petty bourgeoisie. The collective mentality of the middle families is sometimes characterized by a fear of being *déclassé*, i.e. of losing social position, coming down in the world. The growing menace of

3. Cultural nationalism is here defined as a fusion of the economic goals of "Black capitalism" with a utopian "extraterritorial cultural-national autonomy".

permanent unemployment caused by "rationalization", automation, or "modernization" threatens thousands of middle families with sudden fall into the vast army of unemployed and people on welfare considered socially inferior. Well-established in their respective cities in most cases, and intending to remain fixed in residence, middle families are immensely proud of possessing a house. They often use the combined salaries of both working spouses to purchase a home on credit although the undertaking means exorbitant monthly payments. This group of "responsible Negro homeowners", beloved of the white monopoly press, leans toward petty bourgeois social values and moral prescriptions borrowed from white Protestant lower middle class Anglo-Saxons.

There are many fewer "broken homes" among middle families than within the Black community's lower social strata. Middle families pressure their offspring to avail themselves of whatever meagre opportunities monopoly capitalism allows for upward social mobility and most members of this class have a primary education, while a number even succeed in completing high school and college. Prisoners of a basic social ambiguity, middle families shy away from Black political movements that are branded "extremist" by the white press. In 1962 the middle families amounted to no more than 6.5% of the Black community. The watchword of this stratum is caution, its style of life is social mimesis.

*

The same year the U.S. Department of Labour — like all agencies of the U.S. imperialist government a prejudiced and unreliable source — published figures that suggest that the Black *proletariat* constitutes either 10.2% or 33.7% of the total Black national population, according to the occupational categories included in the estimate. Most Black industrial workers are relegated to the cruder tasks and are subject to systematic speedup and compulsory overtime, but the proletariat does number in its ranks a few skilled artisans and some industrial workers with seniority rights. The bulk of the proletariat is concentrated in the six major urban industrial agglomerates of the United States. A highly productive (i.e. super-exploited) segment is that employed in the automotive industry, and also in the construction of aircraft on the West Coast.

The bottom of the social pyramid is occupied by a huge, amorphous, ill-defined *semi-proletariat*, and an already large and growing *lumpenproletariat*. The semi-proletariat can be defined provisionally as that segment of Black America which, like the proletariat, is reduced to selling manual labour power in order to live, but is given work only very irregularly, either seasonal or during periods of economic expansion or "boom", or as an auxiliary, "emergency" or substitute work force during "labour-management disputes". It is the main target of the periodic layoffs that have taken place in the recession-plagued post-World War II U.S. economy. The semi-proletariat has been estimated at 45.3% or 68.8% of the Black community depending on how the calculation is made, and the proportion of Black women in it has always been large, and continues to increase. The semi-proletariat obviously fluctuates between the proletariat and *lumpenproletariat*, but after a period of growth this group of workers will eventually diminish in number in the next two decades as unemployment of large sections of the Black populations becomes permanent and its members are relegated for life to capitalism's ghettoized "surplus" population.

The *lumpenproletariat* is composed in large part of permanently unemployed and "unemployable" school "drop-outs", transients, and recent arrivals in the ghetto. Many *lumpenproletarians* run afoul of capitalism's repressive laws and are arrested and imprisoned at one time or another. Youth is one of this stratum's most outstanding features. A sign of its social and political role in the domestic colony is the fact that the Black university students and radical intellectuals are often allied with the ghetto *lumpenproletariat* in aspirations, organizations and action.

The existence of classes is connected with particular, historic phases in the development of societies based on the exploitation of one human being by another. They reveal a social formation — stripped to its barest essence — in which a group of owners of the means of production, i.e. means to sustain life, stand opposed to people who have no accees to, or control of those same means of production. Violence is the cornerstone upon which this social relation is founded. For in order to maintain their dominance, the monopolizers of the means of production exercise dictatorship over the whole population, i.e. regardless of how it is disguised, a concentration of power exercised by a man or group in the interest of class over the whole. Thus material, economic conditions of life — relation to the means of production, place or role in social production — are the basis for class differences.

Whether their existence is recognized or not, the classes of Black America exist objectively. Classes are comprehensive social categories which influence all aspects of social life and individual behavior. Membership of social class in Black America is determined primarily by economic position. But social class is *expressed* in a peculiar style of life. Life-styles furnish fascinating, though non-essential criteria of class differentiation.[4]

*

The class structure of the contemporary Black community is complex. This complexity is heightened by the community's dispersion in countless urban ghettos. It was not always so. Social structure was relatively simple in the years from the end of slavery to the Great Migration (ca. 1865-1917). For all intents and purposes during the era of Jim Crow segregation in the post-Bellum South, Black America was a two-class community. In contrast to white America, Black America consisted of just two great classes — a numerically small *service stratum* and bourgeoisie and a large mass of more or less differentiated *agrarian peons.* The peons lived in family units which still bore remote traces of the African extended family, and which had partially assimilated the ethos of the European nuclear family — both elements badly scarred and distorted by the demoralizing centuries of slavery.

However, even before the abolition of slavery, the fringes of the population gradually felt the effect of class differentiation. Though it could have no essential social or economic impact in the racist context of the United States, nevertheless the simple legal distinction between Black slave and Black freedman was doubtless one of the earliest social differentiations among Black people. Members of the slave mass were also differentiated according to function or the roles they were called upon to play in economic service or public life; obviously the house servant and plantation artisan occupied — at least potentially — a higher rank in the embryonic Black social hierarchy than a field slave. In public life the Black

4. For a depiction of the ghetto *lumpenproletarian* style of life see "Life with Red Top", by R.L. Fair in Leroi Jones and Larry Neals, eds., *Black Fire: An Anthology of Afro-American Writing*, New York, 1969, pp. 500-509.

preacher or minister soon stood out from the mass of captive Africans.

The process of class differentiation accelerated in the peon society. But before and after the abolition of slavery these social rankings never acquired an objective economic footing independent of white control. It has *not* been demonstrated that when the great majority of American Blacks still lived as peons in the rural "Black Belt", the distinction between landowners — few in number and almost all smallholders — on one hand, and tenant farmers and landless peasants on the other (i.e., those who cultivated the land as sharecroppers, or in return for the payment of rent, or as simple agricultural labourers) made the former superior, and the latter inferior. The existence of landowning Black peasants in the South could not lead to the superimposition of a class of landed proprietors tending to form an indigenous or "national" aristocracy over a mass of peasants because all Black people — landowners and others — were subject to intense racial discrimination and oppression by the ruling class. At the same time, however, Jim Crow segregation fostered the growth of a small Black business stratum consisting of tiny banks and insurance companies, precarious commercial enterprises, fly-by-night small retailers, impecunious artisans, morticians, barbers and beauticians, etc. This "business community" was a parasitic intermediary or epiphenomenal exploiter operating in a marginal, closed residual field of economic activity. It fed on the demand of indebted peons for certain goods and services white exploiters considered beneath their dignity or not profitable enough to supply to Blacks.

*

The dissolution of the peon society, accelerated by the Great Migration which peaked in 1916 and 1917, had lasting effects on more than just the social hierarchy. The vast elimination of the Black farm population — no longer required by capitalist agriculture — continued so that since 1920 more than three-quarters of America's Black farm residents have been erased from the land. The Black family was affected. The shattering effect was so striking that some observers even overestimated the resulting disorganization. At the same time that he left peonage and Jim Crow terrorism, the Black migrant was often also leaving his family behind.

Upon reaching the North he lost himself in the slums of grey industrial cities where he became the prey of a whole crew of professional exploiters led on by slum landlords. Rents were ridiculously high. They were further skyrocketed by a kind of surtax on skin colour that ran from an extra five to twenty dollars per room. In such conditions few could afford immediately to house dependents. Tens of thousands of sharecroppers in search of better work and freedom, either in the cities of the South, or in the industrial centers of the North and West, were forced to abandon their families.

Many never returned home, forgetting first wives and children, only to take new wives and father other children. Others returned, or eventually "sent for" their families to join them in new abodes. However, even when the whole family tore up roots and followed its head, the cohabitation of several ghetto families together in a single apartment — made necessary by poverty and exorbitant rents — distorted family life. Family "breakdown" became commonplace in the aftermath of migration. Many households dissolved without legal divorce leaving some married Black women to live separate from their husbands. The resulting strained confusion has helped to blur the outlines between the ghetto's classes and adds to a picture of already bewildering inter-strata mobility at the lower levels. The blame for this attack on the Black family rests solely with U.S. monopoly capital.

The contradiction between the Black bourgeoisie and the popular masses had its historical origins and its social and economic foundation in slavery. "House niggers" were frequently related by blood to their masters. They formed a privileged caste in comparison with the great mass of field slaves. Quite a few were manumitted, joining the class of "freedmen". Once set free, they benefited from a legal advantage which allowed them to play a leading role in the political life of the Black community in the twenty years before the outbreak of the Civil War. Freedmen were in the vanguard of the struggle for the *legal* abolition of chattel slavery. Prominence led to a desire for acceptance in "white society" and a share in the political and economic power monopolized by whites. The response to this "impertinence" was a violent slap in the face by a surly and racist white America. Disappointed and chagrined, the nascent Black bourgeosie was left with no other recourse but to enter an alliance with the Black slave masses who expressed their opposition to slavery and racist oppression in a blunt, physical manner, i.e. in bloody slave uprisings and wholesale escape.

But the bourgeoisified wing of the service stratum remained equivocal toward the popular masses. It defended itself from the egalitarianism implied in the emancipation of all Black people from chattel slavery by demanding privileges and insisting that it constituted a "better class". Deprived of house servant status, their pretensions were now based on the caste of colour, i.e. on whiter hues of skin. The lighter complexions sported by a segment of the service stratum had been created over the centuries against the wills of helpless Black women forced to submit to systematic rape by white slavers. Nonetheless, the service stratum sometimes boasted that they had become the most mixed race in the world. Until recently the service stratum arranged itself in a hierarchy for social honour and distinction on the basis of colour, those of darker hued skins at the bottom of the pyramid and those "favoured" by light tinted shades occupying superior positions.

*

The only factor to effectively modify or temper this rigid colour hierarchy was the acquisition of substantial amounts of money. Ready cash was the means of rapid upward social mobility for dark complexioned insurance men, gamblers, policy makers and morticians whose dark skins would have otherwise disqualified them. The colour-caste barriers around and within the service stratum could be penetrated, dented, loosened by wealth. However, especially in the South, "jumped up" dark skinned businessmen bent over backwards to marry — an arrangement often tantamount to purchase — light skinned mulatto, quadroon, or octoroon women. Certain New Orleans families almost specialized in the rearing of near-white girls eagerly courted by "successful" darker hued businessmen and professionals, i.e. doctors, clergymen, lawyers and educators at the "Negro" colleges of the South. In the rigidly segregated South the light skinned Black socialities approximated or served as substitutes for white women. Having internalized racist esthetic standards along with other bourgeois values, some men regarded a light complexioned wife as coming as near as possible to that unattainable symbol of prestige — the white wife.

Though exceptional, later on with the shift of a large part of this class to the North and West, fair skinned Black women at times felt threatened by the competition of *bona fide* white women who, in the new urban setting, for the first time became accessible to Black men. The hostility of these daughters of the service stratum was aimed at a legal miscegenation that meant the loss of affluent potential Black mates to white women. Ironically, this hostility to legal miscegenation came from women whose own light complexions show their own ancestry of illicit miscegenation involving the coupling of white men and enslaved and empeonaged Black women.

The service stratum penchant for aping "white society" and inventing and multiplying fine distinctions based on colour caste was compounded by a mentality marked by extreme caution in the fact of oppression and acceptance of the racist ideology of which they are the victims along with other Blacks. The degree to which service stratum youth — and some raised in middle families — are influenced by self-hatred is indicated in the words of Kenneth Clark:

> They are clean, they dress well, they speak well, they strive very hard to make good grades in school and to get a good education. They dedicate their lives to the task of becoming walking refutations of negative racial stereotypes. They are the opposite of the flamboyantly rebellious ghetto youth, more likely to withdraw passively and seek to repress any sign of hostility. Many express a subtle form of self and group hatred by denying awareness of any racial problems, or even by interpreting racial discrimination as an understandable response to the uncouth 'lower class' street Negro.[5]

As the offensive of U.S. monopoly capital grew in strength and spread its tentacles horizontally and vertically through the economy, the petty "Black capitalism" that survived the transition from the segregated peon South to the proletarianized urban ghetto was routed on all fronts. The number of Black-owned restaurants declined by one-third in the short ten-year span from 1950 to 1960. Even according to the Johnson Publishing Com-

---

5. "The Social Dynamics of the Ghetto" in R.P. Young, ed., *Roots of Rebellion: The Evolution of Black Politics and Protest Since World War II*, New York, Evanston and London, 1970, p. 119.

pany's equivocal figures,[6] the further accumulation of capital in fewer and fewer white hands resulted in nearly a twenty-five per cent decline in the number of Black businessmen — from 42,500 to 32,400 in the same period. Those Black businesses still viable are restricted to marginal segments of the economy — in personal services, such as barber and beauty shops and funeral parlors, transportation and retail trade (though the latter is beating a hasty retreat before the advances of white-owned chain stores and supermarkets).

In New York City in the mid 1960s the service stratum's largest contingent consisted of the liberal professions, 31,000 strong — physicians, dentists, lawyers, university professors. That group, swelled by 15,000 to 16,000 "managers and directors", all told amounted to no more than four and a half per cent of Gotham's total Black populace. The only other contingents were a few businessmen, bankers, insurance agents, merchants, public works contractors and Black police officers. The relatively large number of wealthy morticians deserves special mention. Black undertakers take advantage of what seems to be a survival in the collective mind of a traditional concern for the ritual of interment and sumptuous festivities inherited from Africa. They also profit from the monstrous rip-off the "burial industry" perpetrates in both Black and white communities in this country. Throughout the country the service stratum has also shown a predilection for the purchase of real estate, and consequently owns some of the ghetto's slum tenements in which lower income Blacks must seek shelter at exorbitant prices.

*

The Black bourgeoisie enriches itself by catering to the needs of the downtrodden captive clientele contemptuously thrown to it by white prejudice and disdain. Therefore it exists only as a function of the Black popular masses, and only under the patronage, and in the service of white monopoly lords. It is trapped on a social treadmill, having to exert ever greater efforts just to maintain the same relative positions — Black businessmen and professionals are dependent upon other Blacks and can hope to increase

6. See *The Negro Handbook*, Chicago, 1966.

their profits and earnings only if the economic condition of the Black working classes does not worsen. They owe their positions and the degree to which they are tolerated by big business to the buying power of the Black community. Needless to say, that purchasing power suffers a negative jolt each time the over-production crises endemic to capitalism swell the already huge army of Black unemployed workers.

In politics the Black service stratum gives financial support to the Church, the Democratic Party, Urban League, Southern Christian Leadership Conference, and NAACP.[7] In fact, its alliance with the Black popular masses is cautious and lasts only as long as it is able to monopolize the leadership of the "Negro movement", elect "moderate" mayors, sheriffs, Congressmen and judges, act as spokesman for the whole Black community, control and dampen the revolutionary ardour of the working class, and keep the Black liberation movement within boundaries that do no harm to capitalist ideals. The moment the struggle threatens to become revolutionary the bourgeoisie drops its alliance with the masses like a hot potato, makes deals with white ruling circles, vociferously protests its loyalty and demands the maintenance of "law and order". The support voiced for Zionist Israel by the A. Philip Randolph Institute in contempt of the oppressed people of Palestine is a fair measure of the political attitude of the whole service stratum.

*

In a profound sense the roles and historical mission of Black America's popular masses — middle families, proletariat, semiproletariat and *lumpenproletariat* — are at once simpler and more complicated than that of the service stratum.

It has already been pointed out that the middle families share aspects of the service stratum's psychological and political schizophrenia — a schizophrenia caused by social pretensions and fear of

7. The oldest of the three organizations, the NAACP, represents the social interests of the *traditional* service stratum and the Black bourgeoisie. Since it is a class organ for a long time it has been confined to an "elite" of leaders who in more than half the instances across the country are Black clergymen. Hence in the seventeen years from 1946 to 1963 the organization lost some sixty thousand members.

social demotion. Holding down jobs threatened by all forms of "rationalization" from data-processing systems to more efficient office machinery, objective life conditions condemn middle families to administer the very government system that oppresses them. The civilian work force of the federal government — that arch agent of white supremacy — is noted for its relatively heavy concentration of Blacks. Middle families draw a large part of their economic substance from low level and low paying jobs in the federal government bureaucracy. They staff the Government Printing Office, the Department of Health, Education and Welfare, the Federal Services Administration, the Department of Labor, the Veterans Administration, and the clerical sections of Army and Navy branch offices in places like Cleveland. Black faces among the ranks of the U.S. armed forces are by no means an uncommon sight.

The condition of the large, amorphous semi-proletariat is even more bewildering. Everything, its history, collective mentality and present living conditions, hangs the semi-proletariat in dizzy suspension between the proletariat on one hand and the *lumpenproletariat* on othe the other. Black semi-proletarians are concentrated in urban ghettos. Their numbers are legion. When they are lucky enough to be employed, semi-proletarians are garbage collectors, street cleaners, elevator operators, manual labourers. These Blacks are paid wages well below those paid to whites for the same tasks with the gap increasing, growing by seven per cent in the twelve years from 1951 to 1963. In addition, the semi-proletariat — more than any other class in Black America — lacks socio-economic unity, for in addition to the large mass of urban manual labourers, domestic servants and service workers, it still comprises, in the South, a substantial rural contingent of agricultural wage earners, sharecroppers, small farmers, and domestic servants.

*

The Black proletariat requires closer analysis. It has played a crucial role in the historical development of Black America, and its political mood is vital.

In 1890, at the height of the era of agrarian peonage, ninety per cent of toiling Blacks worked in agriculture and in the tertiary sector of the U.S. economy as agricultural producers and domestic and personal service labourers. Fifty years later, migration, urbanization and proletarianization had dramatically reduced the percentage of Blacks in farming and domestic and personal service by forty-five per cent. As early as 1917 — the year of the October Revolution which ushered in a new era in human history — the Great Migration in America had progressed to the point where W.E.B. DuBois could talk of "teeming thousands, if not millions, of Black proletarians" concentrated in urban centers. Thirty years before, the only large class in the Black community were the comparatively dispersed and often isolated peons of the rural towns, villages, hamlets and back-country farmsteads of the old South and Southwest. Thus the class composition of Black America was completely transformed in the generations from 1890 to 1940. The urban proletariat became the *decisive class* in the Black community ousting agrarian peons, most of whom, either personally or in the persons of their children, donned a new social guise by deserting the farms and plantations for the factories, slums and ghettos of the cities. That is, when they were lucky enough to find factory jobs replacing former European immigrants.

However, Blacks were employed mostly as private household workers, manual labourers, farm hands, street cleaners, garbage collectors and other service workers. At the same time mechanized industrial production began to make inroads resulting in stagnation of the ratio of technical workers in the Black population. This predicament is admitted even by bourgeois observers. For instance, based on the assumption that technical and "kindred" workers were to continue to increase at the 1940-1960 rate, Leonard Bloom and Norval Glenn admit that "it would not be for 350 years after 1960 (until the year 2490) that proportional representation would be attained.[8] The overwhelming majority of gainfully employed Blacks in the United States are semi-proletarians and proletarians.

*

Today Blacks are over-represented as mail-carriers, postal clerks, social, welfare, and recreation workers. All occupation of a comprehensive list of forty-seven types of professional and non-profes-

8. "Occupation and Income", in *Roots of Rebellion*, p. 76.

sional, skilled and unskilled employment ranging from electrical and electronics technicians to college professors and instructors to farm hands and wage earners gives incontrovertible proof that Black men — and not just proletarians and semi-proletarians — are paid less than white men for the same amount and type of surplus value appropriated. Racial discrimination has ever remained a mode of exploitation in the United States. When, at terrible cost in effort and emotional stress, Blacks acquired the education and training allegedly requisite to the procurement of employment and occupational upgrading, it was to no avail. The occupational advances of Black proletarians in the last forty years were largely into "intermediate-level" jobs scheduled for elimination by mechanization and automation. The clerical appointments which were tickets to middle family status for many men and women in the 1960s are being made obsolete by electronic data-processing systems. As unemployment swells in the coming decade, more and more Blacks will find it increasingly difficult to get and keep jobs.

This threat to their jobs generates a state of insecurity which influences the attitudes and reactions of workers. In addition, the proletarian is constantly threatened by the morrow. Compelled to live from day to day, week to week, solely on his inadequate earnings, he is ordinarly unable to establish any financial reserve, build any real savings. With each passing day his fragile equilibrium is more and more jeopardized by the progress of the technological revolution now used as a weapon of intimidation by white bosses who can draw on an expanding "reserve" of Black unemployed or "laid-off" labourers. The menace of being "laid off" or fired outright (or marked for "retraining") hangs over his head like the executioner's blade. Any untoward, militant or "uncooperative" action on his part may upset the delicate balance and he and his family are lost. His only hope is unity with other workers and a united, militant fight-back against monopoly capital.

The *lumpenproletariat* does not work because it is kept from working. It does not work because it has been deprived of the opportunity, so it hustles and "scams" for a living. In the past Black people were appropriated or annexed physically by white slaveholders. Now exclusion from the employed industrial proletariat and *lumpenproletarianization* of Blacks is occurring with growing frequency in contemporary America. Among young men aged eighteen to twenty-four, the national rate of joblessness is several times as high for Blacks as for whites. In Black Harlem, for instance, decreases or stagnations are characteristic of industries in which more than 43 per cent of the labour force was employed in 1964, that is, transportation, communication and utilities, and wholesale and retail trades. The only jobs that will increase in number and availability for Blacks are appointments as cooks, servants, waitresses. But even here Blacks will face stronger competition from unskilled whites to procure these marginal jobs as automation continues in the farming and industrial sectors of the economy.

*

Indicative of the special surtax levied on Black women by the white ruling class is the fact that young Black males are often more unemployed than Black females. A Black woman historically was always able to find work as the domestic servant in a white household. The pattern of subordination and deliberate deprivation, and the trend of the economy are further revealed in the fact that younger Blacks are more likely to remain jobless than older ones. The youthful are the most poverty-stricken elements of Black America with destitution concentrated in families with two or more children and in families headed by young adults. Restriction to whites of the "privilege" of holding a job is now one of the chief modes of racial discrimination and a new stage in the developing history of U.S. imperialism.

Black youths are being idled by automated production and computers. But they are not *déclassé* or degenerate like the elements who, in America, have made their name notorious in the Mafia and trade union gangsterism. On the contrary, the restless brooding young *lumpenproletarians* who, in the words of Kenneth Clark, "cluster in the bars in winter and on stoops and corners in the summer"[9] are prisoners of the ghettos. The American Black ghetto *lumpenproletariat* and semi-proletariat are very young social strata in that they are relatively new arrivals in the city. *Lumpenproletarians* cherish recent and intimate relations with the agrarian peons of the South, they have close ties of kinship with the sharecroppers, cotton-pickers and starving smallholders described with

9. "The Social Dynamics of the Ghetto", in *Ibid.*, p. 99.

such force and feeling in the novels of Richard Wright. When they themselves have not "come North" or into the city from the "country", they are the children of those who have. Though many Black youths today are unable to recognize farm animals, the recent rural past has left a strong stamp on both the *lumpenproletariat* and the semi-proletariat: slavery and the frightful conditions of life in the terrorist South after Reconstruction made the great mass of Black peons *the most isolated social component in the Black community* — although it was then the vast majority of the Black population — as well as in the whole United States. Exactly those features that qualify as "national peculiarities and temperament" are most nourished in cultural isolation. However, the estrangement from the process of social production combined with too large a dose of the spontaneity peculiar to the class causes its political spokesmen to set hazy goals.

*

Given these circumstances only the proletariat can take the lead in the Black liberation movement. A prime strategic aim of the Black liberation movement in the United States is the formation of a broad popular coalition of Blacks and whites ready to confront monopoly. The proletariat and the revolutionaries who embody its aspirations must seek to unite all the popular social strata of the nation, and parties, political groups, organizations and individuals willing to accept and support this strategy. Hegemony must rest with the working class. It hardly need be said that leadership by the Black bourgeoisie is out of the question. Although individual revolutionaries have been known to spring from the service stratum, for the objective reasons outlined above this class is not consistent in its dedication to Black liberation.

* * *

65

Chapter 3

THE LUMPENPROLETARIAT REVISITED[1]

The Limits of "Lumpenization"

There is a definite scientific and technological revolution now underway in the United States. Many people cannot understand how it is connected with growing unemployment in the ghetto. Automation and cybernetics foster socialization of the process of production and further concentration of ownership of the means of production at a dizzying pace. The relationship between automation and cybernation and the role of the working class in the United States is even more difficult to grasp. Confusion about these phenomena has made the ultra-Left thesis that the lumpenproletariat has now become the vanguard of revolution popular. Nevertheless, it is the working class, not the lumpenproletariat, which has most to gain from the liquidation of the capitalist system. Most Blacks are working class people, more broadly, ninety-four per cent belong to the toiling masses. This truth is not popular with those forces in the Black community which have been lured by ultra-Left blandishments. Despite that we must proclaim it loud and clear. For the working class goes on and on. It is the most dynamic, the most concentrated, organized and disciplined class in Black America, in Spanish-speaking America, and in white America. In contrast, like the students and semi-intellectuals who purport to lead them, "lumpen" come and go, advancing and receding with the spasms of the capitalist economy and the fortunes of the class struggle.

What Eldridge Cleaver[2] and others who think along these lines

1. This study was originally published in *Political Affairs: Journal of Marxist Thought and Analysis*, Volume LIII, Numbers 5 and 6, May and June 1974.
2. See Eldridge Cleaver, "On Lumpen Ideology", in *The Black Scholar*, November-December 1972.

are unable to comprehend is that *living labour* is the vital agent in the productive forces. Under capitalist relations of production automation can never be more than partial. They cannot conceive that automation, and the mechanization of production in general, are designed primarily to speed up the rate at which surplus value is pumped out of living labour (i.e. variable capital) whose cost of reproduction (i.e. standard of living) is relatively cheapened. Over the long haul of the political struggle for power between the classes (and we must remember, as Lenin has advised us, that in a process of this kind twenty years are like one day), it is not the lumpenproletariat, but the class of wage earners, disciplined and united, which is singled out by the character of the social relations of production to play the crucial part in the revolutionary struggle. In the mid-nineteenth century, wage earners in the world numbered no more than ten million. At that time the overwhelming majority of American Blacks were still chattel slaves. By the turn of the century there were some thirty million workers in the world. But most Blacks still eked out a living in Southern agriculture under neo-slave, semi-peon conditions. Today the international army of workers encompasses hundreds of millions, and the majority of Afro-Americans hire their labour power out for wages. Who would claim the same stupendous rate of growth for Cleaver's "lumpen"?

Given the nature of capitalist relations of production, universal "lumpenization" envisaged by Cleaver and other ultra-Leftists is impossible. It is not even possible for all Blacks, Browns and other "third world" elements to be "lumpenized". The ultra-Left's theoretical grasp of the capitalist economy is simply not advanced enough for its pundits to realize this. It took someone with the genius of Karl Marx to first trace the limits of "lumpenization":

> Now, the concept of capital as a fetish reaches its height in interest-bearing capital, being a conception which attributes to the accumulated product of labour, and at that in the fixed form of money, the inherent secret power, as an automation, of creating surplus-value in geometrical progression ... We know, however, that in reality the preservation, and to that extent also the reproduction of the value of the products of past labour is *only* the result of the contact with living labour; and secondly, that the domination of the products of past labour over living surplus-labour lasts only as long as the relations of capital, which rest on those particular social relations in which past labour independently and overwhelmingly dominates over living labour.[3]

"A development of productive forces", teaches the founder of the science of revolution, "which would diminish the absolute number of labourers, i.e. enable the entire nation to accomplish its total production in a shorter time span, would cause a revolution, because it would put the bulk of the population out of the running."[4] So capitalism sets rigid limits to the mechanization of production and hence to the phenomenon of "lumpenization". Nevertheless, technological development has introduced automation and cybernation. Automation and cybernation, in turn, spur the growth of the number of Black and Latino hands eliminated from production. This has already passed the point where it could have been reversed by measures compatible with capitalism. The Black masses are hit hardest of all. But from the standpoint of the monopoly capitalist class, automation is an unprecedented success in imitating and replacing the skill of man-the-organism with the mechanistic complexities of the machine and, in doing so, in increasing the rate of relative surplus value.

In a public speech on free trade in Brussels on January 9, 1848, Marx showed that under capitalism workers are means of production which in the natural course of development of capital will be superseded in various occupational categories by less expensive means of production. In various occupational categories, but not in all. We can see this in the United States in the way unskilled and semiskilled Black and Brown workers are being done out of jobs by automation in some sectors of the economy while in others they are the victims of automation-derived speedups and intensification of labour. Marx warned workers not to forget that under capitalist exploitation there is no kind of manual labour *in principle* which may not one day be discharged and made superfluous by the progress of technology.[5]

> The very use of machinery historically presupposes .. superfluous hands. Only where there is a superfluity of labour force does machinery intervene to replace labour. Only in the imagination of the economists does it assist the individual labourer ... It does not enter in in order to replace scarce labour power, but rather to reduce the mass of labour available to the

3. *Capital*, Vol. III, pp. 390-391.
4. *Ibid.*, p. 258.
5. K. Marx and F. Engels, *Collected Works*, Vol. 6, p. 461.

quantity tailored [to capital's need — CJM]. Machinery is introduced only where a mass supply of labour is available.[6]

The Impact of Automation

It should be quite clear to us, therefore, that what the Black community is suffering is not a universal "lumpenization", but rather a process of *subproletarianization* in which Black workers are being thrown into the jobless pool to swell monopoly capital's reserve army of cheap labour.

Cybernetics creates a system of control and communications through electrically operated devices. Together with automation it has made a lot of industrial employees more concerned with conceiving, receiving and transmitting orders, and supervising serial production than with actually handling tools and materials. A word of caution, however: no matter how alike the principles of control and communication as they relate to the human brain and to electronic computers, the brain's operations and the physical processes that take place in "control systems" are not identical. *Man cannot be phased out.* That is merely a dream of bourgeois science fiction. A computer, like any tool, is nothing more than congealed labour, labour that has been objectified in the past, a means of production that has been appropriated as capital, as something privately owned, which, by its mastery over living labour, produces a value greater than its own value.

In any case, with automation and cybernation, constant capital (machinery, etc.) holdings can be further increased at the expense of variable capital (wages) in the organic composition of capital. The outlay for labour power sinks in relation to the outlay for capital goods. There is less need — relatively — for cheap labour in some branches of the economy and in some divisions at one and the same enterprise because unskilled muscle power is increasingly obsolete in certain phases of production. Consequently more and more Black and Brown workers are idled. For due to the racist character of capitalism, Blacks and Browns are forced to supply the bulk of cheap, unskilled labour in this country. In addition, they weigh disproportionately heavy in the unemployed reserve

6. K. Marx, *Grundrisse*, p. 589.

army of labour. Blacks are picked out by racial discrimination to stand in the economic wings and wait.

Bourgeois labour-management relations "experts" claimed in the 1950s, when automation and cybernation were catching on, that they would lighten labour and shorten working hours. Not so from the vantage point of twenty years later. Automation and cybernation have proved to be devices for speedup and intensification of the labour process. They have helped to corrode labour power. Their effect has been attrition of labour power resulting in greater mortality among workers. A report in the *Daily World* of 2 November 1972 disclosed that automation most often is a pressure force for greater tensions on the production line. It is a means to squeeze above-normal surplus value from assembly line workers. Speedup and intensification of labour are backed up with ingenious systems of premium time-wages. Again no one has written more eloquently and lucidly on this subject than Marx:

> As a result of the introduction of machinery, a mass of workers is constantly being thrown out of employment, a section of the population is thus made redundant; the surplus product therefore finds fresh labour for which it can be exchanged without any increase in population and without any need to extend the absolute working-time ... One portion of the old [variable] capital is converted into fixed capital, the other gives employment to fewer workers but extracts from them more surplus-value in relation to their number and in particular also more surplus product. The remaining ... [now unemployed workers — CJM] are material created for the purpose of capitalizing additional surplus product.[7]

Usually, only the sections of the assembly line where it pays to automate, are so automated. The speedier operation of the renovated section then sets the norm. It becomes the driving force and quota setter for workers on that line. In the meantime, many experienced workers on the conventional line are ousted and replaced by Blacks and Browns who, because of the race-class situation which prevails in this country, enjoy no seniority and are expected to submit to speedup, poor safety regulations and other devices of superexploitation. The corporations are amazingly consistent in throwing the big burden for speedup on young Black workers. This in turn explains the latter's recent struggles against

---

7. *Theories of Surplus Value*, Part III, pp. 242-243.

automated lines and for "humanization" of the shops in Detroit, in Mahwah, New Jersey and other locations where Blacks are a high percentage of the work force.

Black spokesmen justly talk a lot about the subhuman status to which our people are reduced. What does subhumanity in this particular vein actually mean? Subhumanity draws its full meaning from the *subproletarianization* we are describing — and its most ominous sense. A wage worker who becomes by definition unemployable in a given capitalist formation, or who is regarded as employable only at rates and under conditions worse than ordinarily obtained by employed labour is well on his way to being reduced to subhumanity. For him it becomes the norm for his real wages to be depressed to levels near to the physical minimum. Viewed in this light, we arrive at a statement of meaning of the term subhumanity which for the first time escapes the airy nothings of rhetoric. "By speeding up the supplanting of workers by machinery, and by creating wealth at one extreme and poverty at the other, the accumulation of capital also gives rise to what is called the 'reserve army of labour', to the 'relative surplus' of workers, or 'capitalist overpopulation', which assumes the most diverse forms and enables capital to expand production extremely rapidly."[8] Faced by these conditions ever since he escaped to the city from the old Jim Crow countryside, the Black wage labourer has always had to put up with worse working conditions and poorer wages than his white counterpart. Now with disheartening frequency he is being told that there are no jobs whatsoever for which he is deemed qualified.

This reduction to a status below levels acceptable to humanity would seem to be what Cleaver's rodomontade concerning the "lumpenization of humanity" is really about. But, like so many ultra-Leftists, Eldridge inhabits a topsy-turvy mental world in which mere words become sensate things and acquire a body and substance of their own. He manages to turn phenomena inside out and backwards. "The point", he writes, "is that the Lumpen, humanity itself, has been robbed of its social heritage by the concentration and centralization of technology."[9] Here the influence

8. V.I. Lenin, *Collected Works*, Volume 21, Moscow, 1964, p. 64.
9. "On Lumpen Ideology", p. 10.

of Herbert Marcuse is noticeable. For, like Cleaver, Marcuse's real bugaboo is the scientific and technological revolution. His real quarrel is with computers, not with the monopoly bourgeoisie. In this way the ground is prepared in the ultra-Left's hind-side-before political drama for the working class to surface on the stage of history as the hired auxiliaries of the repressive organs of the capitalist state, which guarantees continued exploitation of labour by capital. All of a sudden racists like "white hunter" Anthony Imperiale and the lynch mobs of skilled craft labour aristocrats who oppose Newark's Kawaida Tower housing project have become the whole working class. The metamorphosis is complete: the victims have become the villains, churlish slave drivers of themselves whom the avenging "lumpen" angels must smite before they smite the master.

The ravages of automated production which are relegating certain categories of workers to long-term unemployment and which increase the weight of the subproletariat in Black America struck Blacks very early. For some economic "obsolescence" began with the Great Depression. As technology evolved in the years from 1929 to 1949, occupation after occupation escaped the grasp of Blacks. An example is the railways where they had long been employed as steam engine stokers. Electric and diesel engines deprived them of these jobs. With each passing week, Black workers lose thousands of job possibilities. A seven-fold reduction has shrunk the number of Black railwaymen. In just a few short years, they diminished precipitously from 350,000 to fewer than 50,000. As unskilled and semiskilled occupations are phased out, so are Blacks.

Black wage earners are concentrated in semi-skilled and unskilled occupations. Employment in the auto industry, for one, is particularly sensitive to overproduction crises and to automation of sections of the production line. The impact of automation and factory closings in the 1960-1961 recession hit Detroit hard. The *New York Times* of March 5, 1961 reported thirty-nine per cent unemployment among Motown Blacks, nearly four in ten. The situation has not improved much since then. The auto industry was the most depressed sector of the national economy in the 1969-1970 recession. Thousands were laid off at year's end in 1973 under the pretext of the "energy crisis" while productivity and profits soared to unprecedented heights. By 1971 unemployment among America's youth in general had reached alarming proportions. Among young whites, 15.1 per cent were jobless, but, characteristically, the figure was a staggering 31.7 per cent among Black and other "third world" groups nationally.[10] In October 1972, 40 per cent of the unemployed and people on welfare were Black. The total number in Detroit either unemployed or on welfare was 250,000. In mid-August 1972, Black unemployment in the Motor City totalled 18.2 per cent of all Black residents, men, women and children.

Due to automation and foreign capitalist competition, made worse by the "runaway" tactics of U.S. supranational corporations, and due to factory shutdowns large numbers of Black so-called "terminal unemployed" have appeared. This is the latest euphemism to describe Black workers doomed to continuous unemployment for the rest of their lives, or prevented from ever entering the labour force. Obviously the latter are mostly youths. In 1970, one in five of the returning Black Vietnam veterans was without a job. It is even worse for Puerto Rican GIs. The trend toward "terminal unemployment" was not slowed by the Vietnamese war "boom".[11] Consequently the ghetto subproletariat grew in relation to the industrial workers in large industrial centers throughout the 1960s.

Let us not forget that machinery — the means of dispensing with living labour — is nothing more than accumulated congealed labour. Thus capital uses dead labour to turn living labour into social pariahs and zombies, into the living dead. The racist aspect of U.S. monopoly capital assures that the bulk of the living dead will be Afro-Americans, Chicanos and Puerto Ricans, Asian-Americans and Native Americans.

The Distinction Between Subproletariat and Lumpenproletariat

In the ghetto it has become increasingly difficult for some to distinguish between unemployed workers, permanently or long-

10. See 1972 *Joint Economic Report*, 92nd Congress of the United States, 2nd Session, March 23, 1972, p. 11.
11. See J.C. Leggett, *Class, Race and Labor: Working-Class Consciousness in Detroit*, New York, 1968, p. 60.

term unemployed and lumpenproletarians. In certain circles it is fashionable to twaddle on about the alleged growing gulf between relatively "well-to-do workers" with steady employment on one side, and poverty-stricken "street" and "welfare" people on the other. Besides highlighting an obvious disparity between a small, predominantly white, labour aristocracy and the Black popular masses, this observation has little relevance to the real situation in the ghetto. On the contrary, there we find less and less difference between subproletarians and impoverished Black industrial workers. However, there is much confusion concerning this phenomenon and many observers have fallen into the habit of mistaking the lumpenproletariat for the class of subproletarians.

Lines which divide classes, especially those which separate segments of the penurious popular masses, are never hard and impenetrable. Classes are not castes. For that reason, the ghetto subproletariat may appear to some to be something less than a class, to be nothing more than a large social collecting basin of class fractions, subclasses and disparate strata, an arbitrary abstraction without real foundation in the social relations of production. However, the subproletariat's lack of coherence is more apparent than real. Social relations of production in U.S. racist monopoly capitalism entail the existence of a ghetto subproletariat. It is one of the necessary conditions for the reproduction of capitalist relations in the United States. The sub-proletariat is a distinct social category with singular features and aspects. On the whole it is a wage labouring class, and not a class of "poverty pimps", lumpen and other parasites. What is peculiar about the subproletariat is that so many subproletarians spend more time hunting for work than actually producing surplus value. Thousands scrape by on make-work, thousands "hustle" and finagle, thousands are forced to live from handouts, thousands more are incarcerated in the ruling class's "correctional" institutions.

If we reduce the subproletariat to its social components or fractions, it would be seen to consist of 1) families on welfare; 2) unemployed youth, most of whom have no prospect of finding jobs; 3) political prisoners in the sense Angela Davis gives to that term; 4) "street people" (i.e. transients uprooted usually by economic need); 5) the whole ill-defined and ill-definable category called "hustlers"; 6) and lastly the true lumpenproletariat of petty criminals, prostitutes, junkies, "poverty pimps" and two-bit pushers. Migrant farm labourers — mostly Browns, but still Blacks in some instances — resemble urban subproletarians in political traits. It is clear that *the subproletariat is the concrete social form the vast reserve army of labour takes in the ghetto.*

When we consider the subproletariat, we are obviously dealing with a very differentiated group of people. One fraction of the group is not very like the other — at least not in life style, collective aspirations and political responses. In this respect there is a distant resemblance between it and the petty bourgeoisie. The sub-proletariat's boundaries are roomy enough to encompass social groups which appear to differ vastly in mentality, and which actually differ in life style.

Thus it is indeed crucial to distinguish between actual lumpenproletarians — prostitutes, hustlers, do-nothings, leeches, petty criminals, drug addicts, muggers, sexual perverts, and other so-called "declassed" elements (so-called because "declassed" elements fully reflect the class traits peculiar to the lumpenproletariat) — and welfare mothers, unemployed workers and decent youth who have never been employed through no fault of their own, but who would gladly work if given the chance.

"The 'dangerous class', the social scum, that passively rotting mass thrown off by the lowest layers of the old society, may, here and there, be swept into the movement by a proletarian revolution; its conditions of life, however, prepare it far more for the part of a bribed tool of reactionary intrigue." This sober judgment appears in the *Manifesto of the Communist Party*. Many events in the Black community in the last few years confirm it — everything from inability of lumpen elements to bear up under the pressure of long drawn-out, day to day political organization, to the rampage of hard drugs in the ghetto. However, this citation applies to the small lumpenproletariat and not to the bulk of subproletarians. Unlike the declassed elements to which Marx and Engels were referring, the majority of Black subproletarians are not the castoffs of an earlier, noncapitalist mode of production. They are the legitimate offspring of U.S. monopoly capitalism, wage workers whose cheap, unskilled and simple labour has been rendered superfluous by the development of the productive forces which, in certain branches of the economy, now require composite, relatively expert labour. Subproletarians are wage workers set aside for capital's future needs. The enlarged reproduction of monopoly capitalism, its advancement to putrefaction, coincided in this country with the shift of the Black masses from the rural "Black Belt" to urban ghettos. Since then, Black subproletarians have been held in *reserve*, as it were, as a vast reservoir of dirt cheap occasional labour power, to be dispensed with entirely when no longer needed, and repressed brutally whenever it gets out of line. Here we are distinguishing, with good purpose I trust, between full fledged workers and subproletarians. The former is defined as one who, with fair regularity, finds in the market a capitalist to purchase his labour power. Though there are those who insist on calling long-term unemployed and permanently "unemployable" Blacks proletarians, I believe it is more helpful to designate this segment of the popular masses as subproletarians. It only adds to the existing confusion to confound them *en masse* with the stable body of industrial workers.

Very many subproletarians are the sons and daughters of rural and southern parents drawn cityward and northward by the pressures of economic development and the lures of big capitalist industries. Many others are the permanently unemployed children of Black industrial workers or semiproletarians who have been living in urban ghettos for one or two generations. In the latter instance it is obvious that the subproletarianization of the off-spring of parents who held steady jobs represents *growing absolute impoverishment* of the Black masses. Welfare is the only means of keeping body and soul together for this segment of the community. In respect of the growing masses dependent on welfare handouts, Marx had this to say:

> The more extensive, finally, the Lazarus-layer of the working class and the industrial reserve army, the greater is official pauperism. *This is the absolute general law of capitalist accumulation* ... It establishes an accumulation of misery, corresponding with accumulation of capital. Accumulation of wealth at one pole is, therefore, at the same time accumulation of misery, agony of toil, slavery, ignorance, brutality, mental degradation at the opposite pole ...[12]

It seems safe to conclude then that the term *"revolutionary ghetto lumpenproletariat"* is misconceived and misleading. More than anything else it obscures that which is most vital — precisely the

12. *Capital*, Vol. I, pp. 644-645.

differentiation between the majority of deprived and potentially revolutionary subproletarians, and a small, declassed lumpen-proletariat. Henceforth, I propose that we use the term *ghetto subproletariat* to designate that amorphous class which occupies the bottom rung of the social ladder in the Black community.

*

Frantz Fanon contended that where the imperialists concentrate the economic and political life of a colony in the towns, large segments of the townspeople eventually draw "benefits" of one sort of another from the colonial character of the economy and society at large. In this way, not only the indigenous bourgeoisie and tribal aristocracy, but the popular masses as well are trans-formed into compradors, handmaidens of foreign monopolists. But, as recent reserach has shown, Fanon was wrong, and he did a grave injustice to the struggle of the African working class.[13] Nevertheless, Fanon's thesis has been widely disseminated and is now widely influential. He contended that the relatively small African working class is an artificial importation, a propped-up excrescence of colonialism which profits from the system. Thus he counted colonized workers among the privileged classes. This is the thesis which Cleaver and some Pan-Africanists have made their own and transposed to fit the American Black community.

Ironically this charge is now redounding against the "lumpen". By the same token that Cleaver's followers may argue that Black workers are "integrated" in the system, and that ordinary white workers have become second line cops, we may insist — with more justice — that the most degraded strata of the ghettos — Cleaver's precious "lumpen" — are living as parasites on the rest of the com-munity without furnishing, and without wanting to furnish, productive labour, pimping off poverty, so to speak. To push this one step further, we might even say that Black lumpenproletarians are "privileged", or at least "benefit" from the system because so many of them live from the proceeds of petty crime. Of course we realize how wrong it is to reason in this way. But merely by borrowing Cleaver's invective and shifting the direction in which it

13. See Jack Woddis, *New Theories of Revolution - A Commentary on the Views of Frantz Fanon, Regis Débray and Herbert Marcuse*, New York, 1972.

is aimed somewhat, we can argue that those who do not work yet are kept alive by mugging working women, pushing dope and running numbers are parasites, obviously not on the scale of the monopoly capitalists, but nevertheless parasites in the full sense of the word. Thieves, tramps, beggars, prostitutes, strongarm men, drug addicts and dope pushers, etc., are all declassed elements of capitalist society. It requires a peculiar mentality indeed to claim that these types are anything positive, that they are anything but a burden on the Black community, particularly on its toiling masses.

This brings us to the phenomenon of organized crime in the ghetto. Organized crime serves the racist capitalist regime both as a *"welfare"* system of sorts for the lumpenproletariat, and as a means of putting lumpenproletarians to work exploiting their own people for the benefit of the white *lumpenbourgeoisie*, the underworld fraction of the ruling monopoly bourgeoisie. The rackets, from pimping to numbers, from scabbing to dope pushing, all provide careers for the jobless. The fact that they line the pockets of the ghetto's *Super-Flies* lends an unhealthy prestige to organized crime in the eyes of ghetto youth. Some interpret it as a means of survival for persons who see no other way. Most of the revenue from the sale of drugs, from gambling, car theft, armed robbery, prostitution and pandering is siphoned off by the white lumpenbourgeoisie, by the gangland bosses. Black lumpenproletarians are left to do the dirty work, and for paltry returns. Organized crime leeches on the Black community. It breeds the "slick" "lumpen" who have caused so much headache for revolutionary movements among Black people.

Much ink has been spilled recently about the "subculture" of organized crime into which so many lumpenproletarians fall. It has its own little hierarchy which parallels the structure of class inter-relationships in the larger society. The "criminal community's" social hierarchy thus overlaps conventional American race-class lines locking Black and white criminals together in a peculiar relationship.

Perched atop the pyramid of organized crime we find the lily-white *lumpenbourgeoisie*. Over the years these lords of gangland have developed a unique set of "social-estate" and political organizations in the form of secret societies and "professional" associations. Individual lumpenbourgeois combine in Mafia associations and La Cosa Nostra "families". However, the group as a whole is merely one fraction of the monopoly capitalist class. The fact that it is a social stratum "on-the-make", and that it is the most unconventional fraction of the monopoly bourgeoisie, does not alter its class character.

One step down in the criminal hierarchy sits the *Black lumpen petty bourgeoisie*. It is squeezed in the intermediate realm between the lumpenbourgeoisie on one side and the Black lumpenproletariat on the other. Typically, the lumpen petty bourgeois pass for the "big shots" of crime among Black people. Actually they appear to be big fish only because the pond in which they swim is economically small. Lumpen petty bourgeois are nothing more than deputized middlemen, supervisors of the criminal traffic on behalf of the big bosses, commissioned exploiters who act only at the behest of the white lumpenbourgeoisie. Because of their money lumpen petty bourgeois often move up into the Black "bourgeoisie" and are assimilated.

Marching in the rear come the foot soldiers of organized crime in the ghetto — the *lumpenproletarians*, the hustlers and petty criminals who serve their petty bourgeois straw bosses and their bourgeois overlords, small time pimps and prostitutes, rank-and-file policy runners, "grass-roots" pushers and addicts, small-time gamblers and crapshooters, alcoholics, muggers, thieves, cut-throats, all sorts of "two-bit" police spies, agents, infiltrators and informers. The bubbling, churning dregs of society.

Many, if not most, lumpenproletarians are irredeemably apolitical. A lot are downright counter-revolutionary. The *immediate* motivations for the lumpenproletarian's counter-revolutionary doings are usually unrestrained egoism and overriding devotion to direct, exciting and immediate pleasure. Admittedly, passing pleasures are a prominent concern also for the popular masses. The difficult, deprived conditions under which most Black people live dictate concern for immediate gratification. But the bulk of the Black masses are not cut-throat or nearly so egoistic in their pursuit of pleasures as lumpenproletarians.

The characters of the ghetto's underworld, the lumpen petty bourgeois distributor of drugs as well as the petty hood and the hustler, all accept the basic legitimacy of racist capitalist society. The hardened assassin, the "strung-out" junkie, the violent street-fighter, usually without being aware of doing so, all bow down

79

before the white monopoly capitalist's "divine" right to rule. They acquiesce in the basic assumptions and give tacit consent to the power relations upon which monopoly capitalist domination is based. Vehement denials are no counterweight to objective facts. When it comes to fighting effectively for the overthrow of capitalist relations of production even the "baddest dudes" are not so bad. This does not mean that Black lumpenproletarians are "nice", well-behaved, "proper" people who will shy away from felonious transgressions, from breaking the "white man's law". Lumpenproletarians break the law every day. But — paradox — they break bourgeois laws while affirming capitalist morality.

Events have proved that very few lumpenproletarians ever rise above individual protests against the system which oppresses and declasses them. Flying in the face of the legal code, most of them objectively uphold and accept the ultimate legitimacy of capitalist law. That is why, unlike revolutionaries, they are tolerated by the authorities. Not just tolerated, for, on the whole, they are *useful* to the regime.

Mugging, robbery, murder and rape may have made some streets unsafe for "law abiding" Americans, but these infringements represent no essential danger to "law and order", for the jungle code they impose is a capitalist code. And "slick lumpen" are would-be entrepreneurs-in-germ. Rough and ready pillars of the system of oppression and exploitation, underworld elements are adept at capitalist techniques and methods which predominated in a bygone period in this country's history. Both the white lumpen-bourgeoisie and the Black lumpen petty bourgeoisie are proficient in arts which served the whole capitalist class well in the days of its infancy and adolescence, methods and techniques which suited bourgeois society and tastes perfectly in capitalism's competitive period, and during the era of J.D. Rockefeller Sr., J.P. Morgan and other "robber barons". However, these methods have since been declared illegitimate and "uncivilized" by today's "respectable" financial oligarchs, the children and grandchildren of the old robber barons. To the extent that they succeed in reviving the rough and ready methods of earlier capitalist accumulation in a moribund imperialist society, the underworld, white and Black, is at once utterly reactionary and right up-to-date. Organized crime serves a "useful" purpose in racist capitalist America, organizing the production of goods and providing services to supply the corrupt

80

"needs" of a degenerating society. Criminal enterprise generates lucrative surplus profit for monopoly capital. The conventional "business community" would be unthinkable without its unconventional counterpart in the form of crime czars, dope peddlers, prostitutes and killers-for-hire.

However, a word of caution. We must be very careful not to confuse professional criminals with the many thousands of ghetto youths harried and hunted by the police for no other reasons than for being poor and nonwhite. For instance, fifty per cent of all Black youths born in Philadelphia are arrested on trumped-up charges at least once before the age of nineteen. These are obviously not hardened criminals. They are the child-victims of the system. Per capita there are more heroin addicts, more drug-ruined young men and women among Blacks than among any other group. Many of these youthful victims of repression are untutored, spontaneous rebels against racism and capitalism. They would tear down the system, not turn it to their own advantage like the "slick lumpen". Angela Davis has this to say about crimes committed by this kind of person: "Spontaneously produced by a capitalist organization of society, this type of crime is at once a protest against society and a desire to partake of its exploitative content. It challenges the symptoms of capitalism, but not its essence."[14] In other words, the youthful offender is a rebel, but an ineffective one. He is pressed by economic need and psychological mistreatment. Once under lock and key, he is very susceptible to radicalization through political education and organized resistance for survival. We can find no more eloquent testimony to this effect than the life of George Jackson. The revolutionary potential of these elements was manifested in the great upsurge of prison movements led by political prisoners but supported by class conscious rank-and-file convicts locked away as common-law felons.

The life style, the social characteristics of the young street subproletarian in today's metropolitan ghetto readies him for desperate adventures and hair-raising schemes. But he can go either way — with the proper leadership he can learn to move in a disciplined revolutionary way; without it he will either fall victim to self-destroying nihilist gestures or move into criminal exploitation of

14. *If They Come in the Morning*, New York, 1971, p. 35.

his own people. The kind of leadership he receives will decide his path. Now from the standpoint of the class struggle, reliable leadership can come only from the proletariat. Left to themselves, Black lumpenproletarians have proven to be prone to "revolutionary suicides" and individual criminality. If they are to be prevented from preying on the community, or from becoming the armed henchmen of cultural nationalist "chieftains", Pan-Africanist bigwigs, religious obscurantists, Black would-be capitalists and other rightist forces which act objectively as the instruments of the monopoly bourgeoisie, then the street sub-proletarians must be given leadership by the vanguard of the class conscious proletarians.

The Black Panthers and "Lumpen Ideology"

For a time the Black Panthers alleged to be the cutting edge of the lumpenproletariat. Before the much-publicized split, Cleaver belonged to the inner core of Panther leaders along with Huey P. Newton and Bobby Seale. For several years the originally united Panther Party spread across the country claiming to guide politically-conscious lumpenproletarians. It swept lumpen and other subproletarians up in its membership along with militant representatives of the Black "bourgeoisie" and the middle strata. The Panthers even won the loyalty of some young Black workers. Following the break between the Peralta Panthers and the Cleaver faction, the two successor organizations, in a storm of mutual recrimination, both claimed to voice the demands of the lumpenproletariat. Thus both before and after the split the Black Panther movement defined itself as the organized political representative of the lumpenproletariat.

Note: at no time have the Panthers spoken for the whole subproletariat, nor for any of its other fractions, although Panther spokesmen often claim to represent all the Black popular masses. This does not reduce the movement's importance for an understanding of the political question of the "lumpen". However, it does mean that we will understand the class composition and political philosophy of the Panther Party *only* if we study it in its proper function — i.e. as the party of the "lumpen" and not as something which it is not. "People always have been the foolish victims of deception and self-deception in politics", wrote Lenin, "and they always will be until they have learnt to seek out the *interests* of some class or other behind all moral, religious, political and social phrases, declarations and promises."[15]

The Panther Party was the creation of young Blacks, mostly first generation descendents of migrants from the South. The Party appeared first on the West Coast as an indigenous northern Californian political phenomenon, parochial at the outset. It was a phenomenon of urban Blacks who knew no other environment but the ghetto, whose parents, however, had but. recently migrated from the South. Perhaps it was these circumstances which lent the Panthers their *populist* aura. Certainly they were a main reason why most of the top leadership was unable to grasp the significance of the application of scientific method to the theory of society. Like most populists in a new urban setting, the group around Huey P. Newton believed implicitly in the socialist instincts and inexhaustible spontaneous revolutionary spirit of the masses, but at the outset understood the masses to be mainly the lumpen-proletariat. In a sense the rise of the Black Panther Party was a symptom of a temporary shift to the West of the political center of gravity of the Black community from the old South and the industrial Northeast and Midwestern quadrangle.

But the temporary shift in the center of gravity westward represented by the sudden rise of the Panthers left a strong Black political focal point in the East, particularly in New York. This, coupled with the large populist ingredients in the Panther movement, had two consequences: 1) it affected the way the Panthers represented the lumpen in the political class struggle; 2) it paved the way for the eventual split.

In a way, the destiny of the Panther movement was marked out in advance by the fact of its West Coast origins, and by the fact of its being the creation of first generation descendents of migrants. But it was conditioned even more by the heterogeneous *class* origins of its leaders. For though the Panther Party was the organ of the lumpenproletariat, Black "bourgeois" elements and representatives of the ghetto's middle strata have always been prominent among its leaders. This explains, in part, the admixture of anarchism and other petty bourgeois doctrines in Panther "lumpen

15. *Collected Works*, Volume 19, Moscow, 1968, p. 28.

ideology". The close marriage of the most radical sounding "lumpen" rhetoric with meekly reformist Black capitalist schemes in the Party's program and actions is no accidental occurrence. I do not wish to create the wrong impression, however. The Panthers did not spring from the "Black elite", as the Black "bourgeoisie" is sometimes called. SNCC, CORE, and NAACP, etc. were and still are the prime political organs of the Black "bourgeoisie" and middle strata. The Panthers were not. They were anchored firmly in the lumpenproletariat and in the rebellious youthful street sub-proletariat. The great majority of the rank-and-file membership belonged to those social strata. However, the fact remains that as one proceded upward through the party hierarchy, one encountered more and more Panthers of "bourgeois" and middle strata background. This laid the social groundwork for the conflict and doctrinal split between so-called "grassroots" Panthers, mostly concentrated along the Atlantic Coast, who were enamoured of ultra-"Left" adventures under the influence of Eldridge Cleaver, and the West Coast leaders, devoted to reformism and Black capitalism. Radicalized former students and prison intellectuals dominated the early Panther organization. Merritt Community College was the training ground for Bobby Seale and the first crop of Panther leaders.

The germ of internal struggle was slow in fermenting, but it was probably inevitable that it would eventually bear fruit given the divergent class interests and the resulting petty bourgeois-radical and lumpenproletarian political lines represented by the Panther Party from the very start. Moreover, both trends in the movement were strongly influenced at first by the political writings, "people's war" strategy, language and style of Mao Tse-tung. The divergent political lines which intersected briefly in the Panther Party emerged from the differing class forces which made the party their common organ — petty bourgeois reformism and Black capitalist ideology were rooted in the militant bourgeois nationalist fraction of the Black "bourgeoisie" and in radical forces in the middle strata; ultra-"Left" populism and nihilism were the authentic expressions of the lumpenproletariat.

From the very beginning the nucleus of what has become the Peralta Panthers was the chief representative of the petty bourgeois radical nationalist tendency in the original Panther Party. But Cleaver is himself a Californian. He is also tarred with the petty bourgeois radical brush — his resurrection of Bakuninist anarchsim calls to mind the classical radicalism of the petty bourgeoisie in European history. This petty bourgeois line reflects not only the middle strata and student background of many Peralta Panther leaders but equally the objective interests of a radical-nationalist fraction of the Black "bourgeoisie". The Panther Party was actually a composite class organ — at once the political organ of the lumpenproletariat and of radical fractions of the middle strata and the Black "bourgeoisie". For a time no one seemed to notice this. That the Party has been a coalition of divergent political tendencies only became obvious once it had split in two.

Momentarily, until they fell to fighting among themselves, the Panthers enjoyed great success in organizing and working with the volatile ghetto subproletariat. For a while the Party was a real force for revolutionary change. It was inevitable, however, that they would exhibit in their political agitation many of the social characteristics of their essential class affiliation. The Panther Party originated as the political organ of the lumpenproletariat. Lumpen-proletarians are extremely violent and erratic in expressing their frustrations — personal or social. Discipline is their weak point. Through no fault of their own, subproletarians are usually estranged from the concrete discipline that springs from involvement every day in social production. The longer one is cut off from the industrial ·proletariat, the greater is the tendency to lose the patience required for effective working-class action. For others there is no prospect of any kind of job after years of being institutionalized in jail-like, racist schools. On all hands the subproletariat grows in size. Hundreds of thousands depend on welfare to survive. They must fend for themselves in a voracious, heartless economy whose values are purely monetary, whose god is private profit. Forced to live by their wits, from hand to mouth, compelled to hustle a living in the streets, many subproletarians go under, giving up entirely. Deprived of the basic human right of existence by racist capitalism, subproletarians are driven to all sorts of schemes — often unrealistic and hairbrained — simply in order to survive.

Demoralization is the lumpenproletarian disease. With it goes the illusion of personal salvation at any cost. Those who trip off into lumpenproletarian individualism are the most short-sighted and scattterbrained.

As representatives of the "lumpen" the Panthers could not fail

to contract the disease. Telltale traces of the Party's shaky foundation soon began to show. When it came to concrete political
action, these conditions and this atmosphere encouraged voluntarism and the worship of spontaneity. Extreme impatience with
theoretical analysis resulted in hasty adoption of political tactics
which turned out to be flimsy and erroneous. Dead-end militarism
and an overemphasis on guns led to adventurism. Rickety mergers
with Pan-Africanist student leaders were frantically pasted together
and just as rapidly collapsed. At a later juncture, the "Black bourgeoisie" was discovered to be "alive and well"; its capacities to
lead Black people were overestimated, and suddenly alliances with
"healthy", "public spirited" Black capitalists were the fashion.

The very possibility of an ideology for a lumpenproletarian
movement caused the stickiest conundrum. For according to the
theory, revolutionary "lumpen" are motivated by anger and outrage and move instinctively. They should not think, investigate or
analyze. Reflection is the straw caught at by overcautious, "integrated" workers. This doctrine makes the revolutionary "lumpen"
ideologist something of a contradiction in terms, he becomes a
logical impossibility. Yet it was obvious that there were active
lumpenproletarian ideologists — led on by Eldridge Cleaver. In
effect, this doctrine created for the Party a surfeit of ideologists,
for every Panther who fancied himself as a theorist came forward
as an "expert" on strategy and tactics. The best of these propa-
gandists were prone to a distorted populist rhetoric. The worst
were a mere breath away from demo-fascism. The most coherent
presentations of Panther philosophy rarely rose above a rough-and-
ready bandit's egalitarianism, a demand for social equality for non-
producing "have-nots". In a way, Cleaver's refrain calls to mind
the beggars of the Three Penny Opera. Even before the rift in the
Party, the Panthers were a prey to instability that degenerated
into political opportunism. Given the class nature of a lumpenproletarian movement, this was to be expected. One wing of the
movement succumbed to the lures of Black capitalism and "re-
analyzed" favourably the prospects of the Black "national bourgeoisie". Its leader repudiated Marxism. The other, lickspittling for
Herbert Marcuse, Jacques Ellul and company, wrote off Black
workers as "integrated" neocolonials, offering humanity as an
alternative the uninspiring vision of universal "lumpenization".

The wiser members of the party, its most consistent revolutionaries, left the sinking ship before it could drag them down with it. Those who realized that the Panthers' inability or refusal to adopt consistent Marxist-Leninist ideology made it impossible for the Party to offer real solutions to the immediate problems of Black working class youth joined the Communist Party of the United States. This move, they felt, would give them the opportunity to build Black caucuses in labour unions and help in the united Black-white fight against racism.

Everyone is aware that George Jackson, famous freedom fighter, still identified with the Panther movement at the time of his assassination. His posthumous writings, published in *Blood In My Eye*,[16] confirm this. But he was a very unorthodox sort of Panther. Confined, chained and spied on throughout his years of political awareness, George Jackson was an anomaly in the Panther movement. In all fairness, he cannot be counted a disciple of either the Peralta or the International trend. Jackson was indeed a confirmed Fanonist, but this did not put him in agreement with Cleaver. He was committed to revolutionary violence, but in a way that put him in a category by himself. The fire which shines through his writings, the crystalline lucidity of his thought, make it very doubtful, had he won freedom, that he would have long been able to conform to the meanderings of either faction. George Jackson gave his readers, and all who came into contact with him, the absolute certainty that he was a man of his word. He exhibited none of the opportunism which typifies lumpenproletarian political movements. He would do whatever he swore to do, even at the cost of his life. His bravery and meticulous integrity speared all those who encountered him, either in person or in written word, solidifying the feeling that here indeed was a pure revolutionary. But George Jackson was not a *professional* revolutionary. He was the revolutionary "people's war" incarnate, fierce and spontaneous, wild and unplanned, cunning and impatient. But he was not the trained, theoretically mature, patient Marxist-Leninist professional revolutionary for which Lenin called, and for which the Black community has such crying need. His spontaneity and ferocity were at once his strength and his weakness. Thus he was both a superb inspiration and a faulty theorist whose doctrine is riddled with voluntarism and subjectivism. George Jackson combined nihilism

16. New York, 1972.

87

and glimmerings of historical materialism in a never-to-be-forgotten personality. But while extraordinary in a personality, such a mixture is unstable politically. Great he was, but not the omniscient theorist the Panthers claimed him to be. Yet he was the best of the adherents of the Panther movement.

The final word rests with Lenin:

> ... the 'spontaneous element', in essence, represents nothing more nor less than consciousness in an *embryonic form*. Even the primitive revolts expressed the awakening of consciousness to a certain extent. The workers were losing their age-long faith in the permanence of the system which oppressed them ... But this was, nevertheless, more in the nature of outbursts of desperation and vengeance than of *struggle*.[17]

17. *Collected Works*, Volume 5, Moscow, 1961, pp. 374-375.

Chapter 4

THE FUNCTION OF RACISM IN CONTEMPORARY AMERICA

Racist philosophy is currently enjoying one of its spasmodic revivals. Once again the public is being deluged with all sorts of racist filth. Well-known scholars and scientists are busy revisiting the eery underworlds of racism, "re-evaluating" inherited racial traits. While a general phenomenon in all the imperialist countries, nowhere has the campaign been as strident and virulent as in the United States. People are led to believe that human behaviour is decipherable only through an examination of its roots among the lower animals. Man is a "naked ape", we are told, with inbred propensities for violence and aggression, and with a "territorial instinct" which stems from his evolutionary heritage. It is now the vogue for bourgeois anthropologists to say that all the traits we exhibit — even sexually or at play — prove our close relationship to the savage animal world. *Homo sapiens* is degraded to the level of a carnivorous predatory killer ape whose most precious "instinct" is the affinity for war. Every effort is being made to convince those whites who are not already so convinced that Black people (and other "third worlders") are racially inferior. Although fully aware that racial distinctions have no bearing on ethnic or cultural matters, the ideologists of imperialism, in their efforts to rationalize class and racial oppression, have kept alive the centuries-old lie of the physical and mental inequality of the races of mankind, of the existence of so-called "lower" races that are incapable of independent socio-economic and cultural development.

Yet despite this powerful reactionary counter-offensive launched by monopoly capital, it is still possible to arrive at a scientific conception of race, a Marxist conception. The Marxist-Leninist understanding of race is vital at this moment when the last remaining bulwarks of the imperialist colonial system are collapsing in Africa and elsewhere, when the general crisis of the capitalist world system has grown critical, when the balance of world power is shifting more and more to the advantage of the socialist community of nations led by the Soviet Union, at this moment when the Black liberation movement in this country is entering a critical new phase. The Marxist conception of race is an efficient weapon of defense against the current racist campaign.

*

Science has established that no "pure races" of men exist on this earth. "Racial purity" is an enormous lie invented by racists, just like the myth of racial "inferiority" or "superiority". Both notions contradict established fact. More germane, the degree of racial "purity", like the degree of racial mixture in a people, has no influence in the history of social development. This was true of ancient Egypt,[1] and it is equally true of the contemporary United States. The early stages of the evolution of hominids − i.e. the family of the primate order of which only modern man survives − took place in East Africa more than three million years ago. This region has been identified by Dr. Leaky and others as the starting point for the gradual dispersal of early men.[2] Later on people settled throughout the globe. The need to adjust to different environmental conditions diversified them into the modern great races − Black, Yellow and white − and several transitional groups.

Human development was influenced by various factors, but relatively early in man's history socio-economic factors won the upper hand over biological factors. Racial specifics were ousted completely as *determining* factors, and certain general biological factors even ceased to function at all. "Migration, isolation, increase in numbers, the mixing of anthropological types, and change in

1. For this reason there are grave doubts about the validity of the theories of Cheikh Anta Diop whose projection of a Negro racial determinant into the early history of Africa is at least anachronistic and unscientific. See his *Nations Nègres et culture*, Paris 1955; *L'Afrique Noire Pré-Coloniale*, Paris, 1960; and *Antériorité des Civilisations Nègres: Mythe ou Vérité Historique?*, Paris, 1967.

2. See L.S.B. Leakey, "The Evolution of Man in the African Continent", in *Tarikh*, Volume 1, Number 3, 1966; and J.D. Fage and R.A. Oliver, eds., *Papers in African Prehistory*, London, 1970.

food habits were, together with natural selection, the main factors in the process of race formation among the ancient hominids."[3]

As soon as each distinct human "race" was formed it began to mix with others. The process of intermingling and intermarriage started during the Upper Paleolithic period (Old Stone Age) which covers probably 99 percent of man's life on earth, and which ended about 8000 B.C. — i.e. about 10,000 years ago. This intermingling of the races has grown more, not less, intense down through the millenia.

As people spread over the earth, they encountered different natural conditions — there is little similarity, for instance, between the rain forest climate of the lower Niger river and the temperate climate of the Paris basin. But unlike other animals, all human beings battled the environment that surrounded them. Man transformed nature in the process of collective work. If these early human collectives had been sufficiently small and hermetically isolated geographically and socially for hundreds of thousands or perhaps millions of years, then differentiation would have intensified racial specifics, and guided the different groups along divergent lines of development, i.e. towards the formation of *different species*, thus breaking the single family of man into *unrelated branches*. *But that simply never happened in the evolution of mankind*. Although waterless deserts, broad seas, dense forests and towering mountains hampered movement, they did not prevent human migration. Adverse climatic conditions increased the parochialism of some hordes and tribes, but large groups of people were never completely isolated. From the collective labour of primitive men arose social organization, and the rudimentary means of production — fire, tools, weapons, and later means of transport — which served to nullify those natural factors which, if they had been unchecked, could have differentiated mankind into different species. The constant mingling of groups, life in the horde and then in the community, and, above all, the influence of collective labour, levelled and obliterated the differences that arose and differentiated consanguine groups as a result of natural and social causes. This prevented the racial differentiation of mankind from being anything but superficial and, in the long run, transitory.

Natural selection in particular influenced primitive man less and

3. M. Nesturkh, *The Races of Mankind*, Moscow, 1963, p. 58.

less as millenia passed. Performed collectively by the community, human labour made human evolution *sui generis*, unique from the very beginning. It was steered on to a path far removed from that followed by the animal kingdom. After a while natural selection ceased altogether to be a factor in the evolution of man. The unending process of intermingling that has gone on throughout human history shattered frozen hereditary features; changing features became man's permanent feature.

As Frederick Engels explained, therefore, the true place for the study of the races of mankind is in the science of the transition from the morphology and physiology of man to *history*.[4] Morphology is the study of the form and structure of animals considered *apart* from function, the study of the form and structure of an organism regarded as a whole. Physiology treats the processes and mechanisms by which living organisms function under varied conditions. When free of racist distortions, the anthropological studies which stand between morphology and physiology on one side and history on the other, lend a scientific sense to the notion of race. History is the science of man as human, i.e. as a social being. *Social* factors are the prime determinants of the evolution of mankind, of the development of human groups and relations between people formed in the course of eons of "species-survival", and, more recently, in the process of social production.

It follows then that heredity in man differs from heredity in other animals. There is a qualitative difference between the races of mankind and the races of animal species. "Mankind constitutes a single biological entity, and each of the races is the result of a qualitatively specific course of development taken by one part of that single whole; the race, therefore, differs in essence from the species or sub-species of animals".[5] Intermingling has given birth to all sorts of human physical types transitional from one of the great races of mankind to another. Hence the concept of racial purity among human beings is berserk as well as anti-historical. Anyone silly enough to carry out a racial diagnosis of the population of the U.S., or any other modern society, would find that for

4. See "The Part Played by Labour in the Transition from Ape to Man", in *Dialectics of Nature*, New York, 1940, pp. 279-296.
5. M. Nesturkh, p. 61.

a majority of the people the diagnosis would either not apply in full or give no results at all.

Both the "great" races of mankind and the "lesser", intermediate or "contact" races have arisen from a single stock — primitive man as he emerged in Tanzania's Olduvai Gorge and surrounding territories. Thus from a scientific point of view the races are biologically identical human *subvarieties*. No race stands higher or lower than the others in its level of physical and mental development. Cultures vary from people to people according to historical circumstances and uneven rates of development, but not races, for representatives of all races can be found in all cultures and at all cultural levels. Single origin makes the races basically identical. They are identical not only in the specifically human peculiarities of their physical structure, but even in many tiny details. The few racial differences that still exist carry no weight. This is proven by the ease and frequency with which intermingling gives birth to healthy, intelligent children. The crucial personality traits, e.g. industriousness, cooperativeness, courage, purposefulness, love of family, class and country, and willingness to struggle against exploitation and oppression are common to all mankind. Man's cultural achievements and his social and historical experience are not transmitted through the genes. We cannot inherit culture biologically from our mothers and fathers as we inherit blood plasma factors or eye-colour. Historical experience is transmitted from one human generation to the next only through a process known as the "socialization of the individual".

In the course of human evolution many racial features arose originally as adaptations to conditions, only to become functionless residues as social factors increased in weight, and as history gradually downgraded and then obliterated the factor of natural selection. In the remote past, race may, under specific conditions, have exerted a certain influence over ethnic processes. But this was exceptional and owing to eons of isolation. At the very most it effected only tiny primitive hordes, and pre-capitalist tribes, lost in inaccessible, undeveloped reaches like Borneo or the Shetland Islands.

The residual racial features in modern man are not adaptive. There is nothing in nature or in the social environment for which they are designed to conform. Skin colour, hair texture, eye shape, lip formation, blood plasma type, etc. — about the only remaining

93

noticeable racial specifics — are no longer of any help in the struggle against adverse natural conditions. Instead, men have designed major artificial means of protection against natural conditions, i.e. means of production which are the powerful artificial limbs of man and which undergo constant improvement to meet growing social requirements. The efficiency of these artificial protectors depend on the level of the productive forces available to man. Productive forces are means of production and people equipped with production experience and skills, with people being the main productive force. *Normally* the productive forces undergo constant development, particularly the tools of work. This determines the necessity for the development of the relations of production formed between people in the process of social production. When relations of production lag behind the level of development of the productive forces, they become outmoded and are then thrown off in those cataclysmic social revolutions which have thrust mankind forward in the course of its evolution.

The technical term for inter-racial procreation is a word of French derivation — *métisation. Métisation* is the process by which populations of mixed racial ancestry have been formed throughout the ages. The fact that there are no anatomical or physiological barriers to hamper the crossing of different races, and that history traces the unbroken, easy intermingling of the races, proves how groundless are the theories that deny the blood kinship of people of different races. In fact, *métisation* is the reason human races never turn into separate species. Due to endless displacement of population, migration and resettlement, resulting in exogamous sexual contacts, people bearing intermediary racial traits are constantly being born throughout the world. This is a phenomenon that is increasing in frequency, not diminishing. "The ease with which the races intermarry and the ever-growing numbers of people involved is evidence that they have a common origin."[6] The children of *métisation* are perfectly healthy, as are the offspring of one-racial unions, and their offspring, in turn, are normal and strong. More than half of mankind today consists of people who are to a great extent racially mixed. Most of the remaining peoples are mixed racially to a lesser extent.

6. *Ibid.*, p. 63.

Métisation is thus leading to a progressive increase in the number of the so-called "racially intermediate". Ultimately, in the distant future, it will lead to all races once again coalescing in a single physical type. The modern great races — Black, Yellow and White — therefore are not developmental stages on the road to three or more separate human species. That is a phoney bill of goods some racist pseudo-scientists would like to sell us. Moreover, the mixing of races has also ceased altogether to be the race-forming factor it was during much of the Old Stone Age. *Métisation* has become instead a factor that tends to eliminate racial differences.

Now the quantitative factor is very important in the process of racial-national assimilation: if the minority racial group makes up only a small fraction of the population, assimilation proceeds relatively quickly — as was the case, for instance, until recently with those Canadian Blacks who lived outside of areas of Black concentration like Nova Scotia and Ontario's Chatham region. But if the racial minority accounts for a fairly large proportion, as in the United States — even without the artificial barriers raised by the ruling class — assimilation is more difficult and requires a longer historical span. Due to the supremacy of racism, for a long time legally-recognized *métisation* has been restricted in the U.S. usually to the fringes of society, and underground, as it were, and even then only against huge odds. In the future, when communist society prevails everywhere on earth, the elimination of all barriers will eventually result in universal *métisation* in which the racial units of mankind will merge into one, once again becoming a unified global community of *Earthmen*, such as they were in appearance and socially when dispersal from East Africa began during pre-historic times. Even now it is extremely difficult to suggest even theoretically a universally valid scheme of racial analysis acceptable to all true scientists. In view of the recent findings of investigators who hold to the *populationist* concept of race formation — a trend best represented by the scientists of the socialist countries[7] — it is already doubtful whether races in the biological sense exist at present!

7. See N.N. Cheboksarov, "Human Races and Populations", in I.R. Grigu-levich and Y.S. Kozlow, eds., *Races and Peoples: Contemporary Ethnic and Racial Problems*, Moscow, 1974, pp. 45-62.

Anyway, the recognition of incontestable racial distinctions does not create racism. Racial distinctions like skin colour and hair texture are minor and insignificant. Racism arises from the *idea of the inequality of races* fostered and fomented by the ruling class to divide the exploited and ensure high profits, which is a different matter entirely. American bourgeois sociology has invented a mythical "racial identity" which it blames for feelings of racial antipathy. But the most that can be said for this "identity" is that members of the same racial or ethnic group are conscious of themselves as group because of historical circumstance and social pressure. Boiled down there is not much else to "racial identity", for after all it makes as much sense to observe that dogs know dogs from cats, and that a football team can distinguish its members from the opposing team. When checked carefully, "race consciousness" turns out to be nothing more substantial than a feeling — obviously difficult to measure — and this feeling, in turn, is circular, based, as it is, on individual consciousness of membership of one specific "race".

*

Thus to really take cognizance of racism and racial prejudice, as they exist today, we must turn to something substantial like concrete *social* reality, i.e. to social relations of production and the methods by which monopoly capital dominates the working masses. 130 years ago Marx and Engels demonstrated that a person's consciousness is always social, and social consciousness in class society is based on just that — class. Whether we like it or not, class interest and class-related objects are the building blocks of our awareness. In as much as social class is thus the starting point for *ideology* — the systematized views held by social classes — then class relations must be the root from which racist ideology springs. Racist ideology constitutes a whole system of views and ideas: political, legal, ethical, aesthetical, religious, and philosophical. While it possesses a certain relative independence, racist ideology, like all ideology, ultimately reflects economic relations. It is reactionary class interests which nurture race prejudice. Hence race as a scientific notion has nothing to do with racism.

In the political economy of U.S. capitalism, race describes a social status determined by capitalist relations of production. An

American conceives of himself as belonging to a certain race not because of the racial features he sees in his mirror, but because he is regarded and *treated* as a member of a certain race. No Caucasian perceives himself as "white" apart from the social condition of being a white man in a society which discriminates against non-whites. Each toddler discovers, or does not discover, that he is one race or another solely from the behaviour of his elders. What actually crystallized in the course of American history were hitherto non-existent categories of people — *socio-political races* or "race-classes" — whites, Blacks and others — which have nothing to do with the scientific concept of race. In this country, a Black person is simply that human being who other people — white people (especially the ruling class) — designate Black and treat as Black. There is nothing inherent about "Blackness"; there is no "*Africanité*" — no inborn African character. It is a situation. A situation that one discovers at birth or shortly thereafter. Race in the social sense is a socio-political inheritance. Socio-political race can be abolished only by abolishing the exploitative and oppressive situation. "Race-class" will disappear with the abolition of the exploiting classes.

In ethnically heterogeneous societies the ruling class proclaims part of the population to be a "separate racial group" in order to facilitate the collective oppression and super-exploitation of that group and swell the number of recruits for capital's reserve army of unemployed labourers. Only under these circumstances do quite incidental physical traits become *stigma* exposing the designates to degrading mistreatment. Assuming no differences in skin colour, etc., it is conceivable that the imperialist bourgeoisie could designate eye colour, and eye colour alone, as the degrading stigma.

Usually racial stigmatization and enforced membership of a "race-class" are codified in law; even more often they are customary, but just as binding on those subject to the conventions established by the ruling classes. Millions internalize the do's and don't's. These "projections" represent social relations of production, i.e. class relations, transposed to the ideological (and social psychological) sphere. In an advanced capitalist society with long standing traditions of racial discrimination, the direct relationship between racial stigmatization and its economic base tends to blur. Race prejudice seems to work free of economics and to live a life of its own, independent of profit-making imperatives. But that is an illusion. Autonomous-seeming social "projections" are actually indirect, roundabout means of strengthening the socio-economic status quo. They are essential components of the prevailing ideology in capitalist society. Division along racial lines serves to divert the attention of white workers away from their real concerns and to consolidate the existing system. That is a main function of racism in the political economy of the United States. By freezing Blacks in a caste-like position, by keeping them a super-exploited Lazarus-stratum of the working class, by treating non-whites like pariahs and subjecting them to all sorts of desecration, the U.S. class system prevents antagonism between the monopoly bourgeoisie and white workers from crystallizing at the level of struggle for control of state power.

The rites and rituals of racial stigmatization (e.g. the procedure by which American children are taught to abhor intermarriage) lend an aura of sanctity to and mystify what would otherwise be recognized for the fraud it really is. Take for example the I.Q. and other "intelligence" quotient tests. These merely indicate the level of mental development of the subject depending on the level of education and the kind of social conditioning. The questions are designed to elicit answers which indicate the level of mental organization and power to conceptualize. But these faculties, in turn, depend on language skills. The test results themselves never tell us anything about the race of the individual tested. It would be indeed peculiar if affluent white suburbs with well-funded schools did *not* have higher formal language skills than impoverished Black ghettos. Yet these test results have been used to justify the streaming of Black youngsters into "low-achieving" school classes and segregated schools.

These myths and rites hinder the growth of class consciousness among white workers and channel their frustrations into activities acceptable to the ruling class — like attacking Black school children in south Boston, Louisville and elsewhere.

While it is not worthwhile to chart the nuances between racist sentiments, there is a big difference in the power of human beings to cause others to suffer because of their racist sentiments. The means to oppress racially, and the consequence of prejudice, invariably depend on one's class position. The monopoly capitalist has great means to do harm, the bigoted worker comparatively little. Ultimately much of the harm inflicted by the worker's prejudice is done to the worker himself. The monopoly capitalist benefits from, and foments, and encourages racist myths which he personally may or may not believe. In contrast, the petty bourgeois — conformist and fearful — is racist from a misplaced yearning for personal security, and a need to feel superior to someone. The white worker's prejudice may spring from deprivation, anxiety and misdirected fear for his job. The racist cop may hate and despise Black people perhaps because he doubts his own worth and is tormented with self-contempt — by abusing Blacks he hopes to appear tough and win the approval of his superios. But the problem is that Blacks and other minorities experience racist behaviour as an *absolute*, as an irreducible datum — as an evil which causes pain and suffering. However racist behaviour may vary in motive and expression according to class, it makes little difference in the way the victim perceives it.

*

Let us look at some of modern imperialism's practical uses of racist ideology.

The defeat of fascism mainly by the Soviet Red Army in World War II dealt racist ideology a devastating blow. Nevertheless, racist ideas continued to have many followers in extremely influential circles, particularly in the most powerful capitalist country — the U.S.A. — where national minorities, led by 30 million Afro-Americans, now make up almost 22 percent of the population. In fact, along with Nazi Germany and the Republic of South Africa, the United States provides one of history's most notorious examples of the elevation of prejudice into an officially-sanctioned form. In the U.S. racism is both institutionalized and "demo-popular". In South Africa racial discrimination is official state doctrine. The former British colony of Southern Rhodesia has been turned into a shameful white settlers' police regime. West Germany, with its neo-Nazis, and Chile are other horror spots. International Zionism, and its Israeli shock brigade, after having colluded criminally with the fascists during the Second World War, now torture the Palestinian people with a terrorist "New Order" and fully employ chauvinist ideology and racist methods both against the Arabs and against non-white Jews. Brazilian fascists practice genocide against Indians. British reactionaries are known for their outrages against Britain's "coloured" minority. An outspoken racist program is supported by Enoch Powell and a very influential wing of the British Conservative Party. French racists hound immigrant Algerian and Black African workers. Throughout the imperialist camp belief in the right of one race to dominate over another masks imperialist aggression, and is used to justify war between nations, including preparations for a nuclear world war.

But racism is being squeezed by the world's progressive forces. So its proponents now either put up a frantic open resistance or attempt subtle ploys designed to camouflage its rottenness. The socially-derived tension and stress which breed high blood pressure in Blacks, for instance, is explained away by the "discovery" of a simple "racial difference" — Black people's hearts allegedly beat faster than white people's hearts! Or the sting is taken out of racial hatred when it is served up as a "cultured", politically neutral "psycho-racism". "Today, with the increasing ascendancy of the world socialist system, imperialism merges with anti-Communism and racism ever more closely in its efforts to stave off extinction."[8] The whole of current social relations as exemplified by the non-socialist world shows that there is the closest link between racism and imperialism.

More than anything, the tolerance shown racist gangs, the deliberate cultivation of racial prejudices and racial slander reveal the hypocrisy of bourgeois democracy. The Carter Administration's phoney "human rights" campaign and search for "dissidents" in the socialist countries failed to conceal this fact. Even today the United States, Britain and other imperialists try to create the impression in the United Nations Organization that the struggle against racism and racist ideology runs counter to the freedom of speech and the right of association. The precious "liberties" of the racists must be protected against the "encroachments" of the victims of racism, so say NATO diplomats. This is the basic philosophy behind the hands-off policy towards the subversion of school integration in Boston and elsewhere and the Ku Klux Klan's recent Know-Nothing drive to burn school books in West Virginia's Kanawha county.

8. Henry Winston, "Front-Rankers in the Class Struggle [II]", in *Political Affairs*, Vol. LIII, No. 11, November 1974, p. 12.

The imperialist system, based now on state-monopoly capitalism, incorporates in the American setting — along with the familiar features of monopoly capitalist class exploitation of workers — the super-exploitation and racial oppression of a Lazarus-stratum of workers descended from slaves. The heart of super-exploitation remains the wage discrimination which imposes a racial hierarchy in wages paid to equivalent workers. American capitalism has a deeply ingrained racist strain. In the U.S. system of political economy, racism and capitalism are inseparable aspects of one and the same reality. This is not to imply that the capitalist mode of production as an economic category *per se* is inherently racist, but that history has made the *American* brand of capitalism racist, and imperialism, capitalism's monopolistic and final stage, being inherently reactionary, does exhibit a natural tendency to espouse racism.

A given mode of production is manifested only in the particular — in concrete, historical social formations. Capitalism came into being in the U.S. with a large admixture of chattel slavery, i.e. the extraction of a surplus from slave labourers by non-economic coercion, and the slaves were captive Africans. After the Civil War, U.S. capitalism forgot nothing of its slaving past. The traits, habits and peculiar ideology of the slaveholding oligarchy survived the Confederacy as an essential support for monopoly capital.

Now it may be true as some have argued recently,[9] that the roots of some of the racist ideas in the heads of American whites, and some of the details and forms of racist behaviour — the folkways of racism — are holdovers from a pre-capitalist Anglo-Saxon (early Protestant?) legacy. It is also clear that certain transmittable features of pre-capitalist ideologies have shown a capacity to live on through the centuries. There is no question but that the peculiar vocabulary of U.S. racism, its "apple-pie" and "mint-julep" style, clearly bears the mark of bygone plantation slavery. Nevertheless, racism as a system by which the non-white minority is super-exploited and oppressed in this country is thoroughly up-to-date, and thoroughly monopoly capitalist.

The result is the uniquely American social setup. Although the American system of government, like the British, French, West

9. See for example W. Jordan, *White Over Black: American Attitudes Towards the Negro, 1550-1812*, pp. IX, and 3-43.

German, Canadian and Japanese, is now dominated by state-monopoly capitalism, unlike the others it exhibits peculiarly Dixiecrat traits. An ethos reminiscent of slavery pervades the state. This is so because the slavocracy dominated the federal government from independence to the Civil War, and because the Bourbon South was left "unreconstructed", and because today's monopoly lords find racism so useful in dividing the working class along colour lines. The U.S. state apparatus was capitalist from inception, but for nearly ninety years it was administered and controlled by the slaveholders and their "doughfaced" lackeys. American bourgeois society was impregnated at that juncture with slavocratic features which survived the abolition of chattel slavery. Even now the Southern Dixiecrat ex-slave power wields great might and influence in federal and state politics. Because racist super-exploitation is so profitable, U.S. monopoly capital perpetuates and propagates racist attitudes and opinions. Why else would the likes of George Wallace still be a force in national politics?

Racism thus has a class basis, modern racism has its material foundation in the monopoly capitalist class. It continues to generate and guarantee super-profits. Despite its unscientific nature and because of its reactionary character, racism fulfills the social demands of the ruling class. It is a *unifying* political factor which cements the non-monopoly bourgeoisie, the petty bourgeoisie, and the "labour aristocracy" to the reigning monopoly capitalist class. Racism still narcotizes millions of disinherited working class whites who believe what the monopoly media tell them. It thereby helps the reactionary politicians of the Democratic and Republican parties to suppress any independent political initiatives that could lead to a mass anti-monopoly third party. To deny this is to deny the conditioning effect of the past on the present.

*

Racism has been so traditionally effective that it has enabled the ruling class to suspend in respect to Black people, or permanently eclipse, most of conventional bourgeois morality's own prescriptions in matters of work, freedom, personal sanctity, and life itself. Marx observed that the sanctimonious apologists of the bourgeoisie have always tolerated the most shameful violations of the "sacred rights" of property and the grossest violence to persons, as soon as such transgressions are seen to foster capitalist profits.[10] Control of opinion is a fundamental means of power. Propaganda and "public relations" control the formation of "public" opinion. They increase the efficiency of ruling class power. In recent years, it is precisely in the field of media conditioning of the masses that there has been the most incredible refinement in the methods of racist oppression.

No class is more enthralled by the "Establishment's" information monopoly than the white petty bourgeoisie. The media try to keep the petty bourgeoisie walled off from everything progressive and revolutionary. The media either suppress the truth or distort it beyond recognition, and petty bourgeois are trained to follow the media like rats the Pied Piper. NBC, CBS and ABC — all three networks controlled by the Morgan and Rockefeller finance groups — have been "enriching" the racist imagination of petty bourgeois whites for an entire generation now. TV and the monopoly press, Hollywood and bourgeois publishers, prescribe what our petty bourgeois must think and how he must feel, who he must worship and who he must hate. Archie Bunker has made bigotry respectable, while instilling contempt for workers in "lower middle class" youth. Maude condoned white liberal hypocrisy, while creating the impression that there is no alternative to monopoly two-party Democratic and Republican politics. Police Story and a hundred other cop melodramas show "red-blooded", "law abiding" Americans how to deal with petty crooks, radicals and other dangerous social "deviants". Redd Foxx, Flip Wilson and Sammy Davis Jr. project comforting images of contented, or at least funny, "achieving" Negroes into petty bourgeois living rooms. The film industry has dedicated itself to the cult of mindless violence and pornography. Add the endless sports events on TV· — annotated with the racist homilies of the Curt Gowdy's and Howard Cosell's.

The inhabitants of white suburbia and exurbia are brainwashed into believing that in order to retain a relatively comfortable level of material consumption, existing capitalist relations of production must be preserved — at all costs. This opinion sanctions the

10. *Capital*, Vol. I, p. 727.

egoism and self-centered complacency of many ordinary "main-stream" whites. They are blinded to evidence which shows that decent living conditions for "middle class" people are compatible with the eradication of poverty and misery for minority peoples, and that only capitalism prevents this. To keep the so-called "free enterprise" system intact, it is necessary alas — so runs the refrain — that the world continue to be divided into "rich white nations" and "poor coloured nations", and that Afro-Americans and other minorities live in squalor and under repression, and it is necessary even that hundreds of thousands of Africans, Chileans and Indo-chinese be slaughtered to "protect" American investments.

However, for many petty bourgeois whites the bubble burst in the turbulent Sixties and the Watergate Seventies. As the "bad news" about their country rolled in — Black ghetto insurrections, peace demonstrations, urban blight and pollution, unsafe streets, defeat for U.S. aggression in Indochina, balance of payment deficits, dollar devaluations, galloping inflation, energy ripoffs, collapse of the Angela Davis frameup, soaring unemployment and economic depression, loss of jobs even for white employees as plant after plant shut down, Watergate and Nixon's run for cover, the CIA and FBI scandal, etc. — many petty bourgeois shuddered in consternation and bewilderment.

Typically, some of the disillusioned seek a way out in mis-anthropy. Increasing numbers are taking refuge in Neo-Malthusian-ism. Talk of "zero population growth" has grown in petty bour-geois academic circles. A chorus has swelled, counselling vasectomy and sterilization for the poor, the jobless and the Black. This cantankerous misanthropy has much to do with the latest round of not-so-"new" conservatism and with the "silent majorities" of the Nixon-Ford years. Nixon's "southern strategy" and right-wing election coalitions drew much support from this mood among white petty bourgeois voters.

With the aid of bourgeois social psychology, Freudianism and similar theories, the archreactionary slander of "mass psychoses" and other lies are churned out for petty bourgeois consumption whenever people of colour fight against racism, especially when they come to realize that *capitalism* must be overthrown for racism to be done away with. The lie that revolutionaries and anti-racists are crazy, or at least emotionally unstable, is supposed to paralyze the fight for a better future, for the abolition of the

104

exploitation of man by man; at the very least it is supposed to scare the "lower middle class" away from the fight. That is why anti-communism and racist philosophy are recognized subjects of instruction in American universities, instead of being the subject of criminal jurisprudence as in the socialist countries. That is why the Shockleys and the Jensens attract such loud publicity. Social therapy and "behaviour modification" are used to rationalize racist repression and reactionary brutality towards the revolutionary movement. For years now, psycho-racism, neo-Malthusianism, geopolitics and other reactionary sociological theories have been used to fan the flames of the Cold War and set the "middle class" against the idea of international detente.

We should suffer no illusions about exactly what the racists intend to do if they have their way in our country. For at least three decades the aim of the KKK, U.S. Nazis, and certain Pentagon brass has been fascism.

We know that fascism is a specific political phenomenon, but many progressives still wonder as to its class character and social content in the American context. The class essence of home-grown fascism is exactly the same as that of the infamous Nazi German dictatorship. Georgi Dimitrov, the great revolutionary who faced down Hermann Göring and the whole Nazi frameup at the Leipzig Trial in 1933, branded fascist dictatorship as the most brutal offensive of capital against working people. *"Fascist power"*, he explained, *"is the open terrorist dictatorship of the most reactionary, most chauvinistic and most imperialistic elements of finance capital."*[11] Fascism is a "servant of the big bourgeoisie". As early as 1928, the Sixth Congress of the Comintern had already defined fascism as the terrorist dictatorship of big capital, and Dimitrov, speaking with the hindsight of two years of Nazi rule, added in 1935 that "the accession of fascism to power was not an ordinary succession of one bourgeois government by another but the replacement of one *state* form of class domination of the bourgeoisie — bourgeois democracy, by another form — open terrorist dictatorship". Dimitrov stressed that fascism is not an *ordinary*

11. W. Pieck, G. Dimitroff, P. Togliatti, *Die Offensive des Faschismus und die Aufgaben der Kommunisten im Kampfe für die Volksfront gegen Krieg und Faschismus. Referate auf dem VII. Kongress der Kommunistischen Internationale 1935*, Berlin, GDR, 1957.

bourgeois dictatorship but a *barbarian* bourgeois dictatorship, manifested under concrete historical conditions and supported by concrete social forms. Facism is marked by savage cruelty, decadence, and an absence of culture. It burns books, foments racist pogroms, enthrones lynch law, fosters obscurantism, spreads myths, glorifies instinct, and dotes on the charismatic. Note: these are already traditional elements of the American scene — elements which could facilitate the transition from bourgeois democracy to fascist dictatorship. All fascist leaders — even those who do not style themselves *Führer* — claim supernatural dispensation, or at least some extraordinary talent or superhuman quality designed to realize some mysterious social-historical destiny or other (usually to combat communism).

It is wise to distinguish between a fascist state and fascist movements in a bourgeois democratic state — the Third Reich, for instance, was a fascist state, the Ku Klux Klan and John Birch Society are neo-fascist movements in a bourgeois democracy. The fascist state is a particular form of the bourgeois state. It should not be confused with other forms of the capitalist state. *Imperialism*, not capitalism *per se*, gives rise to fascism. Imperialism is capitalism's highest and final stage. The record of history shows that fascism appears during this stage.

Although there were exceptions, as a rule the classical form of government of competitive capitalism, of pre-imperialist capitalism, was bourgeois democracy. *"L'Homme politique"*, the typical politician of bourgeois democracy and constitutionality, was the venal liberal, not the Storm Troop demagogue.

Fascism is thus tied with an umbilical cord to imperialism. Lenin's classic analysis showed that imperialism is characterized briefly by: 1) the concentration of production and capital, the formation of monopolies which play a decisive role in economic life; 2) the merging of bank capital with industrial capital, and the creation, on the basis of finance capital, of a financial oligarchy; 3) the great importance acquired by the export of capital; 4) the rise of international capitalist monopolies, and, lastly the repartitioning of the available world among the great capitalist powers. Based on these features which characterize our contemporary scene, there is a tendency of all the bourgeoisie's political institutions to undergo a reactionary transformation, and this tendency appears in its most coherent forms with fascism. Why? Because

106

given the class relations and the need to safeguard monopoly superprofits, the bourgeoisie must find forms with which to exert heavy pressure on the workers. Furthermore, the monopolies, that is to say, the bourgeoisie's leading forces, reach their highest degree of concentration, and the old forms of rule become impediments to their further expansion.

Palmiro Togliatti, veteran leader of the international communist and workers movement, and an outstanding anti-fascist, focused his attention on fascism's two elements − 1) the dictatorship of the most reactionary, chauvinistic and imperialist elements of the bourgeoisie; and 2) the movement of the petty bourgeois masses. Togliatti recognized that fascism can take different forms in different countries, but warned against the Trotskyite habit of dismissing fascism as a kind of so-called "bonapartism".[12]

But Togliatti's greatest insight was to realize that imperialism does not *necessarily* have to give birth to the fascist dictatorship. Granted that the tendency toward the fascist form of government is present everywhere in state-monopoly capitalist societies, but this still does not mean fascism must perforce be arrived at everywhere. The probabilities of establishing a fascist dictatorship depend on the degree of the working class' militancy and its ability to stage a united defense of democratic institutions. This is the reason why the fascist dictatorship works so hard to build its own *mass* movement by organizing the bourgeoisie and the petty bourgeoisie. And this is why the observations made above concerning the present mood of the white petty bourgeoisie in this country are so crucial and portentous.

Thus we must be careful not to regard fascism as simply the equivalent of capitalism, or capitalism *per se* as merely the same thing as fascism, really or potentially, a mistake made by men like Marcuse and Horkheimer, for this mistake suppresses the qualitative difference between the two, it makes fascism an *irresistible* tendency and prevents any anti-fascist alliance between the working class movement and other strata, including those fractions of the capitalist class whose perspective is bourgeois democracy, but not socialism. Fascism in power is a *form* of the bourgeois *state*. It is

12. See Palmiro Togliatti, *Lectures on Fascism*, New York, 1976, pp. 1-12. Also useful are André Gisselbrecht, ed., *Le Fascisme Hitlerien, Etudes Actuelles*, Paris, 1970.

the open terrorist dictatorship of the most reactionary fraction of monopoly capital and its job is to foster the development of state-monopoly capitalism.

The Sixth Congress of the Comintern which met in 1928, with nothing to go on but the models of Mussolini's Italy and lesser fascisms, then felt that fascism represented a *defensive* strategy of capitalism, it was regarded as a phenomenon springing not from the strength but from the *weakness* of the bourgeoisie. A bourgeoisie solidly in the saddle and the master in the class struggle, sure of its mass basis, can make do, it was said, with traditional liberal democratic methods, and has no need for the risky extravagances of fascism. In this view, fascism, if it is not an outright counter-revolution against a popular revolution, is at least the response of the monopoly bourgeoisie to a *perceived threat* of revolution (Chile would be a model).

But seven years later, surveying the Nazi rise to power, Togliatti modified the proposition to show that fascism results from the *strength* of the bourgeoisie as well as from its *weakness*. It is true that fascism develops because class contradictions have reached such a point that the bourgeoisie is compelled to liquidate the democratic forms. It means that society is confronted with a profound crisis, that a revolutionary crisis is brewing which the bourgeoisie wants to nip in the bud. This is a sign of the bourgeoisie's weakness, that it is unable to go on ruling in the same old way. But fascism's second element, the succesful mobilization of the petty bourgeoisie by the fascists, *strengthens* the monopoly bourgeoisie. The mass mobilization of the petty bourgeoisie fortifies the bourgeoisie inasmuch as it permits it to govern with methods different from bourgeois democratic ones. More than anything this second element is part of a *process of fascization*, for fascism does not spring to life overnight. In 1935, at the Seventh Congress of the Comintern, Georgi Dimitrov noted that most fascist regimes had emerged from a reciprocal struggle, sometimes bitter, against the old bourgeois parties. This struggle to oust the traditional bourgeois parties and transform their followers into neophyte fascists, along with the more vital struggle to enslave the working class and exterminate its communist vanguard, constitutes the process of fascization and is greatly fostered by the spread of racist philosophy and racial hysteria.

German history from 1918 to 1933 also shows that *anti-com-*

munism — the main ideological weapon of modern imperialism — was the decisive means of splitting the working class and exerting anti-democratic pressure on the farmers, the petty bourgeoisie and bourgeoisie, thereby preventing the unification of the popular masses in the struggle against reaction.[13] It is obvious that *racism* served the same purpose objectively.

The experience of Germany also shows that if the leaders of progressive forces surrender the way the right-wing Social Democrats of the Weimar Republic did, and fail to struggle aggressively against fascism and for democracy, then a large part of the proletariat becomes embittered, resigned, disarmed ideologically, and susceptible to fascist indoctrination.

A contributing factor to the Nazi victory was the total impotence and breakdown of all non-fascist or not outspokenly pro-fascist bourgeois parties. All the traditional bourgeois parties abdicated and practically disappeared from the political arena. Their erstwhile members and their voters were sucked into the maelstrom of the fascist movement. The lesson is that without strong pressure from the progressive forces organized in a powerful anti-fascist movement, bourgeois democratic political parties simply cannot be trusted to ward off a reactionary onslaught leading to fascist dictatorship. In 1932, imperialist reaction succeeded in harnessing all German political forces but the Communist Party for the last phase of the fascization process.

That bourgeois democratic elections, even when based on universal suffrage, are neither proof against the establishment of fascist dictatorship nor a reliable gauge of the needs and desires of the electorate, is confirmed by the German presidential elections (as well as by the re-election of Richard Nixon in 1972). Although the majority of Germans wanted neither monopoly dictatorship nor another world war, nearly 90 percent of the voters cast their ballots for the two ultra-reactionary candidates — Hindenburg and Hitler. Granted, they did so under the ideological, terrorist, and economic pressure of monopoly capital's political agents, and because they were told to vote for Hindenburg by the right-wing Social Democrats. Nevertheless, German history from 1918 to 1933 proves once again that ultimately the question of power

13. See Joachim Streisand, ed., *Deutsche Geschichte*, Volume 3, *Von 1917 bis zur Gegenwart*, Berlin, GDR, 1968, pp. 116-164.

cannot be decided through bourgeois elections, that such elections, held under the influence of reaction, may serve merely to legitimize anti-democratic measures.

The monopolies which owned the costly mass media used them to spread Nazi propaganda. The fascists owed their mass following and election victories to the monopolies. The arch-nationalist Hugenberg controlled the press and cinema, Siemens and Telefunken monopolies the radio. Publicity created the mass support which is an inseparable component of any real fascism. In this vein we should take note of the way the U.S. mass media is making Ronald Reagan a "superstar" and providing a mass following for his proto-fascist movement. In the process which led to the startling transformation of the Nazi party from a tiny sect into a mass party, there was no real spontaneity, no "great crisis" which impelled the masses toward fascism. Neither was there from 1930 to 1933 any "point of no return" in the process of fascization. There was no point beyond which the rise of Adolf Hitler became irresistible.

Furthermore, the example of Germany prior to Hitler's takeover shows that part of the process of fascization is a *day to day increase* in the aggressiveness of fascist groups, the racists grow more cheeky by the hour, there is growing street terror by fascist bands, more and more physical attacks, threats, intimidation, murders, bombings, assassinations of left-wingers and minority people, mob or sneak attacks on the premises of the Communist Party and other leftwing and labour organizations. Strike breaking becomes a common occurrence, as do assaults on pickets. Fascists paint racist slurs in public places. Progressive rallies are disrupted and peaceful demonstrators beaten. Police murder progressives and minority people with growing impunity. Racist outrages against racial minorities increase in geometrical progression. Bankrupt politicians exploit issues like busing to foment hatred.

Once in office, fascist governments can be depended upon to foster, protect, and speed up the concentration of capital and production — to help the giant monopolies grow even bigger and stonger. This despite all the populist rhetoric aimed at the petty bourgeois, despite all the promises to protect the "little man" and integrate him in the "national community". One reason fascist regimes insist on a free hand to suppress the working people and forbid free speech and thought is that the draconic anti-social

110

measures they must take on behalf of finance capital are sure eventually to cost them whatever popularity they may own among the petty bourgeoisie. Like Pinochet's regime today, German and Italian fascism worked to consolidate the dominance of state-monopoly capitalism, and this one aspect of the tragic legacy of Hitler and Mussolini, more than any other, has outlived their defeats in post-war West-Germany and Italy. The fascists "fight" unemployment by introducing compulsory labour, i.e. forced labour for little or nothing, thus worsening the penal servitude for the working class which, especially during time of war or severe crisis, is a general feature of state-monopoly capitalism. Jobless youths are drafted into the armed forces, locked in barracks, marched out to break strikes, mercilessly exploited, militarized and poisoned by racist indoctrination.

It is impossible for a fascist state not to make war sooner or later, war in one form or another. They may be civil wars, wars of aggression against socialist countries,[14] imperialist wars against imperialist rivals, colonial or neo-colonial wars. The cold-blooded repression which terrifies the people at home — the racist persecutions, anti-labour outrages, intellectual witchhunts, police spying, concentration camps and murder — serve to prepare the people psychologically, to harden and accustom them to violence, to ready them for war against foreign states and peoples, and for the *genocide* of entire peoples.

We should suffer no illusions about exactly what the racists intend to do if they have their way in the United States.

Apartheid would become the socio-economic law of the land. Under South African apartheid wages are kept so low that the means of subsistence derived from them are not enough normally to provide for the replenishment and reproduction of Black labour power. The South African racists rely instead on starvation-wracked Bantustans (homelands) to supply an endless stream of landless peasants to the mines and other enterprises. Following that example, racists would like to press the earnings of America's non-white workers below the subsistence minimum while depending on the huge army of unemployed as a reserve of dirt cheap

14. For Hitler's plan to annihilate the Russian people from a "racial-biological" standpoint see Grigory Deborin, *Thirty Years of Victory*, Moscow, 1975, p. 103.

labour. Not only would they like to reverse the unenforced school desegregation ruling of 1954 and reinstitute total school segregation throughout the land, they are also lusting to pass federal and state racist legislation and add racial discrimination to the U.S. Constitution in the form of amendments. A *de jure* racial ghetto is a section of a city or town formally set aside by legislation as a segregated territory in which a single racial group is forced to reside and is forbidden to live or own real estate outside its boundaries. At the present time this country's racial ghettos are *de facto* rather than a legal imposition. If the more savage racists take power and establish fascism, residential segregation ordinances and covenants backed by the full authority of the state will transform America's *de facto* racial ghettos into *de jure* ghettos like the homelands of the Republic of South Africa.

The racists also want a Constitutional amendment declaring sexual relations between persons of different races a punishable felony. Like the Nazis, the South African racists, and many states of the Union in the past, they want to prohibit mixed marriage. Since the days of Count Gobineau — the founder of modern racist ideology[15] — racists have regarded *métisation* leading possibly to the birth of children as the ultimate offense. Merely because the sophisticated racist now wears professorial garb instead of the Confederate uniform, speaks in Harvard accents instead of with a cracker drawl, and is a Nobel prize laureate, we should not conclude that he is any less devoted to preventing intimate contact between whites and Blacks.

Beyond that, Jim Crow legislation would purge federal, state and local government of non-white officials — elected as well as appointed. The racists would like to prohibit non-whites from practicing law within the confines of the United States and reduce the already small number of minority physicians. Non-whites would be ousted from teaching positions in "white" universities and other institutions of higher learning. Large numbers of foreign-born "third worlders" would be deprived of American citizenship by law, and hundreds of thousands deported as "illegal immigrants". Racist pseudo-science, incitement to racial discrimination and the preaching of racial separation would become obligatory in all

15. The four volumes of Gobineau's racist opus were first published from 1853 to 1856.

institutions of learning. If the likes of Ronald Reagan and James Schlesinger had their way, "Americanism" and anti-communism would be required courses in every school in the country. Full segregation in public places would be reinstituted and stringently enforced. Laws would reserve certain types of jobs solely for whites. Equal pay for equal work would be prohibited for workers of different races. Neo-Nazi "race improvement" laws and eugenics would impose the sterilization of millions of Blacks and other poor people. Politically-active progressives of all races would be rounded up as guinea pigs for "behaviour modification" institutes. Concentration camps would appear everywhere. In the effort to control the non-white population and shape its demographic profile, an openly racist regime would subject Black and other "third world" people to massive birth control. Repression, massacre and genocide would keep them in line.

*

The effect of race prejudice, as it bounces off the injured victim, is insidious. It creates a grave political danger for the Black liberation movement. For this reason we must be circumspect in our approach and take care to differentiate in our condemnations between the duped bearers of racial prejudice and the fomenters and beneficiaries of racism. As Roscoe Proctor of the Communist Party's national Black Liberation Commission has stated,

> There is a very important distinction between bearers of racist ideas and attitudes. On the one hand there are whites possessing a highly sophisticated and well thought-out racist ideology, but racists in the United States are those who are highly organized and becoming more active, with racism as their main focus, and who enjoy the support of the nation's leading politicians and elected officials, beginning with the President and backed up by official Government propaganda. On the other hand, there are white workers who have not been exposed to working-class ideas, who are also racist, but most of these are not consciously racist.[16]

However, the reverberating or echo effect of the mounting campaign of racism obscures this fundamental difference in the eyes of many Black people, and this is what makes it so timely for a ruling

16. *Daily World*, January 4, 1975.

imperialist clique in hot water at home and in foreign affairs. Racial prejudice not only separates workers and causes frictions among nationalities in the patchwork of nationalities which is the United States. It also actively helps to isolate the minorities politically and generate fiery separatist nationalist sentiments among them, thereby weakening the working class-led struggle for Black liberation. It produces exaggerated emotional attachments to one's own ethnic group and to real or imagined "traditional" values and culture.

Thus just as it is incumbent upon white workers and other white progressives to wage a constant priority struggle against white racism, it is equally important for Blacks in the "Movement" to realize that they can and must work together with white workers and progressive elements inside and outside the workshop in a joint struggle to counter the monopoly attack on their living standards and rights.

* * *

Chapter 5

MANCHILD IN THE LAND OF LENIN:
OR, THE ALTERNATIVE TO CAPITALISM[1]

In 1922, under the guidance of Lenin, the Union of Soviet Socialist Republics was formed as a unique kind of federal state. It was
the first state in the history of mankind in which all peoples,
regardless of race, colour or nationality, were equal and able independently and freely to determine their own destiny. Today the
250 million citizens of this fraternal family consisting of all races
and over a hundred nations and nationalities live and work together
in astonishing harmony. Their labour and working class power
have created a socialist economy in which the entire national
income is utilized in the interest of working people.

It was no great surprise to me that a large share of the national
income in the Soviet Union goes for expanding production in
industry and agriculture. Like others, I had read and heard very
much about the land of Lenin. I had heard tell fabulous tales about
its two-fold resurrection from ruins, once after the Civil War and
foreign capitalist intervention, and once after the Nazi holocaust.
I had heard that racism had been wiped out and that harmonious
assimilation is far advanced. I had read the statistical reports. I
knew that one of ten families in the Soviet Union is an "inter-
nationalities family" — family unions that Americans would
designate inter-racial or inter-ethnic. I had learned that these mixed
marriages are the consequence of enlightened Soviet policy,
especially of the affirmation of woman's equality, and I had seen
the divorce figures showing that mixed marriages prove more
lasting than one-nationality marriages.

Yet it is one thing to read about and study a society that lies far

1. This essay was originally published in *Freedomways: A Quarterly Review
of the Freedom Movement*, Volume 14, Number 1, 1974 (First Quarter),
under the title "Travels in the Soviet Union - Manchild in the Land of Lenin".

yonder, and another to see for oneself how wealth may be used to improve the people's material and cultural standards. Above all, it was important for me to see for *myself* how the Soviet Union's many non-white, non-European citizens were faring.

Who am I? No one outstanding. Just the manchild of Black worker parents from Alabama and Louisiana whose wanderings north from Jim Crow took them first to a small·racist Ohio steel town, and finally, like so many others, to Cleveland, the industrial "mistake on the lake". I was a boychild who became a stripling and then a man in Cleveland's dreadful eastside Hough ghetto, a fellow who, like many of his compeers, hustled for an education and who, after various, not-always-purposeless meanderings, is roosting now in his late thirties in an Ontario university trying to teach Black Studies. Who am I? Just a manchild who knows that racist America is *not* the promised land.

Anyway, it was time for me — a Black American — to go and observe at first hand the rising real wages of the Soviet Union's Brown people I had heard reports of. The moment had come to verify for myself the increasing expenditures for social security and public health services of the USSR's Asian citizens. It was with a critical eye and a sensitive ear that I set out then, at the beginning of October 1973, to test the educational, scientific and cultural advances of Soviet Central Asia and the Caucasus, but mostly to see whether it is possible for a society to solve the racial-national question.

On my itinerary I crisscrossed three of Soviet Central Asia's five Union Republics, a journey spanning thousands of miles. It took me deep into the Caucasus Mountains and to the shores of the Caspian Sea, cheek-by-jowl with the Shah's Persia. It took me to the legendary cities of Tashkent, Samarkand, Bukhara, Dushanbe, Penzikhant and Ashkabad, Arabian Nights oases strung across golden desert sands. It threw me into challenging, person-to-person contact with real people, with Uzbeks, Tadjiks, Tatars, Karakalpaks, nationalities of which little is heard in the United States, and even with Soviet Germans. I penetrated to the very heart of ancient Central Asia and saw a rejuvenated land. I came away with the firm realization that the peoples of the Soviet Union have indeed solved the racial and national questions. There are vital lessons for Black Americans to learn in Soviet Central Asia. Soviet Central Asia provides the most positive and relevant kind of proof for

Blacks in this country that socialism and socialism alone eradicates racial discrimination. The example of the Brown people of the Soviet Union indicates the road to salvation for Black people from their life-long crucifixion under monopoly capitalism. The future of American Black people is writ at the foot of the Pamirs.

Industrialization in Soviet Asia

Production is the cornerstone of social living. Fifty years ago the peoples of Soviet Central Asia realized that if they were going to bring to life the Leninist principle of voluntary state alliance of equal peoples they had to make it in production, and in productivity of labour. They not only made it, they were a thundering success.

Before Soviet power was established, productive forces in the region languished at one of the lowest levels on earth, and some of the most degrading social relations of production to be found anywhere tormented the people. Soviet power came in a purifying storm and the Central Asian Republics made a breath-taking leap from backwardness to progress. The people were determined that the earth should rise on new foundations and rise it did. Compared with 1922 the volume of industrial goods increased 228-fold in Uzbekistan, 500-fold in Tadjikistan, 130-fold in Turkmenia, 381-fold in Kirghizia, and 558-fold in Kazakhstan. In the lifetime of one generation the five Union Republics of Soviet Central Asia have become highly industrialized countries with a well-developed agriculture and advanced science and technology.

I tasted this tremendous achievement by going right into Central Asia's factories and talking with Uzbek, Tadjik and Tatar workers directly.

Even in Moscow, before setting out for Central Asia, I got a presentiment of the new world of work relations I was about to enter, work relations light years removed from those known to most Americans. I glimpsed some Moscow textile factories in passing. I was struck by the fact that the factories of one of the world's largest and busiest capitals show a humanized aspect. Moscow factories looked so clean, so unassuming and so un-factory-like, so unlike the horrible, dark, filthy and forbidding premises in which American workers, especially minority workers, must toil, that the manchild began to wonder — had he finally found a society

117

in which labour is indeed being transformed from an onerous burden into a truly creative activity for the individual?

Tashkent, the capital of Uzbekistan and a metropolis of a million and a half, reinforced this impression. This city, more than a thousand miles distant from Moscow, closer to Afghanistan than to Russia, was ravaged by a terrible earthquake in 1966, a short seven years ago. Now it is one gigantic construction site. No phoenix ever rose from ruins more swiftly or more gracefully than Tashkent. All the fraternal nations and nationalities of the wide Soviet land pitched in to rebuild the stricken city.

From Tashkent we winged south and west, until we came to Samarkand, in the Middle Ages a city of Khans and conquerors, now a modern industrial center of 600,000.

Here I toured my first Central Asian plant — the Samarkand Silk Factory. Its name is a concession to the past. Actually the enterprise's 3,000 textile workers — mostly women and mostly youthful — now turn out nylon and other artificial fabrics to meet modern consumer needs. Only one small department still manufactures natural silk fabriks. Although the productivity of the average workers in the plant is understandably lower than in fully automated Soviet textile factories, these Uzbek, Tadjik and Tatar women workers approach the productive standards of similarly equipped textile mills throughout the country. They now produce in a single day the same amount as in the whole of 1935. They know that improvements in output result in better wages and higher living standards for themselves, their children, husbands and sweethearts. These Asian women have long since freed themselves of the parasites who siphoned off the fruits of their labour as owner's profits.

Right now there are three categories of wages in the USSR: a) piece-wages, b) time-wages based on hours of work, and c) time-wages plus bonus. The last is the most widespread system and predominates at the Samarkand Silk Factory. Thus each worker's pay is based on his productivity. The enterprise's annual gross social product is subdivided and allocated in a manner that is grasped by every worker. There is no hocus-pocus by management, no one tries to pull the wool over the eyes of the workers. A fund is set aside to replace means of production consumed in the course of the year and to finance enlarged production in the next. Naturally a portion of the new value accrues to the Soviet state to meet

118

national requirements and provide for socialist economic planning. The remainder is divided into a fund for workers' remuneration and a fund for cultural and social expenditures. The sum for workers' remuneration contains employees' wages and bonuses and a special emulation fund shared out annually and based on yearly performance. There are job norms for all work places. Through their trade union the workers have a large say in the allocation of funds realized from the social product. When I was visiting, the minimum monthly wage in the Samarkand Silk Factory was 90 rubles, the maximum 230 rubles. The factory average was 130 rubles. But a factory worker pays less than 7 rubles a month for a two-room apartment with kitchen and bath, electricity, water and gas. Since 1926 there has been a single rent rate in effect throughout the Soviet Union. Tenants pay 13.2 kopeks a month per square meter of living room space (100 kopeks = 1 ruble). No rent is charged for the kitchen, bathroom, corridors and other auxiliary premises and large families pay 15 per cent less than the standard rate. Government taxes are almost nominal (the highest being 13% for earnings beyond 100 rubles). Medical care is free, accessible and good.

Women as Leaders

However, women not only work in the Samarkand Silk Factory, they also run it. Although a few departments have male chief engineers, the secretary of the party committee and the factory's head engineer are women. The party secretary, the plant's first lady, is a charming Uzbek woman in her mid-forties. Workers themselves, the women who head the enterprise keep a sharp eye on the well-being and cultural advancement of the workers. It is their duty to see to it that the plant provides them with the facilities to enjoy leisure time. The factory has a library (and it is much used, as I discovered), a drama group, various sports clubs, a literature group and a chess club. Fifteen per cent of the workers are members of the Trade Union's "Communist Schools". These school workers in the principles of scientific communism while giving them the opportunity to learn advanced skills. Naturally, social life centers around the work place and the factory is spotlessly clean. There is no speedup, no slave-driving foreman. The

119

work pace I observed was relaxed and free of the pressures that cause nervous disorders in American workers.

From a personal standpoint the high point of my visit to the factory was a brief encounter with a young Tadjik woman operative. In passing, I noticed her standing at her machine which she had decorated with fresh flowers — a widespread habit of Soviet workers. She glanced at me, took a second look, returning my smile. Then suddenly came a spontaneous, unrehearsed act of friendship and attraction. She snatched the bouquet of flowers from the vase on her work machine and sped toward me. Shyly, warmly, with trepidation she held the bouquet out to me and then fled back to her work place. Here was an act extraordinary in a factory work situation. For the first time I sensed the Soviet workers' deep friendship and solidarity with Black Americans. For years they have been schooled in the best traditions of internationalism and brotherhood, and here in a small way I encountered the result of that teaching. My enchanting acquaintee was not exceptional. Themselves Brown people, Soviet Central Asians — Uzbeks, Tadjiks, Tatars and others — feel they march shoulder to shoulder with Black Americans. This was evident in the wild welcome they gave Angela Davis upon her visit to Tashkent in 1972. Aglow, stammering tongue-tied thanks, the manchild stumbled away, clutching his bouquet of flowers.

The next plant toured was much larger. It is located in Dushanbe, capital of the Tadjik Union Republic which borders Uzbekistan on the southeast. Across the mountains lie Afghanistan, Pakistan and China. Before the October Revolution there were only a handful of miserable enterprises in the country and the proletariat was minuscule. The Tadjik working class formed only after the Revolution when state enterprises were set up. The Civil War was very bitter in this part of the Soviet Union. For years White Guards raided over the border from China and Afghanistan, and the armed struggle dragged on long after it had ended in other parts of the country. After the Civil War many young Tadjiks were sent to other parts of the Soviet Union to be educated. They returned to train those who remained behind. Even the aged went to school. Those were difficult, raw years, but illiteracy was eliminated and the people acquired higher work skills. Aid in the form of machinery and trained personnel poured in from all over the Soviet Union, and the year 1929 marked the real beginnings of the Tadjik working class. Great difficulties were experienced in convincing backward Tadjiks of the superiority of collective labour. Beliefs rooted in Islam also stood in the way of progress. Women who discarded the veil were often murdered by reactionaries. It was a tough struggle to persuade women to join the labour force. It was an even tougher struggle to prevent chauvinist males from standing in their way.

The enterprise I entered is a textile mill constructed during World War II at a juncture when many industries were moved from the west to Central Asia to escape the Nazi invaders. Sprawling over 146 acres, the mill employs 8,500 workers of all races and nationalities. In 1972 more than 1,930,000 yards of cotton fabrics spun from its looms. The domestic market absorbs the cottons and only velvets are exported. Six thousand looms with 267,000 spindles operate around the clock. In one highly mechanized shop there is one machine maintenance man for every eight operatives, but the plant-wide ratio is 650 to 7,850. The whole complex nestles in lush parkland with buildings scattered among apple trees. Most Americans would find it a most improbable setting for a textile mill. It gave me the impression of a small, serene, self-contained town.

Production and the Unions

This graceful setting conceals the most modern techniques. The production process in this mill is almost fully automated. Workers need only oversee the procedure and supervise the workings of machinery. I saw no humans turned into appendages of machines, only machines lightening labour, and I noted the leisurely pace at which automatic machines were tended. Workers spontaneously broke away from their machines, came over and welcomed us, spoke to me of friendship and peace, and then moved away with slow dignity — masters in their own house. There was no one to harass them, no one to hurry them back to work. Production norms are negotiated between union and management with the union always having the final say. No agreement is valid unless it bears the signature of the head of the mill's trade union committee.

Production is continuous. The looms spin without stopping. There is never a break, so the plant runs on the shift system. Actually there are two shift systems — one section of the plant lays on three shifts a day, the other only two at the moment. The shortfall is due to a shortage of labour. An additional two thousand hands are needed, a shortage that will be filled by labour-saving investments combined with enlivened recruitment. Further mechanization and automation are underway, designed to free workers to staff third shifts in departments now limited to two.

Meanwhile the available hands work a forty-hour week. Those who work six days a week have a seven-hour day. The working day lasts eight hours for persons on a five-day week. Operatives begin a shift by working three hours steadily, with a fifteen-minute rest period midway, then break off for a forty-minute lunch or dinner interval, returning to complete the remaining three and a half or four and a half hours. The last stint is interrupted by another fifteen-minute break.

The trade union committee, headed by a competent, no-nonsense Tadjik woman, shows unstinting concern for the workers' health and well-being. Meals are taken in a well-stocked canteen and cost only 40 kopeks. But night shift workers pay nothing at all. The food is hearty and the portions are large. Work places are kept spotlessly clean and safe working conditions are an overriding rule. Before it can harm the lungs of workers all cotton lint is sucked up by automatic vacuum devices. In one shop, rather than walk, women charged with replacing empty spindles ride up and down the line of spinning machines in small, comfortable buggies. The harmful effect of din is recognized and noisy, old-fashioned looms are being phased out in favour of quiet, pneumatic machines. More than 2,000,000 rubles were laid out in 1973 for the new machines. No worker ever need fear being ousted by machinery. He can always count on being reassigned to a new task in keeping with his skills, or having his skills upgraded.

The plant is equipped with excellent recreational facilities to accommodate vacationing workers and those merely out for a leisurely weekend. There is no absenteeism other than for illness. The plant's own kindergarten and pioneer camps relieve working mothers of most of the burden of child care. The mill has two libraries and two large halls set aside for concerts and other cultural events. The evening school is well attended. Astonishing to an American is the way the plant's system of transportation works. Buses carry workers from their doorstep to the job and home again. There is none of the nerve-wracking scurry of U.S.

122

workers left to their own resources to get to and from work.

I found essentially the same working conditions, the same respect and concern for working people in the great oil city of Baku, the capital of the Azerbaijan Union Republic, a country situated in the Caucasus bordering on Iran. Though Uzbekistan and Tadjikistan are Central Asian Lands, while Azerbaijan is in Asia Minor, in regard to the ruling class status of workers they are the same. A quick side-trip to an offshore oil field in the Caspian Sea linked to the mainland by a giant causeway resting on trestles (Baku itself anchors a peninsula which juts out into the Caspian), and a frank discussion with some of the oil workers confirmed my findings.

Education of the Young

This manchild was not foolish enough to leave Central Asia without sampling the system of education. I simply could not overlook the schooling of Soviet citizens knowing as I did that people, human beings, are the most dynamic ingredient in the forces of production. Lenin's great love and solicitude for children are the precious heritage of the Soviet Union. I had heard tell that a deep-reaching cultural revolution was the very basis for the building of socialism in the U.S.S.R. So I went in search of kindergartens, schools and universities.

First the kindergartens, the homes away from home for millions of Soviet children between the ages of three and seven. Although these child care centers release countless mothers for gainful employment, their purpose is to provide for the physical, moral and aesthetic education of very young children.

In Samarkand, the desert oasis, I found a combined nursery and kindergarten for babes from six months to seven years. Like most such centers it was open for at least twelve hours a day. But it also had a special section, a five-day kindergarten, where the children spend only weekends at home, going home on Friday night or Saturday. Regardless of the section in which a tot is enrolled, his parents pay only a tiny fee. The State bears the burden of the cost.

I watched the little ones learning to work and to become independent. Each child is assigned regular duties. The older children

123

see that the younger ones keep their room tidy, make their own beds and put away toys after play. Others help their teachers to set and clear tables at mealtimes. Several times a week, or every day, if necessary, a doctor or medical nurse examines each child and records his temperature. A woman physician heads the kindergarten I saw. By the time a child enters school a precise medical case history has been compiled.

What fascinated me most about the kindergarten in Samarkand is the way art and music are used to impart socialist values. We watched the little ones singing and dancing at their music lessons. Then I remembered the allegation of some American New Leftists that the Soviet Union is not traning "revolutionary successors", that it neglects the ideological moulding of the young. How hollow and ludicrous that claim now seems! It is slander, rubbish of the worst kind. Here in remote Central Asia I found pre-school children surrounded by pictures, displays and lessons about Lenin's life. They recited poems about Lenin to me, sang songs about Soviet power and were learning to live in comradely friendship with children of all races, colours and nationalities. I looked in vain for disturbed children.

Primary and secondary schools continue the training in the finest traditions of the working class. I was invited to Tashkent's School No. 110 by its principal, a beguiling Uzbek woman who voiced special affinity for Black Americans. I met tranquil, purposeful youngsters from seven to seventeen years, and it was a wonderful, inspiring experience. They have absolutely no drug problems and the school officials do not know what a "dropout" is.

In Dushanbe I had a bit more time. I spent it in a Tadjik-language high school. The city's population of 600,000 is served by 78 secondary schools. The one I checked out has 1,500 pupils. In a room adorned with revolutionary flags and pictures of Lenin as a child and as an adult, the principal, a Tadjik woman, welcomed us and told us something about the school and its close-knit community of teachers and pupils. She herself is the proud mother of six children. Four have already completed higher education and are working, while the two youngest are still in university. Though she was too modest to mention it, we discovered that she wears an *Order of Lenin* awarded by her countrymen for her services to the people. The math teacher, another Tadjik woman, wears the medal of an *Honoured Teacher of the Republic*. In all, forty nationalities are represented on the teaching staff. There are two vice-principals, both men, both married, one with five and the other with two children. The spouse of one is studying to be a physician; his colleague's wife is employed at the local textile mill.

Tadjik is the main language of instruction, but Uzbek runs a close second. Russian ranks third. Each child is taught in his native tongue by teachers trained in local teachers' colleges. Tadjik, Uzbek and Tatar boys and girls learn German and English from teachers of Tadjik nationality in beautifully equipped language labs. The curriculum includes a sound grounding in mathematics, biology, chemistry, physics and social science.

I watched a 7th grade physics lesson in progress. The youngsters were very advanced for their age and I was astounded at the neatness and precision of their notes. When I looked in, the history class was busy learning how fascism was defeated in the Great Patriotic War (1941-1945). The 9th grade has more girls than boys, but all wear red ties to show that they are Young Pioneers, active helpers of the Young Communist League and the Communist Party. Girls predominated in the home economics room with only a few lads. I was told that most boys prefer shop, but the choice is left to the youngsters and there is frequent interchange. There is no pressure on the girls to confine themselves to endeavours traditional for women and vocational counselling is both competent and sympathetic to individual preferences. An air of intimacy reigns in the school library; there I found Tadjik translations of the works of progressive American writers.

Before departing we were given a special treat: to the accompaniment of native instruments, a small troupe of very tiny Tadjik girls performed an enchanting and graceful national dance — a ballet of stylized hand and shoulder movements.

Extracurricular Activities with a Purpose

It is the task of education in the Soviet Union to train children ideologically, to give them a dialectical, materialist concept of the various phenomena and processes in social life. It must reveal to them the inevitability of society's transition from capitalism to socialism, and it must impart the ideals of communism. The Young Pioneers' Organization, uniting practically all children from ten to fourteen, is a great help in accomplishing these lofty aims. In Baku, the oilman's capital, I got a look at one of this organization's out-of-school centers — a Young Pioneers' Palace.

Young Pioneers' Houses and Palaces arrange competitions, reviews, exhibitions, rallies of young technicians and naturalists. They take charge of festivals dedicated to the outdoors and organize hikes. Young Pioneers' Palaces have special sections specializing in physics, chemistry, mathematics, literary criticism, and more. It is the duty of Palace instructors to arrange visits by writers, poets, scientists, actors, leading workers and war veterans, while at the same time introducing youngsters to the arts of singing, dancing, drama, painting and sculpture.

A large, stately building houses the Baku Pioneers' Palace. I counted no less than eleven voluntary hobby interest groups. Though the size of each activity group is limited, for obvious reasons, to 15 to 20 youngsters, the only restriction on a child's participation is passing marks in school; a youngster with poor marks is expected to spend more time at homework than with hobbies. In any case, there could be no question about the seriousness of these young buffs. Each pursues his hobby with passion, developing it to the fullest potential. After graduating from secondary school, many of the pioneers, I was told, go on to develop their skills professionally — today's bird watcher, tomorrow's ornithologist. They get a good start, for each group is instructed by a qualified teacher. For instance, the astronomy workshop — in many ways the most interesting in the Baku Palace — is led by a math teacher who, though self-taught, has become famous in his own right as an astronomer throughout the Soviet Union and abroad. His young charges, mostly boys from the 6th to the 10th grade, were busy grinding their own lens for a telescope with 0.01 micron accuracy. When finished, the telescope will weigh more than a ton. Manipulating lathes and other machinery, these youngsters manufacture sophisticated instruments and regularly photograph and study the moon and stars with them. In the radio shop teenagers from 14 to 17 handle sensitive radio transmitters. Not only are they competent Morse code telegraphers and short wave radio operators, but they also have built all their equipment themselves. A proud map display traces a network of radio contact with hams from all over the globe. Although this was Azerbaijan and not Russia, we even found a ballet group, the youngest ballerina a tender four years. Three proud little lads added a masculine flavour to a roomful of future prima ballerinas — they were not intimidated or embarrassed by the girls in the least.

In Tashkent I met Komsomols and in Samarkand had a delightful evening with university students who entertained us with a musical variety group. Today the Leninist Komsomol — the Young Communist League of the Soviet Union — has a membership in excess of 23 millions. I was invited to sit on the presidium at a Tashkent branch meeting. It was thrilling to see the Komsomol at work teaching its members to be purposeful, to show initiative and to study and work well. This branch, like others, gives voluntary assistance to building projects, sending its best members to construction sites.

Samarkand has six institutes of higher learning and one university, founded in 1927 with just 60 students and a single professor. Now it numbers 15,000 students, 11 faculties, 65 professorial chairs. The entire teaching faculty is more than 700. The library contains two million volumes. Thirty nationalities are represented among the student body, but since this is Uzbekistan, the majority of students are Uzbeks, Tatars and Tadjiks with a leavening of Russians and other nationalities. No racial or ethnic friction upsets the tranquility of the university.

My host was the International Friendship Association, a student body most of whose participants are enrolled in the Foreign Languages Faculty. The Faculty specializes in English, German and French. The languages of instruction are Uzbek, Tadjik and Russian. Foreign language training is top notch. I had fluent discussions in English with students who have never in their lives set foot out of Central Asia. Others speak excellent French and German. The more outstanding students win special scholarships of which there are three at graduated levels, the highest being the Lenin Scholarship. With or without a scholarship, all students are paid stipends and no student pays more than 30 kopeks a month for dormitory accommodation.

Higher Education

Soviet universities are composed of separate Faculties. A student matriculates in the Faculty of his choice for five years and

127

then must pass a taxing State examination for a diploma. Post-graduate study is not unlike that in the United States. The second degree, known as the Candidate of Science, is awarded at the end of three additional years of study and successful defense of an academic thesis. The Doctorate of Science is the highest degree. Both Candidate of Science and Doctor of Science are academic degrees which qualify one to teach in institutions of higher learning. The Doctorate of Science resembles both the American Ph.D. and the German *Habilitation*, but, unlike the latter, is granted in recognition of outstanding contribution to science and not for any prescribed academic dissertation. Thus the author of any particularly brilliant book or article may be recommended for a Doctorate. Academic rankings among the teaching faculty at Samarkand University are very like American rankings. The lowest grade is that of Instructor, a scholar who holds a diploma and who, in most cases, is preparing to defend a thesis for the degree of Candidate of Science while teaching. The middle rank is Candidate of Science. At the top are the Doctors of Science. There are several hundred Instructors at Samarkand University, 76 Candidates and 43 Doctors of Science. The most reputed Faculties are Biology and Mathematics. The Faculty of History specializes in Uzbek history, but also gives its students a firm grounding in the general principles of historical materialism. Scientific communism is one of the subjects of the State exam all Soviet students must pass at the end of five years. I was informed that each Faculty in Samarkand includes specialists who teach dialectical and historical materialism to students of the Faculty in a manner specially related to their subject. However, these specialists are themselves trained in the main universities in the capital city of each Union Republic — e.g., Moscow, Kiev, Tashkent, Alma-Ata, etc. Only there can separate Faculties of Philosophy (Marxism-Leninism) be found.

Scientific research, teaching and scholarship all merge in the Soviet Union's great Academies of Sciences. In Moscow sits the headquarters of the All-Union Academy of Sciences, but each Union Republic has its own Academy. In Dushanbe, capital of Tadjikistan, we were invited to the Tadjik Academy by the Director of its History Institute. He received us in his study where he remarked with modest pride that his colleagues were churning out scientific books and articles at the "rate of a conveyor belt." The

Academy has its own publishing house. Altogether the Tadjik Academy of Sciences has 3,000 members.

The History Institute is a working collective of 130 scientists. Research is divided among seven sub-divisions. The brunt of the work is carried by the archaeological division, the pre-Revolutionary division which handles the history of Tadjikistan up to the October Revolution, and the Soviet division which studies the period from 1917 to the present. The latter is by far the most important division. It is headed by a woman historian and recently published a pioneering five-volume history of the Tadjik people which sold out immediately. In addition, there is a division of art history, a division devoted to Tadjik culture, an ethnographic division, and a restorations laboratory. With this elaborate set-up there is no danger that the history of this Brown Central Asian people will ever be lost or ignored. Accustomed as I am to struggling to teach Afro-American history on a shoestring budget, I was floored by the facilities available to my Tadjik colleagues. I was one flabbergasted manchild. The archaeological division stages expeditions to remote parts of Tadjikistan. There are ample funds for research trips both within the Soviet Union and abroad. The Institute has a wide network of international contacts. Its members appear prominently at international conferences.

The director likened the staff to an "international brigade", for it is a multi-national body of historians, all enjoying equal rights. Current research programs include the history of the working class in Tadjikistan and the development of the now-flourishing Tadjik intelligentsia. The chairwoman of the Soviet division is researching the Tadjik people's share in the Great Patriotic War against Hitler. Of great interest to me personally is the work on the history of the establishment of collective farms in Tadjikistan. We learned there was a gap in time between the collectivization of farms in the rest of the Soviet Union and in Tadjikistan. Collectivization in this Moslem country began in 1928 but dragged on for a decade. The process finished only in 1937. First attempts took the form of mutual aid teams and remained stuck at that stage for quite a while. Fierce class struggle roared back and forth throughout the countryside. At first collective ownership was restricted merely to land, tools were exempted, farm animals and implements remained private property. But at that stage it did not matter, for there were very few tools in existence in backward Tadjikistan anyway. Today ninety per cent of all farms are collective farms and most have modern equipment.

Museums and Political Education

Everyone knows the Soviet Union is filled with monuments to Lenin and the world is familiar with the great Lenin mausoleum on Moscow's Red Square. Overlooked by many foreigners, however, is the large Lenin Museum situated close by the mausoleum, an incomparable collection of mementos from the life of the leader of the first victorious proletarian revolution. The museum houses graphic and visual displays of the history of the Bolshevik party, the working class movement, and the Soviet Union since the October Revolution. A walk through it is as good as a short, concentrated course in political education — the history of the class struggle in Czarist Russia and Leninist strategy and tactics unfold before the viewer.

Although the Moscow museum is a must for foreign Communist Party delegations and representatives of the national liberation movements, what even fewer foreigners seem to know is that each one of the fourteen other Union Republic capitals has its own Lenin Museum, exact replicas of the Moscow collection supplemented by unique reminders of the local revolutionary past (e.g., Lenin with the leaders of the Peoples of the East, etc.). The love for Lenin and the desire to learn from him carry over into remote Central Asia. There the Lenin Museums, magnificent edifices, serve the ideological needs of the working people and their children. Soviet Central Asia's Lenin Museums are priceless schools in the principles of scientific communism. Tashkent, Dushanbe, Ashkabad, Frunze, Alma-Ata — each has its Lenin Museum and into each one stream Uzbeks, Tadjiks, Turkmen, Kirghiz, Kazakhs, Tatars and Kara-Kalpaks, workers, collective and state farmers, and intellectuals. I observed rapt Central Asian school children, whole classes, being guided on political lecture tours through these museums. Once I came upon deaf-mute children, a little silent band enjoying a lesson about Lenin and the struggle against capitalism in *sign language*. Some Lenin Museums even have foreign language guides who give expert commentaries in English, German, French and other tongues. The layout is modern and attractive. For easy com-

130

prehension the display is divided into sections corresponding with distinct periods in Lenin's career (e.g., 1895-1903).

All in all, it is awe-inspiring proof of the Soviet Union's determination to realize Lenin's legacy concretely. If ever he is fortunate enough to revisit the land of Lenin, this manchild will make a beeline to a Lenin Museum.

Everywhere I went in the Soviet Union I found the same concern to preserve alive the memory of the Revolution and the centuries-long fight against oppression. For instance, the most striking work of art in all of Azerbaijan is the huge, sparkling monument in Baku to *26 Bolshevik Commissars*, among them Shaumyan and Japaridze, butchered in 1918 by British and Turkish imperialists and Azerbaijanian counterrevolutionaries. While in Baku, I attended a superbly-danced ballet whose plot would stun Americans — it depicted the anti-feudal class struggle in medieval Asia.

The People — Educated, Wise, Unforgettable

What more need I say? That the land of Lenin is gorgeous? From all I have said that is obvious. That the Soviet Union's nonwhite citizens have made the leap from poverty and illiteracy to well-being and advanced culture? Everything I saw testifies to that. That the national question has been solved and that racism is just a bad memory? No one who actually sees Soviet Central Asia can honestly think otherwise.

Naturally I registered kaleidoscopic impressions, some more lasting than others. I remember Tashkent, for instance, shimmering in the sun, limpid and resplendent in reconstructed elegance. Along its boulevards, umbrellaed by leafy trees, stroll folks for whom the horrid memory of the earthquake is beginning to fade. I remember its graceful fountains and its gracious people, mostly one remembers the people — it is they who are truly unforgettable. The Uzbeks are a hearty, handsome people, strong stock cradled in Asia's midriff, the kind of people who, once they were rid of their exploiters, were able to make the arid steppe bloom and the desert surrender its secrets. An engaging and spontaneous people now preparing to reverse the flow of the rivers to water the desert. I remember their heartfelt sympathy for bleeding Chile, their pain

131

at the thought of the fascist murders going on there, their solidarity with valiant Vietnam, their determination to aid the embattled Arab peoples and fighting Black Africa (Guinea-Bissau, Angola, Mozambique).

Tashkent is noted for its great open-air market with fixed stalls and concrete canopy for all-weather service. There on a Sunday morning I made instant friends with collective farmers vending fruits and vegetables. Shoppers elbowed one another good-naturedly, the crowd ebbed and flowed, people milled about at a row of haberdashery stalls — a riot of colour and animation. Above the roar I heard what sounded like haggling, but do not be misled. There were no wheeler-dealers here, no slick young men on the make, no private enterprise greed. The goods on display in the haberdashery stalls are State-owned and the stalls are run by employees of the State. I wandered across to the pomegranate counter and ran upon an ordinary-looking Uzbek collective farmer. He was a collective farmer all right, but he also turned out to be a foreign language specialist. We conversed in French, his much more fluent than mine. I came away feeling there is more to be learned about real social equality in the Tashkent marketplace than in all the leaden volumes of bourgeois sociologists back home.

One evening I wandered into the hotel bar in Dushanbe, the number one hotel, and was immediately approached by two truck drivers, one Tadjik, his partner a *Volksdeutscher* German, born and raised in the Soviet Union. They patted my back, shook my hand, and insisted that I drink a fiery toast with them to peace, friendship and international worker's solidarity — at their expense. Not only did they make me welcome, these two workers were themselves well at ease. The bar was filled with ordinary Tadjik and Tatar working men taking their pleasure. Thunderstruck I remembered that this was the most exclusive hotel in the Union Republic capital. It was the equivalent of Black workers hanging out at the bar in the Waldorf-Astoria, not only being served but actually being able to afford the expense!

When the manchild left the land of Lenin, he left knowing that at the foot of the Pamirs, in remote Central Asia, he had indeed read his own people's future. For the first time he knew where the "promised land" lay.

Part II

REVOLUTION IN AFRICA AND U.S. IMPERIALISM
PROBLEMS OF THE NATIONAL LIBERATION MOVEMENT

Chapter 6

THE ANATOMY OF IMPERIALISM[1]

More and more, as Afro-Americans — locked in their own class struggle against U.S. monopoly capital and racism — look around the world, they are at once encouraged and baffled by the emergence of so many new states and great liberation struggles in Africa, Asia and Latin America. They feel drawn towards Africa, but do not know what to make of some of the regimes there. They hear much of the effect the general crisis of U.S. capitalism is supposed to be having on the "third world", but really have not made up their minds whether a "third world" exists at all.

In the flood of rhetoric concerning the "third world", basic questions are left unanswered, questions, like the difference between colonialism and neo-colonialism, like whether a non-capitalist path of development is feasible in "third world" countries, and whether non-capitalist is identical with socialist development. How does the political economy of raw materials work in the developing countries? Exactly why and how does the imperialist world system go about exploiting and oppressing Africans, Asians and Latin Americas? What are the scientifically-verifiable prospects for improvements in the "third world"?

This essay will probe these and related questions, and suggest some answers.

*

We must begin by understanding what the term *imperialist colonial system* means. A product of history, the imperialist colonial system is the totality of colonies, semi-colonies, dependent countries, and neo-colonial states, oppressed and enslaved by the

1. This essay was originally published in *The Black Scholar*, Volume 6, Numbers 7 and 8, April and May 1975, as "Imperialism and Third World Economics".

135

modern imperialist powers. At one time this system enveloped most of the people on earth, today it is badly battered and much reduced, but still has notable vestiges and powerful capacities to assume new forms. Colonies are best defined as countries lacking political independence which belong to a monopoly-capitalist-dominated metropolis (an imperialist state). In the narrow sense, a colony is any inhabited territory whose sovereignty rests with a distant state.

In imperialism's current phase, the colonial system consists, in addition to full-fledged colonies, of various types of semi-colonies, dependencies and neo-colonial states. Dependencies are poorly developed, formally independent countries which have become the objects of colonial exploitation and which are subject to imperialist economic and political control. A semi-colonial state is one in which pre-capitalist local ruling classes share the exploitation of the popular masses with the foreign imperialist bourgeoisie. Neo-colonial states are formally independent countries still subject to colonial exploitation, but in which, owing to the national liberation movement, the worsening crisis of capitalism, and the growing weight of the socialist world system, the imperialist masters are forced to resort to modernized and more sophisticated methods in order to hold on.

Colonial conquest and the establishment of great world empires by enslaving weaker peoples existed before imperialism dawned in the 1870s and 1880s, in fact, long before the appearance of capitalism. After all, Rome and the Hellenistic states — ancient slave-holding societies — were empires, and Genghis Khan, the Arab Caliphs and the Ottoman Turks ruled over military despotic empires. Western European commercial capitalism, capitalism in its simple cooperation and manufactory stages, which from the sixteenth to the nineteenth century created the world market and enslaved Africans, set up huge colonial empires in the Western hemisphere, India and Indonesia. However, as Lenin proved, colonies acquired new significance in the era of monopoly capital and imperialism.[2]

2. See V.I. Lenin, "Imperialism, the Highest Stage of Capitalism. A Popular Outline", in *Collected Works*, Vol. 22, pp. 185-304. This is the basic, indispensable work for the understanding of imperialism and will remain so for the rest of our epoch of transition from capitalism to socialism.

The change in the role of colonies was caused by the ousting of free competition by monopoly domination in the advanced capitalist countries (ca. 1873-1895) which were just then in the process of subjugating colonies and semi-colonies. Exploitation of colonies, semi-colonies and dependencies became one of the most lucrative sources of superprofit for the emergent monopolies. Imperialist colonial policy was historically inseparable from the completion of the territorial division of the world among the imperialist powers and their struggle to redivide it. In 1919, colonies and dependencies herded into the imperialist colonial system occupied 72 percent of the world's surface and contained over 69 percent of its production. The methods by which this empire was exploited included the export of capital, control of raw material sources, and competition between the monopolies for spheres of influence, economic regions and military bases.

*

As it overran the globe, capitalism thus brought to a culmination the tendency to integrate separate countries and regions economically. It tended to abolish national isolation, gradually uniting huge territories in an integral whole. The method employed was unfeeling oppression and exploitation of colonial and dependent peoples by the metropolises. The so-called "third world's" separate national economies — most of them pre-capitalist[3] and with weakly-developed productive forces — were transformed into links in a connected chain called the "world economy". This "integration" actually split the world into a small group of imperialist powers which exploited and oppressed colonial and dependent countries, and the great majority of colonial and dependent countries whose inhabitants had to fight to free themselves from the imperialist yoke.

3. Primitive-communal, slaveowning, feudal, small-scale commodity, and transitional and intermediate forms of these social formations, prevailed in Asia, Africa and Latin America at the time of the conquest. As everywhere, the motor of history in these class societies was the antagonism which arises between people in the process of social production, exchange, and distribution of material wealth. See I. Andreyev, *The Noncapitalist Way. Soviet Experience and the Liberated Countries*, Moscow, 1977.

Imperialism condemned colonial and dependent peoples to economic and social backwardness. Robbed of the prerequisites for progress, hundreds of millions fell victim to unparalleled cruelty, poverty and ignorance. Arbitrary imperialist disposal of the labour power and resources of the colonies for a long time froze productive forces in Asia, Africa and Latin America where the majority of mankind lives. The colonies were drained of everything from the blood of humans to raw materials. In the First World War almost a million and a half Blacks from the African colonies, cheap "cannon fodder", were mustered to fight as soldiers on the side of France. During both World Wars, the metropolises shifted a large part of the financial burden off on the colonies.[4]

The extent to which British capitalists enriched themselves at the expense of their raw materials producing overseas colonies showed in the gap between the value of British imports and the value of exports. Taking the price of producers' goods in 1913 as a basic index of 100, by 1920, following World War I, the increase of the export prices received by British imperialism had outstripped the import prices it paid by 61 percent. Colonial conquest also caused a tremendous growth of racial discrimination and national oppression. Thus from a historical standpoint, imperialist colonization is an enormity which cannot be overestimated. As Lenin noted, it transformed capitalism from the liberator of (European and North American) nations it had been in the centuries of struggle against feudalism, into the greatest oppressor of nations and nationalities in modern history. It is the cause for the backwardness of the "third world" today.

A striking feature of the general crisis of capitalism is the crisis and collapse of the colonial system we have witnessed over the last three decades. Of course we cannot fathom the crisis of the imperialist colonial system unless we first understand the general crisis of capitalism, the main features and tenets of which were revealed by Lenin.

*

4. See Jean Suret-Canale, *Afrique Noire Occidentale et Centrale*, Volume II: *L'ère coloniale*, Paris, 1964.

Long-awaited, capitalism's general crisis exploded on the scene in 1917. It is a comprehensive crisis of the capitalist world system, marked by imperialist and anti-imperialist wars and social revolutions, by the struggle between moribund capitalism and rising socialism on a world scale. The chief characteristic of the general crisis of capitalism is the establishment of the dictatorship of the proletariat first in one country, then the division of the world into two antagonistic social systems — the capitalist world system and the socialist world system.

Capitalism's general crisis encompasses all aspects of bourgeois (capitalist) society, economic and cultural as well as political, long term morbidity as well as crises of everyday living. One aspect means growing weakness for the capitalist world system in relation to emergent socialism, the other growing economic and political power for the countries which have broken away from capitalism. The general crisis began during the First World War and developed as the aftermath of Russia quitting the capitalist system. The first stage in capitalism's general crisis coincided with the inter-war years, 1917-1939. The second stage of the crisis opened with World War II and the subsequent revolt against the capitalist system of the People's Democracies in Europe and Asia. The third (present) stage of the crisis began in the late 1950s and has featured the Cuban revolution, the Vietnamese people's victory over U.S. aggression, the collapse of the Portuguese colonial empire, and the orientation on socialism of a growing number of African states.

Against this background we can understand the crisis of the *imperialist colonial system* which appeared during the imperialist World War of 1914-1919, only to grow in scope and profundity thereafter, stimulated by the 1917 October Socialist Revolution. It is punctuated by terrible aggravation of the contradictions between the imperialist powers on one side, and the colonies, semi-colonies and dependent countries on the other. A series of violent turning points, and critical collapses of one empire after the other, the crisis of the colonial system is manifested in the growth of the national liberation struggle of the oppressed peoples, culminating in independence, and in post-independence struggles against imperialism. The crisis of the colonial system is further caused by the development of industry and native capitalism in the colonies, a process which worsens the capitalist world's marketing problems and leads to the rise of an industrial proletariat in the colonies.

It was during the second stage of the general crisis of capitalism that the crisis of the colonial system reached its exploding point. World War II exposed the cancer of colonialism, it subjected the enslaved peoples to sore trials, yet by the same token destroyed the myth that the colonial masters were almighty. As the national liberation struggle revived and swelled in intensity after 1945, the colonial system disintegrated.

Lenin was the first to realize (August-September 1917) that, under imperialism, monopoly capitalism has a tendency to develop into state-monopoly capitalism and that this was bound to affect the mode of colonial exploitation. State-monopoly capitalism is imperialism's ultimate phase. Despite uneven development, today this process has gone so far that the bourgeois machinery of government is subordinate to the monopolies, and, as a glance at Washington, D.C. will tell us, big corporations merge with the state. The only article of faith worshipped by the state-monopoly capitalists is the extraction of the maximum superprofits. Though it deepens the main contradictions of the capitalist system, state-monopoly capitalists pursue their aim with an obstinacy worthy of the damned. Exploitation of working people intensifies in all advanced capitalist countries.

What remains of the imperialist colonial system is transformed into an integral economic system consisting of a *center* — the imperialist powers — and a *periphery* — a belt of super-exploited underdeveloped countries. Territorial division of the non-socialist world between the imperialist powers and the struggle to redivide it now largely take the form of neo-colonialism. Basically neo-colonialism is a system of state-monopoly measures aiming at maintaining the economic positions and restoring the political privileges of imperialism in new forms in former colonies. Forcible suppression of national liberation movements has become a fundamental imperialist doctrine. The Mussadiq government of Iran was overthrown for daring to clash with the international oil cartel, and the Arbenz government in Guatemala for facing up to the United Fruit monopoly. Israeli militarists were unleashed against progressive Arab regimes. Patrice Lumumba, the father of independent Zaire, was murdered, and Santo Domingo invaded by U.S. marines. Chile's President Salvador Allende was brutally assassinated for having exercised sovereignty against the profits of

ITT, Anaconda and Kennecott. Racists terrorize Zimbabwe and South Africa. Franco-American imperialists and the Chinese leaders intervene in Zaire's copper-rich Shaba province to preserve the puppet Mobutu regime. Protracted colonial wars rage everywhere.

Such is the history of the emergence and the content of the imperialist colonial system.

*

Let us seek to strengthen our theoretical grasp of the success of the national liberation movement.

Following the defeat of fascist imperialism in World War II, the struggle against imperialist colonialism proceeded in a new, favourable world-political environment. Consolidation of the socialist world system and the strengthening of the world's democratic forces promoted the national liberation movement globally. The expansion of socialism beyond the confines of a single country and the formation of a socialist world commonwealth radically altered the correlation of class forces in the international arena. A situation was created propitious to the collapse of the imperialist colonial system. Thanks to the moral, political and material solidarity of the socialist states, the national liberation movement succeeded in holding its own and turning back the united counter-onslaught of the imperialist powers and international monopolies. As the bond between the national liberation movement and the struggle for socialism tightened, the progressive elements of the post-war world proved decisive for the disintegration of the colonial system in its traditional form. Imperialism was thrown on the defensive historically.

Hence no matter how limited and imperfect, political independence creates better conditions for colonized peoples to develop the class struggle and strengthen the anti-imperialist alliance. Merely for this reason, political sovereignty should never be underestimated; it is essential for the progress of "third world" countries. Meanwhile factors like the rise of multinational corporations and the internationalization of production under the sponsorship of state-monopolies have accelerated the breakup of one of the colonial system's traditional features — "closed reserves", i.e. colonial territories protected by the flag of *one* specific imperialist power and reserved exclusively for its financial oligarchy to exploit.

Thus we see that it is the national liberation movement which draws the overwhelming majority of the world's population — oppressed by the financial oligarchy of a few large capitalist powers — into the historic struggle against imperialism. Without it, this majority, the third stream in the world revolutionary process,[5] would stand apart from the international class struggle.

*

We have now laid the groundwork for an examination of present-day colonial economics and exploitation of the "third world". Our next step will be to understand how the basic economic law of capitalism works under imperialism, and how monopoly superprofits are extracted from imperialism's "third world" periphery.

Monopoly superprofits include, in addition to average capitalist profit, a *surplus* profit which monopoly extracts in one or the other sphere of production or exchange because of its dominant position. A monopoly is a corporation or other business enterprise whose concentration of capital and production is large enough to enable it to make regular superprofits. The big corporations like Ford Motor Company, General Electric, United States Steel, Morgan Guaranty Trust, Exxon, etc., whose names are household words for us, are all monopolies. Now, although the main component of monopoly superprofits is the extra surplus value[6] obtained at monopoly enterprises in the metropolis as a result of their higher rate of exploitation of workers, compared with non-monopoly enterprises (i.e. small- and medium-scale capitalist businesses),[7] a lot of monopoly superprofit is extracted from the

5. The socialist world system is the first stream in the world revolutionary process, the struggle of the proletariat in the advanced capitalist countries, the second.

6. Rooted in surplus labour, that is, the unpaid labour of hired workers, *surplus value* expresses the relations between the capitalist class and the working class, relations of the exploitation of hired labour by capital. The extraction of surplus value is the basic law of capitalist production. Profit is a changed form of surplus value.

7. A caveat against assuming automatically that the rate of surplus value (i.e. rate of exploitation) is always higher in monopoly than in non-monopoly

142

sale of commodities. Commodities owned by monopolies are, as a rule, *not* sold for their prices of production (cost price plus average profit), but rather for *higher* monopoly prices. *The monopoly price is equal to the cost price plus high monopoly profit.* Monopoly price lies above production price, and, as a rule, exceeds the value of the commodity. This is an essential phenomenon which determines the necessary, natural development of monopoly capitalist reproduction. Under imperialism, this derivative law of monopoly superprofit functions as a form and development of capitalism's *basic* economic law — the law of surplus value.

How does this affect the "third world"? It affects it in the most brutal and physical manner because huge monopoly superprofits are obtained by appropriating much of the value created by the labour of "third world" people. In colonial and neo-colonial countries the lion's share of the surplus value (along with part of the necessary product) produced by the agonizing, compulsory labour of hundreds of millions is seized by foreign monopolies, while most of the remainder is consumed unproductively by native ruling classes. In fact, the advanced capitalist states achieved a large part of their high development of productive forces and their comparatively high standard of living through looting the economically backward countries. Proof that the "third world" offers U.S. monopoly capitalists fabulous opportunities for profitable investment is the fact that the average profitability on direct investments of U.S. companies was 7.7 percent higher in the "third world" from 1960 to 1970, than in developed capitalist countries.[8]

Governed by free competition, the export of commodities was typical for pre-monopoly capitalism. Imperialism shifts the emphasis to the export of capital. Capital is exported for one reason only — to bring monopoly superprofits back home to the capitalists. Capital is exported in two forms. In one variant, loans are granted to foreign governments, provincial authorities, municipal-

enterprises, is that the selfsame organic composition of capital (C:V) which being higher in monopoly enterprises, elevates the productivity of labour there above that in non-monopoly enterprises, implies in small, backward non-monopoly enterprises a higher rate of variable capital to constant capital, and thus a higher rate of raw exploitation. See note no. 18 below.

8. CIC Brief, *An Examination of the Multinational Corporations*, p. 36.

ities, and banks. In the other, the capital shipped abroad establishes industrial, commercial and banking enterprises in foreign countries (direct investments), or it purchases concessions and constructs infrastructures like railways, port installations, airports and roads, or, in backward countries, it buys up already-existing enterprises at ridiculously low prices.

While most of the capital now exported from the U.S. goes to advanced capitalist countries (e.g. Canada, the Common Market), a lot still finds its way to backward, "third world" countries where little capital is available, where wages are abominably low, raw materials cheap, and the price of land comparatively low. Kenya, Zaire, South Africa, and the West Indies, for example, fit this bill. There rivers of gold are sweated from the backs of superexploited workers and peasants. In 1964 the United States officially repatriated $4,900,000,000 in profits from direct investments in the "third world"; in 1966 it brought home $5,800,000,000, and in 1971 $8,820,000,000.[9] Profits exported from Africa have almost trebled in recent years. In 1970 alone, profit on foreign investments transferred abroad from 19 African states exceeded one billion dollars. During 1970-1971, the Ivory Coast paid the imperialists $36,000,000 in profits, Zambia $38,000,000, Ghana $42,000,000, Nigeria $156,000,000, while $346,000,000 were sucked from Black workers in the apartheid Republic of South Africa.[10] As of 1974, "Nigeria holds first place for the influx of private investments (about $100 million); next come Morocco and Kenya, both at about the same level".[11]

*

The export of capital continues to be closely connected with the export of commodities. Once a country has fallen into their debt, the imperialists who export capital usually force their manufactured commodities on the debtor country at very disadvantageous rates for the debtor. The many puppet states who

9. International Monetary Fund, *Balance of Payments Yearbook*, 1970 and 1971.
10. *Ibid.*
11. L. Alexandrovskaya, "Africa: Some Tendencies in Economic Development", in *International Affairs*, No. 7, Moscow, 1974, p. 66.

144

receive U.S. military "aid" are required by the Pentagon to purchase their military hardware exclusively from American arms manufacturers. In this way, tax monies deducted from the wages of U.S. workers, and delivered to such traitors as General Nguyen Van Thieu, end up in the pockets of American big businessmen. Directly invested capital also enables foreign monopolies to seize markets and sources of raw materials in backward countries. Thus while quickening the development of capitalism in the "third world", the export of capital results in its allround subjugation and pillage by foreign monopolies. The export of capital provides the material basis for the division of the non-socialist world into a tight ring of profiteering imperialists and a large majority of peripheral debtor countries.

Clearly, "third world" countries are subordinates in the international capitalist division of labour dominated by the monopolies. Here it is useful to distinguish between ordinary foreign monopolies which exploit the underdeveloped periphery and the giant multinational corporations which already control one-sixth of the aggregate gross national product of all the capitalist countries, and which have turned neo-colonialism into a nightmare for the peoples of the "third world". They are now the most typical representatives of imperialism in the neo-colonial era. A United Nations study of these new imperialist octopuses showed that the volume of direct foreign capital investment by U.S. multinational corporations in 1971 alone amounted to $4,800,000,000, while they repatriated about $9,000,000,000 in dividends, interest, and payments for managerial services, licences and patents.[12] The annual turnover of ten of the biggest multinational corporations exceeds the national income of two-thirds of the member countries of the United Nations. Not only do they control more than half of the world trade in raw materials, multinationals are also the mainstay of colonialist and racist regimes. Before the recent democratic revolution in Portugal, they lavished handouts to the fascist Portuguese military administrations in Guinea-Bissau, Mozambique and Angola. U.S., British and West German multinationals bolster the white minority regime in South Africa.

12. See United Nations Secretariat, *Multinational Corporations in World Development*, New York, 1973.

145

There are two kinds of multinational corporations — those controlled jointly by the financial oligarchies of different countries (e.g. an enterprise in which, say, U.S., British and West German capitalists all share the pie), and those which operate "transnationally" in various countries around the world (e.g. General Motors, IBM, Unilever).[13] Today about a third of multinational subsidiaries and investments are located in the neo-colonial world. The sales of the major multinational corporations exceed the gross national product of any African country, and only India, Brazil, Mexico and Argentina in all of the "third world" have a greater economic potential than the General Motors Corporation. The multinationals have a steel grip on the international marketing, transport and insurance network that "third world" countries, dependent on foreign trade, must use in order to survive. The forced economic specialization imposed on individual countries and whole regions keeps wages low and enables the multinationals to draw ever larger batches of raw materials and foodstuffs from the periphery.

Multinational corporations preserve the colonial link by concentrating investments mostly in the extractive industry, plantations, the services sector, as well as the preliminary processing of farm products for the markets. This is what makes "third world" economics so one-sided or *monocultural*. Imperialism transforms them into raw material and agrarian appendages of the metropolises. Many dependent countries specialize in the production and exportation of just one or two products. Thus following World War II, coffee and cotton were more than 60 percent of Zambian exports, while 80 percent of Ghana's exports was cocoa beans. Today more than a third of Senegal's exports are peanuts and peanut oil, more than half of the exports of the Ivory Coast are coffee and cocoa, and nearly a third of Malawi's exports are tea and tobacco.

Monoculture teaches the colonial farm worker only a limited number of routine skills difficult to apply to other sectors of the economy, and it subjects the country as a whole to the arbitrary will of the multinational corporations who do the wholesale

---

13. See I. Ivanov, "International Corporations and the Third World", in *International Affairs*, No. 8, August 1974, pp. 31-42.

buying. "The result is that it is not the multinational corporation's enterprises that are 'integrated' into the national economy of the 'host' countries, but rather the 'enclave' sectors of this economy are 'integrated' into the international production of the multinational corporations."[14]

Under capitalism nothing develops evenly, neither the economy nor political activity. The competition and anarchy of production which are inherent in capitalism endow "high growth-rate sectors" of the economy and certain lines of production with a fast tempo of development, while other lines and branches take a slow tempo, or even decline. The scientific and technological revolution enables individual capitalist countries and whole regions to play catch up, to leapfrog one another in stages of development and in the accumulation of capital. In the age of imperialism, this objective law of the uneven development of capitalist countries is a main cause for the export of capital, and thus one of the main forces conditioning the exploitation of the "third world". Since capital is accumulated at different rates in different countries, a relative "surplus" of free money begins to form in one country, say, the United States, faster than in rivaling countries, when the domestic market for a particular line has been saturated. Thirsting for profits, this "surplus" capital begins to look beyond its borders for investments with worthwhile returns. Evidently, different rates of profit cause uneven accumulation. Capital has a tendency towards partial non-reproduction in a market where the effective demand has already been satisfied, a tendency to lose its value (devaluation or devalorization), and this often happens, especially in the USA.

The appearance and export of "surplus" capital have profound negative consequences for the movement of productive forces, especially in the capital-importing countries. In social formations where the capitalist mode of production has made only superficial penetration (i.e. the "third world"), where the spontaneous spread of capitalist relations was hindered by colonialism, and by outright destruction, the distortion of the human and material forces of production is monstrous. The U.S. financial oligarchy in particular, commanding huge sums of "surplus" investment capital, hurls the effects of the overall tendency of the average rate of profit to decline — the result of capital's tendency to lose value — off on

14. *Ibid.*, p. 35.

the weaker nations subordinated to it by the whole network of dependency and "participation" woven by the export of capital. The most common form of imperialist pillage today is the *direct* exploitation of "third world" workers made possible by foreign monopoly ownership of productive. commercial, financial, transport or other enterprises in capital-importing dependencies.

> The capacity of the capitalist market is largely determined by the purchasing power of the two basic classes — the capitalists and the hired workers. In the less developed countries the part of the surplus value used by the foreign monopoly bourgeoisie does not add to the purchasing power on the national market. It goes to the metropolitan countries, where it is used to purchase commodities for the use of the monopolists and top executives. National capitalists also mainly buy means of production abroad and the surplus value they use for personal consumption is often spent on foreign goods.[15]

Under-employment rules local labour markets in the "third world", so labour-power is dirt cheap. The lack of jobs, combined with the surplus of hands created by agrarian "over-population", exposes the working masses to a tremendous rate of exploitation which, in turn, guarantees the high yield on capital invested in the neo-colonial world. Throughout the "third world", particularly in sub-Saharan or Tropical Africa, the labour movement is rudimentary, trade unions just beginning. Super-exploitation is so rampant it results frequently in the physical deterioration and even destruction of labour-power — Blacks are entombed in South Africa's mines every day. What is more, millions of "third world" workers are imported from their native lands into the metropolises where they must perform heavy manual labour for starvation wages. U.S. monopolies import and deport Haitians, Mexicans, and Puerto Ricans like cattle. Hundreds of thousands of expatriate West Indians and Southern Asians work for pittances in England. France draws a large proportion of its "temporary immigrant" workers from a "20th century slave trade" in Africans arranged by the puppet rulers of Senegal and the Ivory Coast who seek to relieve high domestic unemployment by exporting their people to the European capitalists. Canada siphons cheap "third world" labour mainly from the Commonwealth countries.

15. M. Ryndina and G. Chernikov, eds., *The Political Economy of Capitalism*, Moscow, 1974, pp. 272-273.

Once they have set up in dependent countries, multinational corporations infiltrate the local markets so as to entrap the small producers in the towns and villages. They weave a network of relations with the local small and medium native capitalists, smothering the latter in a system of contracts. Partnership, integrated banking and financial pressure are used to subvert and control "third world" economies. There are all sorts of *indirect* forms of monopoly exploitation and domination into the boot — risky, parasitical methods of subsidiary accumulation: usury, speculation, middlemen rake-offs, and so forth. Petty though they may seem, these procedures are necessary to squeeze out and realize every possible ounce of monopoly profit. Indirect exploitation puts brakes on productive accumulation — meaning that it prevents sorely-needed investment of money in the expansion and modernization of "third world" production.

*

The third, current, stage of the general crisis of capitalism which features an increasingly uneven development of the world capitalist economy, and a worsening of all its internal contradictions, is about as old as the collapse of the colonial system. Its general effects are being felt presently in the underdeveloped countries which are following the path of capitalist development, and thus still suffering the pressure of imperialism. Only in the "third world" capitalist crisis features appear in their most primitive forms, as caricatures of the original contradictions. Since it makes a travesty on and grotesquely exaggerates exploitive conditions in underdeveloped countries, direct foreign investment runs too great a risk of devaluation or confiscation. So, rather than increase productive investment, imperialist financiers seek first to get control of local agencies of capital accumulation. In this way, they are able to operate businesses in dependent countries with funds sucked from the dependent people themselves. To accomplish this, the imperialists work through the financial networks described above, and through alliances with local neo-colonialist regimes. International finance capital has come to rely a great deal on government financing and state intervention to extract monopoly superprofit.

To meet the needs of monopoly "business operations" (i.e. ex-

ploitation), roads, waterways, ports and other means of transport
are laid out in "third world" countries. Energy sources are readied.
This "infrastructure" is funded, partially or totally, by the government. The monopolies make the "granting" of private capital
investments dependent on the construction of infrastructures
rigorously adapted to the extraction of monopoly superprofits.
They are not the least bit interested in facilities which meet the
needs of the country's economic independence. They will insist,
for instance, that railway lines run straight from the site of mines
in the interior to port facilities designed to handle export freighters.
The whole operation requires that the local neo-colonialist government raise the funds to construct these facilities from its own
downtrodden people. While there are cases where foreign monopolies lay out infrastructures with monies provided by their own
imperialist governments, most times the peripheral states themselves are forced to collect the funds by taxing their own people.

The rate of surplus value, expressing the degree of exploitation
of the wage worker by the capitalist, is extremely high in the
"third world". This is mainly because labour power is cheap and
the working day lengthy. Imperialists keep it this way by com-
bining capitalist (i.e. purely economic) exploitation with pre-
capitalist coercion (i.e. non-economic, physical constraint). When
the imperialists invaded and took over pre-capitalist Asia and
Africa late in the 19th century, they found common peoples who
were variously subjected by local ruling classes to slavery, labour-
rent, rent-in-kind, and tributary peasant communes. In some countries the colonialists retained the medieval *corvée* (forced labour)
along with the payment of debts by manual labour — landless
peasants were required to pay for leases and repay debts by working several days a week for the landowner. In Mozambique the
Protuguese rounded up young Africans for compulsory gang labour
on the roads or in the mines. Mercenary tribal chiefs helped ship
contract-labour gangs to the South African mines. Grinding
poverty forced peasants to become dependent on loansharks;
there are records of peasants selling members of the family into
slavery to pay debts. The imperialists made wide use of parasitical
subleases in which, between the landowner and the poor tenant
cultivating the soil, there stood a middleman who rakes off a
large part of the harvest. Retention of these precapitalist forms of
exploitation helped create the tremendous agrarian overpopulation

150

which prevails in neo-colonies.

*

Nowhere is the situation worse than in Africa. Imperialist monopolies appropriate about 45 percent of the gross social product of independent African countries. Foreign capital still dominates much of Tropical Africa's trade, industry, construction and services. In 1968, national-democratic progress having been reversed by the reactionary coup which toppled Nkrumah, foreign capital owned 46 percent of the "value added"[16] in Ghanaian manufacturing. Mixed companies jointly owned by imperialist monopolies and the Ghanaian state contributed 30 percent of the new value, leaving a meagre 24 percent of the value added for industries belonging to Ghana's national bourgeoisie.[17] Through its control of the market and its government connections, foreign monopoly capital is reducing peasants, urban and rural craftsmen, and other reputedly independent African small producers to the status of semi-wage earners. It is a ruthless leveller endlessly churning out poverty-stricken semi-proletarians who spend most of their time unemployed. Monopoly domination permits little more than the bare reproduction of the labour-power of these Africans.

An axiom of capitalism's general crisis is that the imperialist bourgeoisie can no longer rule in the same old way. Assailed by all three currents of the world revolutionary process, imperialism must trim its sails, tack and manoeuver in the wind of change. So the structure of the commodity exchange between the imperialist metropolises and the "third world" is beginning to take on a new aspect. The tasks assigned to the "third world" in the capitalist world economy are as onerous as ever, only the emphasis is shifting in the commodity exchange polarity of "third world" raw materials — imperialist manufactured goods to a new specialization exchanging the so-called "science-intensive" output from the advanced capitalist countries for the "labour-intensive" commodities of the underdeveloped world.

16. "Value added" refers to the new value created by workers in the course of a year, i.e. to V + S (the value of the workers' wages + surplus value).
17. See *Economic Bulletin of Ghana*, Accra, No. 3, 1971, p. 21.

Actually there is little that is new in this relationship, for "science-intensive" are merely code words for managerial know-how, patents and goods produced with the advanced technology of capital with a high organic composition[18] and labour with high productivity. "Labour-intensive" denotes old-fashioned colonial commodities produced by super-exploited, low-productive colonial labour. That imperialism has switched in certain select neo-colonies (e.g. Republic of South Africa, Brazil, South Korea) from preserving economic backwardness to rearing a big native bour-geoisie is the other new wrinkle. This class of native capitalists is tailored to keep their countries within the world capitalist econ-omy and link "third world" capital with the multinational corpo-rations. In this version, "modernization" of the "third world" means capitalist assimilation.

Of course, neo-colonies and dependent countries continue in the old fashion to deliver the monopolies raw materials at rock-bottom prices. For example, gold, copper, lead, zinc, molybdenum, platinum and other rare strategic ores are obtainable in the Republic of South Africa from Black labour power paid no more than one-twentieth (1/20) of white mining labour.[19] Monopoly of the source of a new raw material gives a multinational giant a decisive advantage in the competitive struggle. Cheap raw materials enable industrial monopolies to dictate monopoly prices to the world market. For many years the imperialists used the development of synthetic materials and increased farm produce in the advanced capitalist countries to pressure the former colonies into selling their output at a low price. Bad weather and resulting crop disasters altered the picture somewhat. Raw material prices have always been particularly sensitive to changes in the business cycle, as a rule declining markedly as the outlook worsens and soaring when it improves — down during "recesssions", up during booms. As for foodstuffs, demand here is only marginally dependent on change in the capitalist economic outlook, and fluctuations in the size of

18. The organic composition of capital is the relationship between constant capital (production instruments, raw materials, fuel, etc.) and the wage fund (variable capital) determined by the ratio of constant capital to living labour in the production process.

19. In the gold mines, a white miner takes home an average 327 rand a month, but his African counterpart pockets only 16 rand (in 1972).

the crop are usually the most crucial factor, especially for the "third world's" hungry millions. In 1972, the prices of many foodstuffs and basic cereals, particularly wheat, climbed as a result of lower production of the leading grain crops and widened demand on the world market. The "third world's" food bill rose.

The imperialists also grow richer at the expense of the small raw materials producers of the countries which have thrown off the colonial yoke. Since the imperialists are the sole buyers of their products, "third world" producers must accept the price they are offered or none at all. The importance of colonies as market outlets grows during the age of imperialism. Internationalization of production and exchange combined with the aggravation of the domestic market problem prompted the monopolies to seize foreign markets. Before independence the imperialists employed fixed tariffs to cordon their colonial markets off from foreign competition. This enabled the monopolies to dump commodities in the colonies for insanely high prices, and also get rid of inferior wares unsaleable in any other market.

*

The latest wrinkles in monopolistic price formation are much more subtle. The prime consideration is to avoid customs regulations and the prices for export and import goods officially fixed at the national borders by newly independent governments. The first step is to buy up existing facilities, or go into partnership with some local firm, in this way enabling a multinational subsidiary to get itself recognized legally as a locally-registered "naturalized" company. Lever Bros. manufactures soap, margarine, plastic products and detergents in Nigeria. Phillips Oil is now a "partner" in joint companies in Kenya, Tanzania and Nigeria. In West Africa, some of these "naturalized" subsidiaries are actually headed by Western diplomats! Once within the borders, the monopoly buys up goods for export from dispersed and unorganized sellers at lower prices than those of the world market, and sells imported commodities at higher prices to the poor, disunited and ill-informed customers. Not only are high monopoly prices based on the fact of control over the local economy, but also frequently on the prestige of foreign trademarks boosted by advertising. Oftentimes "third world" manufactures of better quality but lesser reputation are neglected by local consumers.

Any landowner whose property is the site for the extraction of mineral resources collects absolute ground rent, irrespective of the quality of the deposits and their location. Now the monopolies sell oil and gas for a price determined by the most *unfavourable* conditions of production. Thus oil pumped under the extremely favourable conditions which obtain in the Middle East (rich deposits plus cheap labour power) is sold by the monopolies on the world market at the *same* price as the oil pumped under worse conditions in the United States (where both wages and other costs of production of a barrel of oil are much higher). Obviously the profit from the sale of Middle Eastern oil is much higher than from the sale of U.S.-pumped oil. This difference in profit forms a *differential rent* which is appropriated by the controllers of Middle Eastern oil. For a long time this enormous differential was largely appropriated by U.S. and British oil magnates, with only a minor part accruing to Middle Eastern governments as concession payments.

According to Algerian President Houari Boumedienne, between 1965 and 1970, multinational monopolies withdrew 25 billion dollars in profits from the "third world". The "third world" foreign debt is steadily growing and is now estimated at 80 billion dollars. It owes seven billion dollars just in interest. Multinational oil delivery speculation cost developing countries more than 800 million dollars in 1973/74 alone.

*

Discussed and rediscussed currently is the role that *non-equivalent exchange* plays in keeping the "third world" poor and backward. Let us delve into the problems of unequal trade and underdevelopment, and the inter-connections between them.

Right off we should note that unequal exchange is an outgrowth of capitalism's uneven development, and hence unavoidable as long as capitalist relations persist in the affairs of men. Uneven development plagues the newly free countries in the form of a non-equivalent trade which exchanges unequal national values, or in other words, a trade in which the weaker partner must surrender a larger amount of embodied labour for a smaller amount of the same. Non-equivalent exchange arises from the great disparity in national levels of labour productivity imposed on the world by capitalism's uneven development. It is unfortunately true at the present moment that it takes a much greater expenditure of social labour (measured in time-units) in one part of the world than in another to produce identical commodities. A disguised procedure, the exchange of non-equivalents is a major extractor of superprofits from colonial and neo-colonial territories for the imperialist monopolies. Through commercial transactions the advanced capitalist metropolis swaps less value for more — the products of a few hours of the socially necessary labour-time of the wage workers in advanced capitalist industry for the products of many hours of the low-productive labour of "third world" workers and small-scale commodity producers.

The fact that the low-productive labour of a "third world" worker may be typical for his community, that it expresses the socially necessary average *within* the backward local economy, does not counterbalance the fact that it exceeds socially necessary labour-time in the *world* capitalist economy, the fact that the equivalent of the "third world" commodity can be turned out with much less expenditure of human energy and time in the advanced capitalist countries. A factor which helps to maintain non-equivalent exchange is the use of armed force — either directly by the imperialist or through puppet regimes — to depress "third world" wages and living standards to the barest minimums. Prior to the collapse of the colonial system, the African rate of surplus value was at times more than 2,000 percent.

The "terms of trade", an expression used in the world market, indicate the volume of commodities an underdeveloped country must deliver in exchange for goods manufactured in an industrialized capitalist country (e.g. x sacks of coffee or cocoa beans, or y bunches of bananas, to get one tractor). The terms of trade at present are deteriorating so rapidly to the detriment of the "third world" that for some countries the loss incurred annually in unequal trade now exceeds the entire sum of foreign productive and loan capital "imported".

The productivity of labour is measured by the quantity of the products created per unit of time. The growth of labour productivity is expressed in an increment in the amount of use-values[20] pro-

20. Use-value is the properties of a material object which characterize its

duced per unit of time. A rise in labour productivity does not affect the value of the total production — whether one hour of labour produces one or one hundred commodities, the value embodied is still one hour of labour — but the value of each commodity-unit decreases as labour productivity rises.

Very simply then, now that they are independent but still burdened with colonialism's legacy of backwardness, the main problem for African and Asian countries, as far as the terms of trade are concerned, is that it takes less and less labour-time to produce, say, a tractor in advanced capitalist countries than it takes, say, the Ghanaians to produce the equivalent in bags of cocoa. The per unit value of manufactured goods is falling much faster than the per unit value of "third world" commodities. The result is the "scissoring" of the prices commanded by imperialist-owned products and those paid for "third world" commodities.

Working this lop-sided international division of labour for all it is worth, the monopolies which engage in wholesale purchase of raw materials and sale of manufactured goods in the dependent countries rake in huge profits. What is more, their commodities are sold at prices which are *above* their actual value, while goods produced in tne backward economy are bought up at prices *below* their value. This means that along with the profits they expatriate every year, the monopolies also pump out of the exploited countries part of the working people's personal incomes. Add to this the earnings on high interest rate loans, and from patent, transport, insurance and banking operations, and we begin to get a measure of the proportions of the non-equivalent exchange between the imperialist powers and the "third world". "Non-equivalent exchange is operating in full force, prices of raw materials and manufactured goods fluctuate, the food situation is deteriorating and the storms of the monetary and the financial crisis and of inflation are raging."[21]

importance to a class, to society, and man. A use-value is any object which satisfies a definite human need, like the need for food, clothing, housing, etc. For example, a spoon, being an eating utensil, represents a use-value. We should not confuse use-value with the concept *exchange* value. A use-value acquires exchange value only when it is a commodity bought and sold on the market and thus exchangeable in specific ratio for other commodities. We discover that the spoon, whose use-value is obvious, has a definite exchange value when we purchase it.

21. L. Lobanov, "Raw Materials and Politics (Results of the 6th Special

This is a strategic point at which to try to correct a misconception. We have seen that large scale non-equivalent exchange is very real. The deterioration in the terms of trade the "third world" is now experiencing is caused primarily by the much faster growth of labour productivity in metropolitan than in peripheral countries. This process further accelerates the unequal accumulation of capital. Unfortunately, the theory of non-equivalent exchange advocated by *The Guardian* and *Monthly Review* theoreticians and by such writers as P. Baran, P. Sweezy, Arghiri Emmanuel, Samin Amir and others, is both untenable and damaging to the anti-imperialist struggle. They begin by imagining something that does not exist − a unified, equalized rate of profit. This fantasy is caused, in turn, by a misconception of the very real law of the tendency of the rate of profit to equalize. It is in fact true that this tendency towards equalization of the profit on equal amounts of capital clears a way for itself through the entire process of social reproduction by means of the flow of capital from one branch of the economy to another, so that at any given moment an average rate of profit is discernible in any capitalist economy.

Waving their magic wands, however, the "non-equivalent exchange" theorists simply ignore the reality of *monopoly* and *unequal accumulation* which now prevents equalization of the rate of profit. They forget that under today's capitalism, the reproduction of monopoly capital is *not* the same thing as the reproduction of capital in the non-monopoly sector of the economy. This oversight is caused by the diverse locales of the realization and accumulation of capital in advanced capitalist countries − banks, manufacturing corporations, commercial enterprises, branches, etc. − which conceal the real dominance of the big corporations. In any case, the deterioration in the terms of trade affects first of all production in the *non-monopolized* sectors of the underdeveloped countries. Ignoring this crucial fact, the "non-equivalent exchange" theorists jump to the conclusion that "third world" workers are being exploited by the *workers* of industrialized countries as well as by the capitalists! The political consequence of this claim is disastrous − it would pit the national liberation movement against the working class in the advanced capitalist countries and split the anti-imperialist forces.

157

In truth, the exploitation of workers in the developed countries and the pillage of the "third world" is a mutually-reinforcing, locked-step mechanism, for the new capitals derived from these two sources demand profit in their turn, profit that will be sweated from the hides of working people *everywhere* in the capitalist world.

We will never understand how the monopolies exploit and dominate us if we restrict our analysis solely to the non-equivalent exchange between the imperialist metropolises and the underdeveloped lands, as some theoreticians of "third world" underdevelopment would have us do. Within large, integral financial groups, prices, more often than not, are merely distorted images of the real values they represent in transmuted form, and the value sucked up in the periphery by imperialism seldom appears on any corporate account book.

*

As for the notorious "energy crisis" which flared up in the autumn of 1973 in connection with the outbreak of war in the Middle East, embittering relations between the imperialist powers and the "third world" more than ever, it has turned out to be a two-pronged weapon for monopoly capital: first, it is a fabulous "energy ripoff" for the companies; second, it fosters an imperialist campaign of anti-Arab racism.

There is no better proof that the newly free countries are still the agrarian raw materials appendages of the imperialist metropolises than the "energy ripoff". Unprocessed primary commodities, including crude oil, account for 88 percent of U.S. imports from the "third world". Almost 75 percent of all U.S. investment in Africa is in the mining industry, with 60 percent in oil extraction. Outrage at this continuing impoverishment and humiliation, coupled with the consolidation of world socialism, gave unusual sweep and unity to recent anti-imperialist struggles in Arab countries. To check Israeli Zionist aggression, Arab oil-producing countries, at the end of 1973, imposed an embargo on oil exports to the United States, the Netherlands, Portugal and other states supporting Israel, and petroleum prices rose steeply. These political events, added to the fact that the Soviet Union and the rest of the socialist camp is not undergoing any "energy famine", confirm that the "energy crisis" is rooted in economics and politics and not in any natural scarcity, as white bourgeois newspapers would have us believe. The acute shortage of oil and other energy sources was artificial and spurious, but the hike in the prices of these and other raw materials and ancillary manufactured goods was real enough.

It is clear, therefore, that the raw materials, or "energy" crisis, is a crisis of the imperialist system of robbing the developing countries. It is engendered ultimately by the nature of the capitalist mode of production, it aggravates the contradictions between such imperialist powers as the United States, France and Japan, and it intensifies social conflicts within the advanced capitalist countries.[22]

With the rate of profit on oil pumped in some Middle Eastern countries reaching 500 percent and more, "third world" petroleum extraction is absolutely vital for the reproduction of monopoly capital. Running a close second and third for the monopolists are the non-ferrous metals extraction industry and certain tropical farm products. To date, the scientific and technological revolution, instead of loosening the ties with the metropolitan countries and increasing the "third world's" options, has merely intensified the latter's role of agrarian raw materials appendage. For the most advanced innovations of physics and chemistry, the new plant biological procedures, improved seeds and artificial fertilizers have restricted the specialization of the peripheral countries as a supplier even more narrowly to raw materials. Instead of more, a dependent country has even fewer commodities to offer the world market, making it even more exclusively dependent on the demand for its products by the imperialist purchasers. Synthetic tires are wreaking havoc with natural rubber producers like Liberia and Malaysia. Artificial fibres are winning out in the market over natural fibres. Plastics are beginning to rout forestry products. The agriculture of the United States, Canada, France and other industrialized capitalist countries regularly yields relative "surpluses" of farm products while the overwhelmingly agrarian, but backward "third world" countries suffer chronic crop deficits. This means not only

Session of the U.N. General Assembly)", in *International Affairs*, No. 7, July 1974, p. 28.
22. See *Ibid.*, pp. 22-23.

that the metropolitan countries are less interested in purchasing foodstuffs from the dependent countries, but also that the "third world" must buy staple grains from the big monopolies, and pay high monopoly prices or starve.

* * *

Chapter 7

AFRICA AND THE POLITICAL ECONOMY OF
UNDERDEVELOPMENT

Colonialism is the exploitation and spoliation of a people by the ruling class of another people. Outward changes in the form of the exploitation, new techniques of spoliation alter nothing in the essence of colonialism. For this reason we must distinguish between the terms *colonial system* and *colonialism*. Seeing one as synonymous with the other is dangerous, for we may be led to believe that since the colonial system has collapsed, colonialism has ended. The evidence shows that this is not true. The collapse of the colonial system meant primarily that the emergent states ceased to be the object of the *territorial division* between the imperialist powers. Colonialism is alive today, however, because of the threat to the very existence of the capitalist system, it appears as *collective colonialism* or *"neo-colonialism"*.[1]

Collective colonialism is a union of finance capital and the bourgeois machinery of government designed to protect and spread capitalism in the "third world" and to make the economic exploitation of Asia, Africa and Latin America even more profitable. Jolted by the national liberation movement, the individual imperialist powers pooled their resources and turned for salvation to neo-colonialist methods. Unlike classical colonialism, which relied mainly on native tribal chieftains and feudal lords, neo-colonialism can no longer prevent the emergence of the national bourgeoisie, of the local capitalist class. So it switches its skirt and actively woos the native bourgeoisie in the hope of perpetuating its domination in a different form. Today the neo-colonialist

---

1. On the emergence and development of neo-colonialism, see K. Brutents, *A Historical View of Neo-Colonialism*, Moscow, 1972. Brutents traces U.S. neo-colonialism from the collapse of classical colonialism through John Foster Dulles and the "New Frontier" to the Nixon Administration.

masters have their homegrown "partners" everywhere in the "third world", from Nairobi to Bangkok to Santiago.

U.S. neo-colonialism is a very special case. It is the richest and most predatory, specializing in "indirect" intervention in newly free lands. It helped Britain engineer the reactionary takeover in Ghana. It stage-managed the bloody fascist coups in Indonesia and Chile. It joined with the Chinese leaders and South Africa in trying to foist FLNA and UNITA on Angola. Throughout the "third world" the CIA foments political instability, sabotages economies, instigates armed conflicts, and conspires to isolate the national liberation movement from the socialist world system, its natural ally. U.S. neo-colonialism concentrates on anti-Sovietism and anti-communism, but it is also very adept in using racist myths to split the anti-imperialist front. It relies heavily on such false concepts as the theses of "North and South", "rich and poor countries",[2] and "two super-powers", paralyzing notions which say that socialist and capitalist countries are the same. The fundamental *class difference* between socialist and capitalist states is obscured, thereby excusing imperialism for its misdeeds.

There is nothing more neo-colonialist than the "foreign aid" extended by capitalist countries, and the United States leads the imperialist camp in "foreign aid" programs. This device was seized as a remedy for the financial headaches caused by "third world" operations. Independence has given emergent states an option they have not had before. When foreign debts become too heavy they may simply decide to suspend payments to their trading partners in the metropolitan countries. Prompted by local anti-imperialist forces, "third world" governments may also refuse to "service" (i.e. pay interest on) debts owed to imperialist creditor-governments. Lastly they can exercise their sovereignty and curtail the profits of the foreign monopolies operating on their soil. It was to avoid these catastrophes primarily, and secondarily to check the "spread of communism", that state-monopoly capital invented the system of government credits and grants which it christened *"foreign aid"*. Naturally, the sums delivered as foreign aid to the ruling elements of the "third world" by imperialist governments come from the

2. See K. Ivanov, *On the "Rich and Poor" Nations Theory*, Moscow, 1973. The author very effectively refutes this "vicious circle" recipe which is a special Maoist justification of colonialism.

slender earnings of working taxpayers in the advanced capitalist countries, and not from the pockets of the financial oligarchs, the ruling stratum within the bourgeoisie, composed of the tiny minority of super-rich who dominate the whole economy through personal or financial control of several groups of finance capital. To keep the system of exploitation afloat in the neo-colonial world, the imperialist bourgeoisie rips off its "own" working people.

For years the U.S. annual federal budget has included fiscal resources to subsidize, finance, and protect the operations of American-owned monopolies in the underdeveloped countries. U.S. military assistance and arms sales to foreign states in the 1973-1974 fiscal year ending June 30, exceeded 12 billion dollars. The outlay was the same for the 1974-1975 fiscal year. From 1962 to 1973, U.S. military "aid" to foreign countries totalled $35,400,000,000. The "aid" program enables the Pentagon to keep some 3,000 special representatives in 42 countries.

Whether bilateral or multilateral, imperialist "foreign aid" has long strings attached. If infrastructural improvements are envisaged, they must first be endorsed by monopoly representatives. If the grant is to offset a young state's budgetary deficit, the recipients must accept imperialist influence on local domestic and foreign policy. If the "aid" is military, then the underdeveloped country must chain itself to the imperialist war chariot and join a war-mongering pact. "Foreign aid" is a weapon also in the struggle between the imperialist powers for market outlets in the "third world". The United States pressures other imperialist governments to cease requiring that the "foreign aid" they grant to underdeveloped countries be spent only in the aid-giving country. In other words, where France, for instance, grants funds to the puppet regimes of, say, Gabon and the Ivory Coast, the U.S. government would like those African states to spend the money buying tanks and jet fighters from U.S. corporations rather than from French arms manufacturers. This would transfer French capital to U.S. monopolies through the agency of African states. U.S. imperialism thus expects to horn in and profit at the expense of its NATO partners in regions where the latters' interests predominate, like Francophone Africa, and the former British sphere of influence in southern and eastern Africa and Nigeria, etc.

"Third world" governments who seek aid are compelled by the

imperialist bankers to "clean up their accounts" and "put their books in order" as a condition of credit. The "house-cleaning" is actually a pretext for extracting more taxes from the down-trodden popular masses, a device for having the local government squeeze every last penny from the peasantry. Once the increased taxes have been centralized in the emergent country's treasury or state bank, the foreign monopolies then step in and drain off these funds through the agency of *mixed companies* — corporations in which foreign capital shares the stock with local private or state-owned capital. East Africa, Kenya, in particular, is a favoured spot for the formation of mixed companies.

Foreign borrowing has put the "third world" so deeply in debt that in some countries the situation has become critical. New in-coming loans are less than the sum spent to pay off the principal and meet interest payments on outstanding debts. Kenya and the Ivory Coast are in this predicament. Foreign indebtedness is a tremendous drain on the material resources also of Liberia, Tunisia and Ghana. They face soaring interest and principal payments. Each year about one billion dollars in hard currency[3] flows out-ward from poor developing Africa.

*

Africa's social and economic structure is backward. Colonialism caused this retardation. The typical African economy is based predominantly on primitive, low-productive farming. The imperial-ists introduced mining and other extractive industries, but neglected manufacturing. Even in places where industry was relatively more advanced, mining and textiles, food-processing and other light industries were the only branches fostered. Heavy industry, the basis of economic self-sufficiency for any country, is weak or non-existent — there is almost no engineering industry. The ruling monopolies took care to prevent production of instruments of production — they flatly refused colonies and dependencies credit for this purpose and would not sell them the necessary equipment

3. Payments between countries in the capitalist world system are made in either gold or U.S. dollars, £ sterling, French francs, or other convertible currencies. "Third world" countries therefore try to accumulate reserves of foreign exchange.

and patents. Colonialism cold-bloodedly prevented the industrial-ization of Africa.[4] Forbidden to undertake any independent industrial development, the colonies and semi-colonies thus remained *agrarian* countries. Farming is the livelihood of the crushing majority of Africa, Asia and Latin America. African agriculture in particular is divided into two sectors – the traditional sector and a sector devoted to export crops. The traditional sector is trapped in simple commodity or subsistence farming and bur-dened with tribal and semi-feudal survivals of all sorts; the other sector is involved in the plantation economy.[5] Stagnation and decay of agriculture keep the domestic market from expanding.

A characteristic of the colonial exploitation which assures that finance capital will get its monopoly superprofits is the merger of up-to-date imperialist plunder with pre-capitalist, especially feudal, forms of exploiting toiling masses. Under feudalism, the basic economic law is production of surplus product for feudal lords in the form of feudal ground rent through the exploitation of depen-dent peasants. Domination by feudal lords is based on their monopoly of large landed estates. Personal subordination of peasants is a secondary factor. Under feudalism, a system of extra-economic coercion, he who lived on the lord's land was servilely subordinated to the lord.

On one hand colonialism developed commodity production and spread money relations, the native population was robbed of its land and small handicraft production was disrupted; on the other hand, holdovers from the feudal and tribal past were artificially preserved. During their stay the colonial lords even introduced forced labour. As "modernization" i.e. colonialism, sank roots in Africa, taxes in various forms were introduced accelerating the ruin of masses of peasants. Yet until the recent revolutionary reforms pre-capitalist rent still predominated in Ethiopia, a country victimized by both British and Italian imperialism. It took the

4. Y. Popov, *Marxist Political Economy as Applied to the African Scene*, Moscow, 1973, pp. 33-43.
5. Plantations are large capitalist farming enterprises which supply plant raw materials like cotton, rubber, jute, sisal, coffee, cocoa and palm nuts. They belong mostly to foreign capitalists, and, under colonialism, were a major area of economic activity for white settlers. Starvation wages, and some-times semi-servile labour, were trademarks of the African plantations.

form either of sharecropping where the landowner appropriated a large share of his tenant's produce as payment for the use of the land, or of labour rent where the peasant performed manual services for the landowner in return for the right to cultivate a tiny plot of soil.

Africa has a variety of social formations. The peoples entered upon their politically independent careers at different levels, some more advanced in capitalist relations, others living in predominantly pre-capitalist societies.

> The emerging countries vary, notably, in regard to their level of capitalist development. Some have reached an average level. Others may be said to be semi-capitalist, with marked feudal and often even tribal relics. Still others are on the lowest rungs of primitive capitalist accumulation. Sometimes yet another group of countries is identified, namely, those whose development has stopped at the feudal or even pre-feudal stage.[6]

Indicative of the incipient character of African social relations is the co-existence of 1) subsistence natural economy, 2) simple commodity, 3) native capitalist, 4) foreign monopoly capitalist, 5) public sector, and 6) many tribal, feudal and capitalist transitional relations, often in one and the same economy. This peculiar situation is due to backwardness and the after-effects of colonialism. Class differentiation is either just beginning or incomplete with no single social class yet capable of establishing sole dictatorship and shaping the socio-economic formation in its own image.[7]

Now when finance capital penetrates African societies, it disrupts pre-capitalist forms — petty handicraft, tribal communities, the semi-natural economy of subsistence peasants — in favour of a *one-sided* capitalism. In order to exploit the country, the imperialists construct railways, ports and industrial enterprises designed to deliver raw materials and foodstuffs to the metropolis. Simultaneously the multinational corporations preserve the socio-economic backwardness of the country, since this underdevelopment is the

6. Y. Zhukov, L. Delyusin, A. Iskenderov and L. Stepanov, *The Third World: Problems and Prospects*, Moscow, 1970, p. 179.

7. See "Socialist Orientation: Theory and Practice", Round Table Discussion, in *Asia and Africa Today*, Moscow, Number 3, May-June 1976, pp. 12-24; and Vladimir Lee, "Problems of Social Differentiation in the Newly-Independent Countries", in *Asia and Africa Today*, Number 4, July-August 1976, pp. 2-5.

basis for their continuing dominance over the "third world" and the foundation upon which their exploitation is seated. Were Africa, Asia and Latin America not backward, they might advance as capitalist rivals of the imperialists and not as their subordinates. Or what is more likely in present circumstances, they might adopt the socialist orientation, the non-capitalist path of development.

But inexorably, capitalist relations and the capitalist mode of production — in the strict sense of those terms — are forcing their way through in many African countries. Millions of small producers are being ousted from farming and animal breeding to become proletarians, semi-proletarians, unemployed, and lumpenproletarians. The monopoly of the land and other means of agricultural production by landowners (Morocco, and Algeria and Ethiopia before land reform), the tyranny of loan sharks and usurers, the pressure of taxation, etc. condemn a large portion of the able-bodied inhabitants (i.e. of the total social labour-power) to stagnation and ruin. Many pre-capitalist forms of livelihood are disintegrating and being dismantled. As that happens, hundreds of thousands of youths stream out of the villages only to circle idly on the edges of Africa's already overcrowded cities. Cairo, Lagos, Nairobi and Abidjan teem with displaced millions. Africa's urban population is growing much faster than its rural population. Given the persisting agrarian backwardness, the growth of manpower without a corresponding growth of the means of production expands the labour supply in the villages, leading to intensified rural-to-urban migration. The influx, in turn, worsens the situation in the cities. The African big cities are now bursting with under-employed hands. The number of unemployed is growing faster than the number of employed workers. For every 100 unemployed in 1974 in Africa, there will be 142 in 1985. Yet the cities will continue to swell because the income from irregular urban activities, occasional jobs, etc., is still higher than the income drawn from permanent farming in the countryside.

Certain local classes and social strata become more and more parasitical. Large scale capitalist industry rarely appears, however, and when it does, then only in restricted sectors and weak proportions. Large scale private capitalist industry never captures the commanding heights of the economy. Narrow limits, consequently, are clamped on the growth of the class of wage earners. The industrial proletariat — the core of the working class — is stunted

167

in "third world" countries, but most of all in Africa. Over this mixture of native capitalism and pre-capitalist relations, foreign monopoly capital imposes its authority.

In the process of economic development there is a widening gap between different structures in labour productivity, in the living standards and so on. This gap, as a rule, is wider in proportion to the greater export orientation of the country's economy and the larger per capita income. In conditions of disunity between the structures, the growth of production in one sector, for example, the foreign, may be high, but this has little or practically no effect on other sectors, for instance, on the traditional African sector. Under such conditions, the growth rates of income must not be regarded as the sole criterion of development.[8]

The ranking of the "third world" in the overall capitalist world economy is diminishing. The "third world's" share in world trade declined 3.7 percent in the ten years from 1960 to 1970, and its annual economic growth rate slipped from 5 percent in the late 1960s to 3-4 percent in 1974, a performance that is clearly inadequate, for its population increases at about the same rate annually. The "third world" is treading water economically. Only 25 percent of the world's protein is consumed (unevenly) by the half of mankind that lives in the backward countries. The United Nations food and Agricultural Organization (FAO) reports that at least one billion "third worlders" suffer from hunger or undernourishment, and that each year 4 million more adult illiterates are added to the 800 million illiterates Asia, Africa and Latin America already have. A "third world" person lives 20 years less on the average than the inhabitants of socialist or imperialist countries. From 1971 to 1974 world market prices of wheat and fertilizers doubled, causing the "third world" a supplementary expenditure of 7 billion dollars and additional privations for its already famished consumers. The daily income of 900 millions is less than 33 cents. From 6 to 17 percent of men, and from 15 to 50 percent of women in Africa suffer from anemia caused by a lack of iron in the diet. Southern Africa is a hell of gastrointestinal, nervous and skin diseases, all caused by pellagra, a niacin-deficiency illness. A third of all African infants die before reaching five years of age. Yet, as a Somali

8. L. Alexandrovskaya, "Africa: Some Tendencies in Economic Development", in *International Affairs*, No. 7, 1974, p. 65.

delegate to the special U.N. General Assembly in Spring 1974 said, the announced profits siphoned out of the newly free countries from 1966-1970 by foreign monopolies amounted to half as much again as the "aid" these countries received from the countries to which these monopolies belong.

Backward economies with weak productive forces and low labour productivity are the special prey of natural catastrophes against which they are never able to defend themselves. The terrible drought that bit into Africa in the early 1970s starved hundreds of thousands of people. Saharan dessication has chewed up so much fertile soil that there is danger of a substantial decrease in the harvest of cotton, cocoa, peanuts, coffee and cereals, as well as continued high prices of essential foods. Dessication threatens at least 17 states or territories located south of the Sahara. In the recent drought it reached tragic proportions in five countries — Mali, Niger, Chad, Mauritania and Ethiopia. The body count of the dead was teeth-rattling: 200,000 in Ethiopia, 100,000 in the Sahel. Symptoms of dessication appeared in Gambia, Cameroons, Nigeria, Dahomey, Upper Volta, Ghana, Guinea, Central African Republic, Sudan, Tanzania, and in that model of the capitalist path of development — Kenya. In some African countries longevity, or average length of life, is *30 years* — the same as in ancient slave-holding Rome and in feudal France's more backward provinces on the eve of the 1789 Revolution!

Yet the crucial problem in underdeveloped countries is not a contradiction between demographic growth and food resources, as bourgeois neo-Malthusians would have us believe. The so-called "population explosion" is a hoax, a modernization of the old "Yellow Peril" myth, dreamed up by racists. As everywhere in the capitalist world economy — and most of the "third world" is still imprisoned in that economy — the problem is that of the *limits* set by capitalist accumulation and the *antagonism* caused by the accumulation of "surplus" capital.

As accumulation of capital we designate the conversion of part of the surplus value into additional capital thus enlarging the original stock of capital. As the total mass of capital grows, the component parts of capital change unequally. The composition of the capital alters. New machinery is purchased and new techniques are introduced. New technology signifies swift growth of the portion of capital which exists in the form of means of production

169

(i.e. constant capital). Variable capital — the wage fund — grows much slower relatively. At the moment there is a new dimension to capitalist accumulation — *"super-accumulation" of capital.* Super-accumulation means that so much excess capital piles up in the hands of the monopolists that its profitable investment becomes increasingly difficult. By the same token, the productivity of labour in the advanced capitalist countries continues to rise. This means that there is less and less labour time (less value) materialized primarily in those commodities which are means of production. This tends to swell chronic mass unemployment in the imperialist countries.[9] The "third world's" fate is more efficient and rapacious exploitation. Imperialist plundering, the extraction of resources, the "brain drain" of trained personnel from backward countries hand in hand with "third world" importation of expensive skilled technicians and commodities from the imperialist metropolises, are seriously aggravating social conditions.

Unemployment, the low skills of the human resources, the poor conditions of the working masses, and the weakness of national markets are major social problems throughout Africa. But *low national productivity* can be singled out as a major contributing factor to economic enslavement after independence.

The entire "third world", particularly Africa, is plagued by a low level of productive forces and resultant low productivity of labour. This is a time when labour productivity is growing in the imperialist metropolises.[10] The overwhelming majority of Tropical African enterprises are equipped with obsolete installations and more often than not depend on manual techniques. While in the imperialist metropolises the 4.5 to 20 percent of the economically active population engaged in agriculture easily feeds the entire population, 80 percent of Africa's economically active population are either peasants or farm hands, yet their output is too small to ward off undernutrition, i.e. starvation for a large part of the population.

*

9. N. Grauzner, *Social Effects of the Scientific and Technological Revolution Under Capitalism*, Moscow, 1973, pp. 120-134.

10. See A. Shpirt, *The Scientific-Technological Revolution and the Third World*, Moscow, 1972.

170

The United Nations designated the 1960s as a "development decade" for Africa and the rest of the "third world", and fixed 5 percent per annum as the target economic growth rate for African nations. By Year Ten it was clear that Africa had failed to achieve the goal, expanding at a rate of only 4.2 percent annually. Although it does not seem like much, the shortfall had serious economic consequences. Africa went right on exchanging its oil, copper, coffee, cotton, rubber and cocoa beans for capitalist manufactured goods. Taking into account the growth of population, the annual per capital income rose only 1.7 percent during the decade of "development".[11] Total farm output per capita increased just *one percent* in Africa from 1965 to 1971.[12] Of the total world production of steel in 1970, the whole "third world" accounted for no more than 4.5 percent, and Africa is by far the weakest part of the "third world" in metallurgy.[13] The gross social product of 325 million people in 41 African states in 1971 totalled a mere 53 billion dollars in monetary value. In other words, because of the colonial legacy and the present imperialist exploitation, gigantic Africa's economy is really no larger than the combined economies of tiny Austria and Belgium whose population, added together, is merely 17 millions. How graphically these figures tell their tragic tale! *17 million inhabitants from two countries that are not even tops in European development are the equals in productivity of 325 million Africans*! The gross social product in 25 African states is less than one billion dollars annually; in 23 of them it is below 500 million dollars; in 16 it is less than 300 millions, and in the four most abject it is below 100 million dollars a year.[14] In rate of development Africa lags markedly behind Asia and Latin America. This is the ugly reality of "development" under the aegis of the capitalist world market.

The 6th Special UN General Assembly Session of April 9 - May 2, 1974, met to consider the grave problems of raw material resources and "third world" economic development. It adopted

11. See *Survey of Economic Conditions in Africa, 1971*, U.N., New York, 1972, E/CN. 14/560. Part I, p. 3.
12. P. Jalée, *Le tiers monde en chiffres, Edition revue. 1974*, Paris, 1974, p. 26.
13. *Ibid.*, p. 47.
14. L. Alexandrovskaya, pp. 64-65.

a significant *Declaration on the Establishment of a New International Economic Order.* Expressedly recognized is the right of every sovereign state to control all internal economic activity without foreign interference, and select its own economic and social system, including the right to begin non-capitalist development, if it so chooses. Implicit in the Declaration is the realization that regardless of what NATO imperialists claim, *industry* — and not agriculture, trade or raw materials extraction — best eliminates the backwardness left by colonialism. Any "third world" nation which fails to nationalize the major means of production and require indemnity and full compensation for the depletion of its natural resources and exploitation of its manpower by the multinational corporations, has only a sham independence. The UN Declaration recognizes the right of control by developing countries over the activities of multinational monopolies, and the need to set up and strengthen associations of producing countries like OPEC which deal with the main raw material commodities.[15] Required most urgently are measures to check the "scissoring" of prices, i.e. to establish an equitable correlation between prices of raw materials and semi-finished commodities exported by "third world" countries, and the prices of the manufactured commodities and means of production they import from the imperialist metropolises. The UN discussion showed that for a "third world" country to break free of imperialism and improve the condition of its working people, it must nationalize natural resources, the wholesale trade, and foreign banks and insurance and mortgage companies. It is essential to construct a state-owned sector of the economy centered on industry. Democratic land reform is spotlighted as the first step toward placing agriculture on a co-operative footing. But even these measures will abort if steps are not taken to establish democratic organs of popular rule, democratize the civil service, police and armed forces, and adhere staunchly to an anti-imperialist foreign policy in close alliance with the USSR and the other socialist countries.

Quite naturally, Africa's neo-colonialist regimes have opted for the capitalist method of development and open their doors to

15. See L. Lobanov, "Raw Materials and Politics (Results of the 6th Special Session of the UN General Assembly)", in *International Affairs*, No. 7, July 1974, p. 26.

foreign monopolies. In order to obtain comparatively high growth rates of national income, Tunisia, Morocco, Kenya, Ivory Coast and others have increased their economic dependence on the capitalist world market by sharply expanding the production of raw materials or tropical farm produce for export. This one-sided expansion brings growth but no real development, and the mono-cultural character of the economy is strengthened rather than weakened. African states whose rulers have chosen the capitalist path have little or no modern industry, their agriculture is mainly undiversified, and unemployment rages.

However, nearly everywhere in the "third world" local capital-ism is taking the form of state-capitalism rather than that of classical "free enterprise". Owing to the economic weakness of the national bourgeoisie and the limited opportunities for capital accumulation described in the following chapter, the bloc-in-power has no other choice but to go in for state-capitalism. Today a *mixed sector* is a common feature of many African economies. The mixed sector comprises state-private companies in which part of the enterprise stock belongs to the government, and part to private owners. The rub is that frequently a large portion of the privately-owned shares is held by *foreigners*. It is indicative of the major role of state-capitalism, however, that, with some exceptions, those African countries which have a large and active public sector and state ownership of much of the national income, tend also to have the more advanced productive forces. For many African nations, then, the appearance of state-capitalism — properly conceived and regulated — is a sign of progress.

All measures taken to foster the growth of state-owned property, and state regulation of the economy under conditions in which private capitalist ownership of the means of production is main-tained, and in which the national bourgeoisie holds power, are state-capitalist measures. The Egyptian system is perhaps the purest example of state-capitalist development in Africa to date. However, the state-capitalism which exists in underdeveloped countries is state-capitalism of a special sort. It differs both from the state-monopoly capitalism in advanced capitalist countries where the imperialist bourgeoisie holds power, and from state-capitalism in lands which are achieving the transition from capitalism to social-ism under the leadership of the proletariat. "Third world" state-capitalism is progressive only when it is directed against imperialism and undermines the economic domination of foreign monopoly capital.[16] Furthermore, where there is a powerful upsurge in the national liberation movement of the popular masses, it can play a positive role in creating the material prerequisites for transition to *socialist* transformation of the society. At the present time, given the powerful socialist world system, a real opportunity arises for underdeveloped countries to take the *non-capitalist* path of development, looking forward to the eventual building of socialism through the establishment of working class power.

An anti-imperialist analyst who specializes in African affairs puts it this way:

> Struggle for economic independence implies a steady reduction in the share of the foreign sector in the property and incomes of African countries and a corresponding rise in the share of the local population and the national state. How far has Africa advanced along this path? ... It is reflected in the nationalization of foreign companies, in the absolute and relative growth of state revenue and expenditures, in the so-called Africanization of some services and types of activity and, lastly, in the greater employment of the African population.[17]

Taxation and income policies can be powerful weapons in the struggle to Africanize and provide jobs for African workers. Leaving aside the imperialist-subsidized budgets of the more blatant neo-colonialist regimes (e.g. Gabon, Sudan, Zaire, etc.), direct and indirect taxes are a main domestic source of budget revenue for African countries. The ability to check the encroachments of multinational corporations depends, to a large extent, on the money at the disposal of the government. The bulk of use-values in Africa is still produced and consumed directly by the subsistence farming peasantry without ever reaching the market or becoming commodities in any significant way. So this leaves the foreign sector of the economy as the main potential source of government revenue. Since a substantial part of the taxed imported and locally-produced commodities are consumed in the *foreign* sector, African governments may structure their policies of indirect

16. For a comprehensive analysis of state property in the economy of the "third world" by an international team of socialist scholars, see V.F. Stanis, G.B. Khromushin and V.P. Mozolin, eds., *The Role of the State in Socio-Economic Reforms in Developing Countries*, Moscow, 1976.

17. L. Alexandrovskaya, p. 65.

taxation so as to regulate the activities of individual groups and classes of the local population, while at the same time stimulating or restricting the profit-making activities of imperialist monopolies. Used properly, indirect taxes can redistribute income for purposes of national development, counterbalancing the interests of national progress against the narrow privileges of the national bourgeoisie and the tribal and feudal cliques.

But let there be no mistake here. These measures toward planned regulation of the economy differ fundamentally from national economic planning in the socialist countries[18] because they are realized under conditions of continued private ownership of major means of production, and as a result fail to encompass the whole national economy. State-capitalist regulations therefore cannot overcome the effects of the *spontaneous* laws of economic development. Only in a socialist economy, where production itself is social and the means of production are publicly owned, does planning overcome the anarchy of production and prevent the laws of commodity production from operating uncontrolled by men.

The positive significance of planning in African states of capitalist orientation consists mainly in the fact that it enables the government to concentrate available funds and material resources on the task of creating *heavy industry*, i.e. production of the means of production.

This is important for if left to occur spontaneously, capitalist industrialization is a long drawn-out affair. Spontaneous development of capitalist industry begins not in heavy, but in *light* industry. It initiates with the manufacture of objects of personal consumption. It takes much less money to open and build a textile factory than an iron and steel plant, thus Black Africa has a fair number of locally-owned textile establishments but not a single steel mill.[19] Capital rotates faster in branches producing articles of consumption than in branches fabricating means of production. Only

18. For a brilliant analysis of socialist planning, including such topics as the origin and development of socialist planning, the relationship between Department I and Department II of socialist production, and sectorial structure of the gross social product, see Anatoly Yefimov and Alexander Anchishkin, *State Planning: Aims, Ways, Results*, Moscow, n.d.

19. The steel complex under construction in Nigeria is state-owned and is being built with the aid of the Soviet Union.

175

gradually will capital accumulated in light industry create a demand for equipment to produce consumer goods. A long time passes before the capitalists in light industry have extracted enough profit from their workers and can be persuaded to invest those profits in heavy industry. Not until considerable capital has been drawn into the production of means of production can the unregulated process of capitalist industrialization be said to have fairly begun. This process stretches over a relatively long period of time and is carried out through ferocious exploitation of the working class and the peasantry. It also involves slavish concessions, and loans begged from foreign finance capital, procedures which strengthen the hand of imperialism in the developing country.

The leading African nations in terms of industrial production in descending order are: 1) Arab Republic of Egypt which creates nearly twice as much new value annually as the second-ranked country; 2) Nigeria whose economy is now probably more than half the size of Egypt; 3) Algeria; 4) Morocco, trailing Algeria closely; 5) Zaire; and 6) Ghana. Together these states account for 63 percent of the value of the output of manufacturing in all independent African countries.[20] These rankings reconfirm the fact that industrialization is much further along in the Arab north than in Black Africa. Egypt already has viable steel, engineering, and petrochemical industries. From 1970 to 1973 Algeria planned and built 150 industrial enterprises, including plants for heavy industry. With their new facilities, independent Africa's industrial leaders are now able to turn out cement, oil products, steel, tires, plastics and precious fertilizers, i.e. shift the emphasis of their output from the manufacture of primary consumer goods to commodities intermediary between light and heavy industry.

*

The best evidence that the imperialist colonial system is disintegrating is the breakthrough in the front of imperialism which has occurred over the last 35 years in a great many colonial and semi-colonial lands. These lands have pulled loose from the colonial

20. L. Alexandrovskaya, p. 68.

system, and in the case of North Vietnam, North Korea and Cuba they have broken with capitalism *per se*, first forming peoples democratic, and then later, socialist orders. These victories, especially the emergence of Cuba a few miles from Yankee imperialism's doorstep, coupled with the triumph of the heroic Vietnamese people, exerted tremendous influence on imperialism's remaining colonial hinterland. Now in Angola and some other African countries serious measures are being taken to create the prerequisites for the transition to socialism.

The disintegration of the imperialist colonial system is further conditioned by the fact that the peoples of more than a hundred other colonial and dependent countries have freed themselves from colonial rule and have set upon the road to at least political sovereignty.

The collapse of the imperialist colonial system has complicated the problem of marketing for the capitalists in two ways. Positively from the angle of international monopoly capital, the struggle of the newly free countries for economic independence and their first steps towards the creation of a modern diversified economy are increasing the demand for certain modern consumer goods, and for equipment and other production commodities from the industrialized capitalist countries. But, given the growing trade between the Soviet Union, German Democratic Republic and other socialist countries on one side and the "third world" on the other, sales conditions have become worse for imperialism, for the monopolies are increasingly deprived of the monopoly which enabled them to dictate to the newly free countries what goods they should import and at what prices. The new balance of class forces in the world compels the imperialists to make some concessions to "third world" countries, Africa included. If they refuse, these countries, now sovereign, can get the credits, machinery and equipment they need from the Soviet Union and the other socialist countries on terms of equal rights and mutual benefit.[21] In 1965 the Soviet Union was the first country in the world to unilaterally abolish customs duties on goods of developing countries.

21. L. Yagodovsky, *The World Socialist System - Its Role in the World Today*, Moscow, 1975, pp. 39-50.

Nowadays emerging peoples no longer face the wrath of imperialists alone. The mighty socialist commonwealth of nations stands ready to aid them. Not only Vietnam and Cuba, but Bangla Desh, Egypt, Algeria, Syria, Guinea-Bissau, Ethiopia, Somalia, Mozambique, and Angola's MPLA have all received the material, moral and diplomatic aid of the Soviet Union and the other socialist countries — aid which has more than once forced the imperialists to back down.

* * *

Chapter 8

CLASSES AND CLASS STRUGGLE IN AFRICA

Imperialist exploitation and the backward economy have created class structures in Africa which are characterized by incomplete social differentiation and irregular class relations. Like all societies composed of exploiters and exploited, African societies are divided along class lines. Although the introduction of capitalism has simplified class structures and relations somewhat, giving birth to the now familiar two main classes — the bourgeoisie and the proletariat — due to the incomplete socio-economic differentiation the African scene is still one of complicated hierarchical structures. The coexistence of a variety of classes, estates, strata and intermediate groups is a legacy of the colonial past.[1]

At the top of society in the states of capitalist or indeterminate orientation are perched the native ruling elites — feudal landowners, tribal bigwigs, politicians, bureaucrats and soldiers, and local capitalists.

The most important element in this ruling bloc is the native capitalist class — it contributed much more actively to the struggle for independence than the tribal elite and feudal landlords, it has growing economic power, and it exerts powerful influence on current policy. The African capitalist class owns means of production and exchange and lives by exploiting wage labour and appropriating surplus value. Its ownership of vital means of production is what enables it to exploit the proletariat and other African working people. Based on its economic and political power, the capitalist class and its agents work to extend its ideological hegemony in Africa.

This class is divided into the *comprador bourgeoisie* and the *national bourgeoisie*. Comprador is a word of Portuguese origin

1. A. Iskenderov, *Africa: Politics, Economy, Ideology*, Moscow, 1972, p. 110.

179

meaning the native merchant or middlemen agent for a foreign enterprise. The comprador bourgeoisie is, therefore, that fraction of the local big bourgeoisie which is closely tied to foreign monopolies. It consists of native big capitalists who function as the agents of foreign banks, industries and commercial firms, etc., and who represent the interests of the finance capital of the imperialist powers. They help the multinational corporations exploit their country's raw materials and markets. Along with the tribal chieftains and feudal landowners, comprador bourgeois are the vassals of foreign finance capital and direct agents of the collective colonialism which enslaves post-independence African countries.

A national bourgeoisie grows up with the development of a dependent country's local industry and domestic market. This wing of the big bourgeoisie has three fractions. The first fraction, and the biggest numerically, is the bourgeoisie of merchants and usurers who are interested in the independent development of the domestic market and credit system. Second ranks the national industrial and planter bourgeoisie which, having exploited native hired workers for the production of some commodity, creates a network of enterprises which are independent of foreign capital. Thirdly, in some emergent states a reactionary bureaucratic stratum of the national bourgeoisie has appeared which comprises civil servants, politicians, and military men who use their position in the government for personal enrichment and participation in private business. Egypt, the Sudan and Kenya are notorious examples. This national bourgeoisie has a dual nature — on one hand the yoke of foreign imperialism and tribal and feudal relics block its path to dictatorship over its own society, on the other hand its own existence depends on the exploitation of the local working class and peasantry. Since the national struggle of the peoples of Africa is aimed objectively at overthrowing the rule of imperialism, establishing national independence and eliminating pre-capitalist relations of production, the national bourgeoisie takes an active part in this struggle.

But the African national bourgeoisie lacks social homogeneity. The fact that it is not a monolithic entity, that it is fractionalized, has important consequences. Each fraction of the national bourgeoisie has its own particular interests which is voices in concrete economic and political demands. The demands are determined by a given fraction's economic and general standing in the community, and one fraction rarely sees eye to eye with another. African bourgeoisies seldom possess more than small and medium capitals. Their funds are too small to open really modern industrial establishments. African private capital finds its way, consequently, more often into trade and commerce than into large scale manufacturing. Bona fide capitalist industrialization is beyond the financial means of the African bourgeoisie. Meanwhile, the foreign multinationals buy out all viable local businesses they can. Therefore, in Black Africa, the merchant and usurer fraction — allied with big planters and prominent bureaucratic capitalists — holds sway over the purely industrial bourgeois fraction.

The whole national bourgeoisie operates in a real economic strait-jacket. There is no doubt that native oligarchs run an enthusiastic second to the foreign monopolies in pillaging imperialism's peripheral zone — their own countries. Princely profits can be obtained in Africa from superexploiting the abundant, poorly-trained labour power of rural origin. Nevertheless, there is a limit to these profits. The problem is the scantiness and the poverty of domestic market outlets. Competing in the local market with imports manufactured in industrialized capitalist countries, the native industrialist simply cannot sell enough of his locally-produced commodities to realize ample profits consistently. Furthermore, with each passing day organic composition of capital goes upward, increasing the ratio of instruments, fuel and raw materials to living labour,[2] and entailing greater advances of money capital to initiate each production cycle. This leaves less and less room for the small capitalist to break into manufacturing. As a result industrialization of the private economy occurs only in very restricted sectors. It affects only those businesses which are lucky to have ideal natural conditions (e.g. abundant materials due to tropical climate) or labour-intensive industries with a low technical level which depend on cheap labour (e.g. textile industries). But even where the extremely low pay of the unskilled native workers prevails over the high salaries of imported skilled labour ("colonial wages") and other costly "inducement allowances" doled out to "expatriates", industrialization of African production is usually held back by the high initial costs of transport, energy and supply the local capitalist has to bear.

2. N. Gauzer, pp. 15 and 19-20.

Hence the national bourgeoisie and the social categories allied to it are prey to sharp ambivalences and contradictions — they oscillate between two solutions. They may opt to support the anti-imperialist movement of the masses. Historically, the anti-imperialist struggle for independence was led by the national bourgeoisie — good examples being Nigeria, Ghana and the Cameroons. In some instances anti-imperialism has led the local bourgeoisie to organize *state capitalism*, which should not be confused with the state-monopoly capitalism prevailing in the imperialist countries. Under bourgeois management, state capitalism allows the national bourgeoisie to carry on business within the framework of mixed private and state-owned companies. Here the bourgeoisie shelters its profit-making under the government's umbrella. The second choice, the one most common in Africa, is a leap into reaction. It means containment and repression of the anti-imperialist mass movement. Here the national bourgeoisie banks for support on the army and police leading to the establishment of regimes like Kenyatta's in Kenya and Houphouet-Boigny's in the Ivory Coast. At times it forms a close alliance with tribal chieftains and feudalistic big landowners, as in Nigeria in the 1960s, where the national bourgeoisie, located mainly in the south, shared power with the Moslem Emirs of the north.

Either way, the local bourgeoisie shows that it is unable to cope with all the difficulties in the way of progress without turning to the state for assistance. It entrusts government with the task of channelling the required financial and technological means into those sectors of the national economy most profitable for the bourgeois elite. The rub is that in underdeveloped countries elements like the military,[3] politicians and civil servants are notoriously fickle and unstable. Frequently younger army officers are influenced by democratic ideals and turn their guns against the bourgeoisie and other ruling classes. This occurred recently in Ethiopia. Uncertainty of this kind, in turn, prompts elements of the embryonic national bourgeoisie to export capital, to hide huge treasures away in European banks, or buy "safe" stock in big foreign monopolies.

3. Yves Bénot, *Idéologies des indépendances africaines*, Paris, 1969, pp. 331-343.

Africa's *urban petty bourgeoisie* is an unwieldy composite of intellectuals, independent artisans and shopkeepers, petty traders (many female market dealers, other itinerants), minor employees and clerical workers, and students. Perhaps the most exceptional stratum of the urban petty bourgeoisie is the intelligentsia. The "third world" intelligentsia is a special social category comprising teachers, lawyers, physicians, technicians and scientists, minor officials, junior army officers, and students. As a special category, the intelligentsia is not an independent economic class and therefore is *not* an independent political force. Its role is complicated by the fact that it holds a position between the classes, adjoining in part the bourgeoisie for its friendships and aspirations, and in part the anti-imperialist common people. Many African intellectuals travel abroad for training in the USA, Britain, France or West Germany and return home agents of super-individualism. Arrogant, pushful, egoistic attitudes are instilled in them at imperialist universities and military academies, along with a love of Mercedes autos and other luxuries. Africa's political corps is still recruited largely from the intelligentsia. However, the intelligentsia, as a social category and not a class, has no sufficiently distinct class interests and can move in either social direction. Historically, it has been extremely active in the national liberation struggle.

A measure of the backwardness imperialism imposed on Africa is the slowness with which its *proletariat* (i.e. the class of hired wage earners) takes shape as a stable class.[4] The weakness of the African proletariat is caused by the inadequate productive forces. Most Black African wage earners are not yet *industrial* proletarians. The majority of the class are still workers in the services industries and plantation agriculture. In some regions plantation workers must still act as the cutting-edge of the proletariat. In Nigeria, the world's most populous Black nation, workers' families continue to till the soil in the bush villages. Male workers migrate back and forth from village to town seeking seasonal employment. Thus a large segment of the African working force are *semi*-proletarians, rather than proletarians, with one foot in the proletariat and the other in subsistence farming. History shows that the workers must first stabilize as a *sedentary, hereditary* class of proletarians in

4. A. Iskenderov, pp. 43-53.

order to develop their political consciousness, organization and revolutionary potential to the fullest. In fact, the agrarian "surplus" population, or latent surplus, is very large in Africa, impinging heavily on the character of the proletariat. This latent surplus is made up mostly of seasonal labourers and poor peasants and subsistence family farmers who eke the barest of existences from the soil. Big capitalist estates (colonial plantations) created fluctuating demands for wage workers and drew them from the rural scene. A segment of the latent surplus attempts to find employment in the towns. Many who cannot find jobs in urban industry return to the village or set out seeking employment opportunities, wandering over hundreds, sometimes thousands of miles, and even across state borders. This latent surplus of semi-proletarians retards the African proletariat's growth of stability, and, forming a large part of the reserve army of labour, it is used by capital to keep wages low.

But as industry develops and capitalist relations spread, the working class is taking root in Africa. Its vanguard, and most sedentary fraction, is the industrial proletariat, although it remains a minority. To the proletariat also belong the bulk of plantation hands and day labourers, workers in small handicraft establishments, along with the countless unskilled workers in the towns who try their hands at any and all types of manual labour. The proletariat is the most consistently revolutionary class in Africa.

In 1971, of a total African population estimated at 325 millions, the International Labour Organization (ILO) counted 135 millions as belonging to the "economically-active" population. In 23 African countries proletarians account for 19 percent of the labour force. The remaining 79 percent are subsistence peasants or herdsmen, or unemployed — typical of a backward agrarian economy which usually has from 75-80 percent of the population tied down in agriculture. 19 percent of the labour force works out to a proletariat of *15 millions* for the whole of developing Africa.[5] But the Arab north is much further advanced in industrialization than Tropical Africa. 8 million workers are concentrated in the Arab Republic of Egypt alone, leaving only 7 millions in all the other African countries together. *So more than half the African proletariat is Egyptian.* With the superior industrialization underway in

5. There were more than 500 million proletarians in the world in 1971.

Algeria and the rest of the Maghreb, it is obvious that a large contingent of the African proletariat is concentrated in the continent's Arab northern tier. When the Black proletarians who labour in racist South Africa are counted, the conclusion is unavoidable that, with the growing exception of Nigeria, there are relatively few proletarians in Tropical Africa.

For the working class colonialism of any kind — old-style colonialism or neo-colonialism — means deprivation of all political rights and merciless exploitation. The working day in the colonies ran twelve to fourteen hours and longer. There are still no safety provisions in most "third world" industry and transport. Plant equipment is outdated and in poor repair, and native entrepreneurs lack the means to repair it or institute safety regulations. "Third world" factories are the scene of frequent fatalities and maiming injuries. Without social legislation to protect them, workers who fall afoul of unemployment, illness or job injury lose all means of support. The wages of African workers are seldom high enough to satisfy even the most basic needs. Due to racial discrimination, the average wage of an African was (and remains) much lower than the wages of a white man working at his side and doing the same job. In pre-independence Kenya it was one-fifteenth, in Rhodesia less than one-twentieth, and in Zambia not much more than one-thirtieth that paid to white workers. In the Katangan copper mines, when Belgium ruled Zaire, the wages of an African miner were between one-fifth and one-tenth the wages of his European counterpart. In South African mines today it is the twentieth part. A portion of these paltry earnings is seized by various middlemen — intermediary entrepreneurs, foremen, supervisors and contract-labour agents. The colonial lords made large use of low-paid female and child labour — the latter as early as six or seven years of age.[6] In South Africa colonized workers have no more freedom of movement than prisoners and are confined in special barracks and labour compounds. Most African workers are drowned in debts and living standards for the overwhelming majority are extremely low. Little wonder that more than 53 percent of all children in Zaire died very young; in fact, the population of this

6. See Jean Suret-Canale, *Afrique Noire Occidentale et Centrale. De la Colonisation aux Indépendances (1945-1960)*, volume I: *Crise du système colonial et capitalisme monopoliste d'Etat*, Paris, 1972.

former colony was reduced to half in the time between its annexation by the Belgians and its independence. Even today the national income per capita in neo-colonial parts of the world rarely exceeds $100 per annum. To top it all, not only is the African proletarian impoverished absolutely, but in comparison with the local bourgeoisie he suffers *relative* impoverishment to boot.[7]

Outside the proletariat, circling tirelessly on the fringes of the towns, camping in dismal shanty towns, is the *lumpenproletariat*, that horde of starving men and women which is prone to stealing, hustling, and which is a sign of the irrevocable decay of colonialism, and which, in the words of Frantz Fanon, "is like a horde of rats".

Peasants are the overwhelming majority of the population in Africa. For this reason, agricultural development is urgent for the whole African national liberation struggle. In Zimbabwe, Namibia and South Africa, where Africans have been robbed of their land, and in countries like Morocco, Algeria and Ethiopia where a class of big landowners ruled the roost, land reform is a burning issue. The peasantry consist in the main of subsistence farmers, i.e. poverty-stricken small and "middle" peasants. But these are not the only kind of peasants to be found in Africa. Different modes of agricultural production prevail over wide areas, and there is a remarkable variety of social relations in the countryside. The peasantry is a group of small producers who carry on their own subsistence farming (domestic economy) with their own labour, most often working with the aid of their own meagre means of production, usually producing few or no commodities. But in large parts of Africa peasants have had to put up with tribal, semi-feudal and feudal exploitation.

The role of feudal exploitation in the African class struggle is often overlooked or ignored entirely, a mistake, given the tremendous revolt in Ethiopia against the feudal lords, and the complicated character of the anti-feudal land reform in Algeria. In the

7. Relative impoverishment of the proletariat means this: as the wealth of society (i.e. use-values) grows, the working class' share of the national income produced in capitalist enterprises diminishes, while the share which falls to the capitalists grows larger. The gap between the augmenting wealth and luxury of society's exploiting upper crust on one side, and the living standard of the workers on the other, widens considerably.

former Portuguese colonies feudal relations were introduced by European colonialists. And Northern Nigeria's Moslem Emirs were authentic feudal lords.

Feudalism implies a natural economy of more or less self-sufficient economic life. Despite variation in detail, feudal exploitation in Africa means in essence that the labour time of the peasant is divided into two parts — necessary labour time and surplus labour time. During the former, the peasant creates the means to keep himself and his family alive. During the other part of the working day, he creates the surplus product appropriated by the landowner, who in Ethiopia was also his *lord*. The surplus in labour or produce is *feudal ground rent*. In one form of feudal ground rent the peasant performs work or personal services for his lord. In the other, the lord appropriates the surplus product of his labour. In Ethiopia and Northern Nigeria the lords were the class of big landed proprietors. With the introduction of capitalism during the colonial era, feudal ground rent, previously a hallmark of feudalism, was transformed into a source of capitalist profit in some instances. Some proprietors leased or rented land to small producers. Even capitalist tenant farming made an appearance.

As the majority of African peasants became the victims of imperialism, exposed to the exploitation of big white planters and tenant farmers, of merchants, usurers and colonial bureaucrats, the development of capitalism broke the peasantry into different groups. Very common is a *middle* segment who farm with their own simple implements and their own personal labour. Their labour suffices to feed their families only when favourable weather and other fortuitous circumstances yield a good harvest. A small minority from this group climbs the social ladder and joins the bourgeoisie. The majority stagnates or slips down into the semi-proletariat, or migrates to the towns to join the lumpenproletariat.

The *poor peasantry* is similar to the middle segment, only they are unable to support themselves and must hire out their labour power to supplement their income. This is the rural semi-proletariat.

The peasants rub shoulders in the rural scene with a *village bourgeoisie* made up of well-to-do farmers, cattle dealers, petty traders and loansharks. The concentration of landed property in the hands of native big estate owners (often tribal chieftains and feudal Emirs) and usurers was worsened by the seizure of large acreage by white settlers. Imperialism transformed a number of African colonies into unbroken plantations, brutally displacing peasant communities. It is the peasant question which has assured the progressive character of national liberation movements even in countries where the proletariat is relatively weak (e.g. Ethiopia, Mozambique, Tanzania). The goal of national liberation is not emancipation from colonial rule alone; it also entails wiping out pre-capitalist relics. Thoroughgoing land reforms, redistribution of landownership in favour of those who actually till the soil, is an indispensable first step toward abolishing the pre-capitalist survivals which depress the yield of African agriculture. Lenin assessed the revolutionary potential of the peasantry in these words:

> The peasantry includes a great number of semi-proletarians as well as petty-bourgeois elements. This makes it also unstable, ... However, the instability of the peasantry differs radically from that of the bourgeoisie, ... Without thereby becoming socialist, or ceasing to be petty-bourgeois, the peasantry is capable of becoming a wholehearted and most radical adherent of the democratic revolution. The peasantry will inevitably become such if only the course of revolutionary events, which brings it enlightenment, is not prematurely cut short by the treachery of the bourgeoisie and the defeat of the proletariat. Subject to this condition the peasantry will inevitably become a bulwark of the revolution and the republic, for only a completely victorious revolution can give the peasantry *everything* in the sphere of agrarian reforms − *everything* that the peasants desire, dream of, and truly need ...[8]

Arising from this peculiar class structure caused by the backwardness of the African economy, are three sets of contradictions which govern political happenings throughout the whole region: 1) bitter contradictions between the imperialist monopolies and governments on one side, and the bloc of classes and social categories which rule newly free Africa on the other; 2) antagonistic contradictions between the African popular masses and the imperialists; 3) deepening contradictions between the popular masses and the local ruling classes.

*

8. V.I. Lenin, *Collected Works*, Volume 9, Moscow, 1965, p. 98.

Given these difficult objective economic and social conditions, we should expect ideological confusion, and there is much that is bewildering about the ideological scene in Africa and the rest of the "third world". The main trend, caused by the requirements of the liberation struggle, is toward scientific socialism, Marxism-Leninism. But, "one of the idiosyncrasies of national liberation revolutions in countries lacking sufficiently clear-cut differentiation of classes is that they are often headed by individuals with little training in Marxism and therefore with an ideological baggage likely to be a jumble of heterogeneous and contradictory views (religious, utopian, reformist, etc.)."[9]

Out of this hodge-podge there has sprung a welter of so-called "third world ideologies", or "theories of underdevelopment", alleged to be uniquely suited to Africa, Asia or Latin America, and designed to check the spread of Marxism. Most of these "third world ideologies" are idealist in philosophy.[10] Regardless of its form or disguise, idealism ultimately considers that mind and spirit are primary, while matter, nature and society are secondary things derived from the mind. Believing that ideas and attitudes determine social reality, these ideologies are voluntaristic, based on myths, and lead to erroneous political interpretations and positions. Sectarian in one way or another, such conceptions usually help to derail the anti-imperialist campaign of the masses.

These "third world ideologies" are reducible to five broad tendencies and demagogic theories which in the final analysis serve only the imperialists.

First, there are the straightforward neo-colonialist concepts of "partnership" and "interdependence" advanced in Africa by such spokesmen of foreign monopoly capital as Felix Houphouet-Boigny, Kofi Busia and Tom Mboya. Neo-colonial apologetics may even assume radical cultural nationalist wrappings as with Leopold Senghor's doctrine of negritude.[11]

Next rank the radical petty bourgeois theories of underdevelopment which insist that the "third world" is unique and has certain options open to it that, for some unexplained reason, Cuba and Asian socialist countries like the Democratic Republic of Vietnam

9. Y. Zhukov, L. Delyusin, A. Iskenderov, and L. Stepanov, pp. 212-213.
10. See Y. Popov, pp. 118-126.
11. See Yves Bénot, pp. 17, 179, 358-359, and *passim*.

(DRV), North Korea and Mongolia did not have. Essentially the underdevelopment theory suggests that newly free countries set out on the path of development hewed by capitalist states during the 19th century. It advocates the Japanese model of development despite the fact that imperialism has long since barred that path for all other countries. Japan's ruling feudal aristocracy was able to merge with the native bourgeoisie and squeeze in on the general transition to the monopoly stage of capitalism. But that was accomplished in the latter part of the 19th century and it is impossible for anyone to turn back the clock. The rise of imperialism, the onset of capitalism's general crisis, beginning with the October Revolution 1917, and the consolidation of the socialist world system have removed the possibility of independent monopoly capitalist development for the erstwhile colonies once and for all.

The third tendency is the neo-Trotskyite "intermediate zone" thesis based on rejection of a class analysis of the relations between nations. It completely rules out all distinction between the countries of the socialist community and the imperialist states. Middle-rank imperialist powers with their policy of aggression are dumped into the same pot with newly free states and smaller socialist countries.

Next there is the ultra-"leftist" theory which sees the "third world revolution" as the last remaining spearhead of world revolution. Rooted in a so-called "three worlds" concept it, like the neo-Trotskyite-Maoist thesis, is totally devoid of a class analysis. Socialism, as it really exists (the socialist world system), is ignored, and the international class struggle is arbitrarily said to be a confrontation between so-called "have" and "have-not" countries, between the "affluent North" and "poverty-stricken South", or between whites and coloureds.[12] One or two socialist states are counted as belonging to the evil clique of rich countries, overlooking the antagonistic differences between the capitalist and socialist camps. Even more than the others, this particular doctrine splits the ranks of the international proletariat and disorients the other classes that are menaced, oppressed and exploited by capital, regardless of whether they live in imperialist metropolises or in peripheral lands.

12. S. Agayev and Y. Oganisyan, *Nationalism as an Ideology and Policy*, Moscow, 1975, pp. 79-81.

Lastly there are various brands of "African socialism", "Islamic socialism", "democratic socialism", etc., all of which share a common rejection of scientific socialism, Marxism-Leninism, and which objectively serve to integrate "third world" Africa in the "first" world — the capitalist world system.

*

Unfortunately, the ideological confusion surrounding "third world" economics is most evident in respect to Africa. Africa is a huge continent and there is no homogeneity among its countries, cultures or peoples. There is wide disparity in socio-political orientation from country to country. The regimes in Kenya and Malawi are far removed from the regimes in Guinea-Bissau and the Peoples Republic of Angola. The R.D.A. of the Ivory Coast is a tool of the imperialists, while Frelimo in Mozambique is staunchly anti-imperialist. *That is why the term "third world", when applied to Africa or anywhere else, is so misleading.* There are at least two things wrong with it.

First, it implies that a "third" world system exists which is neither capitalist nor socialist, and that is simply not true. The majority of underdeveloped countries have not yet succeeded in detaching themselves from the state-monopoly capitalist world system.

Second, the very similarity, or "unity" of "third world" countries is largely factitious precisely because social relations and concrete political and economic problems differ vastly in each region and country. Neo-colonialist regimes seek to resolve socio-economic problems by capitalist methods (e.g. Kenya, Ivory Coast, Malawi). Progressive states effect anti-imperialist reforms, restrict private capitalist enterprise, and carry out anti-feudal land reforms in the interest of the subsistence farmers (e.g. Algeria, Mozambique and Ethiopia). One region differs noticeably from another in level of labour productivity and productive forces. The Arab north is far advanced economically over the territories south of the Sahara. Angola and other countries of socialist orientation are far advanced socially over reactionary Gabon, Sudan, Zaire, etc. Algeria and Egypt particularly, but also oil-rich Libya, and even Morocco and Tunisia, have much wider opportunities for industrialization, agrarian transformations, and raw materials development than most of the tropical states. Within the same frontiers of the racist Republic of South Africa there is a developed capitalist state that has now reached the imperialist stage, and a typical colony of oppressed Blacks. Africa's natural resources are not evenly distributed. Nigeria, Angola, Gabon and Libya are rich in oil. Algeria has immense reserves of natural gas. Guinea has bauxite to match Mauretania's iron ore. Gabon's ore bears iron, uranium and manganese, and the copper mines of Zambia and Zaire have long since been worked. In contrast to these amply-endowed lands there are such dessicated "backwaters" as Niger, Upper Volta and Chad. Young economies which extract valuable minerals and petroleum are in a much better position to accumulate foreign exchange than states which mainly export farm produce.[13] Hard currency buys industrial plants, patents and technical designs.

None of the newly liberated countries have so far actually begun building socialism. The fact that so many people think that they have is simply a misconception of scientific socialism. States like Guinea, the Peoples Republic of the Congo, Guinea-Bissau, Algeria, and Tanzania are currently at the stage of a gradual accumumulation of the prerequisites of a socialist development at a future junction. The most important preliminary stage is that of forming a Marxist-Leninist vanguard party — a stage through which Angola and Mozambique are now passing. It is these states with a socialist orientation which are eliminating most consistently the dependence of their national economies on foreign capital. Algeria, for example, has nationalized 75 percent of the country's industrial capacity. Guinea and Tanzania also have taken over some tangible productive properties. Angola's economy is solidly controlled by the popular forces.

Non-capitalist development of backward countries is a delicate process,[14] prone to fits and starts, and subject to mistakes which undermine the worker-peasant alliance, the shield for the socialist orientation. If one moves too fast in collectivizing small-peasant farming and putting private petty trade and domestic crafts on a cooperative footing, this merely discredits socialism and its principles. Tanzania's scale of industrialization, for example, is very

13. See L. Alexandrovskaya, p. 64.
14. See I. Andreyev, *The Noncapitalist Way*.

meagre, with priority having been given during the 1969-1974 five-year plan to only six average-sized industrial projects. "The pace of reform will obviously be much slower in those countries where the material and technical foundation of socialism is non-existent or all but non-existent than in the economically developed countries."[15] In places like Nigeria, Ghana, Tanzania and Zambia, where the clash between classes is sometimes at razor's edge, there are still numerous groups and elements which have not yet chosen their political orientation and which are still open to guidance. They can be influenced either by scientific socialism or, failing that, by the poison of imperialist ideology.

*

The draft Programme of Action of the 6th Special UN General Assembly states that the remnants of colonial and foreign domination, racial discrimination, neo-colonialism in all its forms, and apartheid continue to be the main obstacles to the full emancipation and progress of the developing countries.

Africa's national liberation struggle is thus still spearheaded against the main enemy — imperialism, and it still requires a broad democratic front of· workers, peasants, petty bourgeois and national bourgeois.

* * *

15. Y. Zhukov, L. Delyusin, A. Iskenderov, and L. Stepanov, p. 255.

Chapter 9

RACISM – THE IDEOLOGY OF IMPERIALISM:
FROM GOBINEAU TO SHOCKLEY

The *Convention on the Elimination of All Forms of Racial Discrimination* adopted by the UN General Assembly on December 21, 1965, says that *racial discrimination* is "any distinction, exclusion, restriction or preference based on race, colour, descent, or national or ethnic origin which has the purpose or effect of nullifying or impairing the recognition, enjoyment or exercise, on an equal footing, of human rights and fundamental freedoms in the political, economic, social, cultural or any other field of public life." Article 4 of the *Convention* declares the dissemination of ideas based on racial superiority or hatred, or any incitement to racial discrimination, a *felony*. Genocide is defined in the document as acts committed with the intent to destroy, in whole or in part, a national, ethnic, racial or religious group.

It is clear, then, that, according to international law, racism is a crime, a criminal offence, equally racist ideas are illegal, the prohibited contraband of the intellectual world, as it were. The United States government is a signatory of this international *Convention*, it has obligated itself by law to implement the stipulations of the agreement outlawing racist practices and doctrines. Yet none but fools would deny that Afro-Americans are now, and always have been, the victims of racial discrimination in the land of their birth. Race prejudice has dominated public opinion in this country for centuries – in fact, there is a sense in which racist views can be said to be the prevailing public opinion in America. Blacks and other minorities have been subjected to recurrent spasms of genocide, lynching, mob attacks, terrorism and pogroms without any of the offenders ever having been punished by the law of the land. Despite international law and the liability of the U.S. government to enforce it, racist practices and racist doctrine rule the roost in this country.

Why is this so? The answer is straightforward – because imperialism has embraced racism as its authentic ideology. This essay examines how this tie-up came about and analyzes the role of racist ideology in the political system of imperialism.

*

Let us begin by explaining what we mean by the term *ideology*.

Ideology is the ideas and beliefs of us all, of human beings who live in society. Ideology is a form of *social consciousness*, which means that it is determined ultimately by social being, by objective reality independent of anyone's mind or fantasy. In a sense then, ideology flows through society free of any one person's consciousness. But it does have firm moorings — it is moored to *class*. Each ideology embodies a specific social class' awareness of actual phenomena, as distinct from imaginary feelings and thoughts. Ideology is thus the aggregate of ideas and theories that express the *main* relation of a class to the fundamental issues of social living. Because of this class character, it is always saturated with a partisan class interest put forward in precise, condensed form in political doctrines, literature, ethics and philosophy. Although internalized by individuals, ideology is a *mass phenomenon*; it does not depend on the way any one individual of a class thinks, lives and acts. However, the key factor in an antagonistic class society like the United States with its reactionary ruling elite is that the folk truths contained in the prevailing ideology (i.e. the ideology of the ruling class) are compounded with *falsehoods*, subtle as well as crude.

In the course of history it has become apparent that certain ideologies incorporate elements which enable them to be taken up, revived at a later date in time by more advanced social formations (i.e. societies), and put to use. By a kind of historical "natural selection", the ruling class of a more advanced society may be prompted by interest to select, internalize and propagate ideas and opinions, myths and prejudices, first formulated by the rulers of a bygone class society who, in the meantime, have been overthrown and have faded into memory. Let us call these salvageable elements which some ideologies possess — *selectable features.*[1]

1. For a fuller discussion of this aspect of ideology, see Clarence J. Munford, "Ideology, Racist Mystification and America" in *Revolutionary World*.

Now modern racist doctrine — an ideology born of the slave-holding anomaly grafted to the manufactory capitalism of the 16th - 19th centuries — happens to be one of those ideologies which possess selectable features. For several centuries the selectable aspect of racist ideology has made it worthwhile for ruling classes to refurbish and give it new leases on life. Today racist philosophy is very much alive, although it embodies the thought of a moribund, or expiring, capitalism. As we shall demonstrate, racist doctrine is the visible philosophical expression of the decay of capitalism, but nevertheless racism has had what it takes to root itself in a new social reality, to survive under altered historical circumstances. It was eminently suited to serve a new master class.

There is no denying the brutish, nasty character of racism, or the churlish temper of racist philosophers. A main feature of racism is the downgrading, or total rejection, of reason. Racists, by definition, are anti-intellectual, oppose instinct to reason, and glorify "irrational" will and intuition. Racist ideology is misanthropic, i.e. it is full of hatred for most of mankind. Racist philosophers preach death and decay, unrelievable gloom is their trademark. What is worse, imperialism during the 20th century has reacted to changes unfavourable to capitalism increasingly with segregation, apartheid and genocide. Racism is the ideological rationalization for these crimes against humanity.

Racism's selectable features are rooted in the general nature of class society. This should cause no surprise for social consciousness is always derived from social circumstances. The glands of the human body secrete hormones which regulate physiological functions. Similarly, in order to function in a way beneficial to their ruling circles, class societies must secrete ideologies, as it were. Class society is split into a minority of favoured characters and a majority of exploited working people; class society is thus elitist. Now it appears that the most selectable feature in racism is precisely its *elitist* class element. The phenomena of class society, "which have hitherto been more or less valid throughout all history really express only those relations which are common to the conditions of all society based on class rule and class exploitation."[2] The feature which has made racist ideology adapt-

2. F. Engels, Letter to F.A. Lange, Manchester, March 29, 1865, in K. Marx and F. Engels, *Selected Correspondence*, Moscow, n.d., p. 208.

able for today's monopoly capitalist class is its doctrinal acceptance and propagation of the idea that society must be divided into classes, that either divine will or Mother Nature has arranged humanity into groups of so-called "superiors" and "inferiors", of which the latter are the servants of the former. This concept of servants and masters makes racism perfectly adaptable in any class society part of whose population exhibits different racial specifics from those of the ruling class. Required only is the clever adaptation that will suit racist ideology to modern conditions. Once the adaptation is effected and kept in good repair by the tinkerings of racist thinkers and pseudo-scientists, racism has the resiliency to persist as long as class society lasts. Not until class society is done away with, therefore, will the basis for the total disappearance of racism exist.

*

Let us scan the past to see how racist doctrine has developed through the ages.

The myth of higher and lower races has a hoary history dating back to earliest antiquity. It first appeared when the primitive community first split into antagonistic social classes, entailing private property and different status in social production. When a clan, tribe or a territorial community (whose members were not related by blood) gained victory on the battlefield, it became customary for its war chiefs or proto-politicians to declare the victors a higher race, and the people that had been defeated a lower race. As yet, however, there was no clear understanding of what the concept *race* meant beyond winners and losers. The ancient Greeks preened themselves as the only civilized men and despised all other peoples (i.e. those who did not speak Greek) as "barbarians". Naturally, the Greek ruling class concluded that the "barbarian" peoples should be annihilated, enslaved, or otherwise exploited. Ancient Greece's greatest philosopher, Aristotle, said the state (polis) consists of settlements composed of families, and that a *normal* family is made up of husband, wife, children and *slaves*. Aristotle was the spokesman of the slave-holding oligarchy which ruled the Greek city-states. For the slave-holders civilization was impossible without slaves. According to Aristotle, a slave was the best kind of property a man could own, and a slave was to be valued as the most perfect of tools. "There are cases of people of whom some are freemen," he wrote, "and the others are slaves by nature, and for these slavery is an institution both expedient and just."[3] A certain category of people were declared to be slaves by nature. The proto-racist tendency of Aristotle's writings emerged in his designation of the "barbarian" peoples as those who Nature intended to be slaves. However, racial distinctions played no essential role in the ancient slaveholding mode of production — Blacks and whites, Africans, Asians and Europeans, all were enslaved without preference.

Racist doctrine developed slowly thereafter, by fits and starts through long medieval and early modern centuries[4] — Crusading fits and Protestant xenophobic starts, and convulsive rationalizations of the lucrative slave trade in Africans. Winthrop Jordan has sought to project racist "attitudes" towards Africans as far back into the European past as when Englishmen were still painting themselves blue.[5] But these notions were still *proto-racist*, primitive and inconsistent. Not until the eighteenth century did the lie of racial superiority get its first pseudo-scientific lacquer. The place — backward, feudal-absolutist Germany; the time — 1786; the guilty party — Christoph Meiners, a Göttingen University professor. Meiners dreamed up spurious "proofs" that "whites" were higher in the "hierarchy of creation" than "coloureds". Nineteenth century racists, including the American slaveholders and their ideologists, then seized Meiners' baton and raced headlong. Josiah Nott twisted the science of anatomy into a panegyric on Caucasian "superiority".[6] The tirades of Harvard naturalist Louis Agassiz "proved" the Negro incapable of competing with the white man. A New York publishing firm printed drawings illustrating the beauty of whites and the depravity of all other races.[7] These racist circles were strongly influenced by the pseudo-scientific scribblings

3. Aristotle, *Politics*, London, 1944, pp. 24-25.
4. See Pyotr Shastitko, *The Crime Called Racialism*, Moscow, 1973, pp. 12-14.
5. *White Over Black*, p. ix.
6. J.C. Nott, *Indigenous Races of the Earth: Or, New Chapters on Ethnological Inquiry*, Philadelphia, 1857; and J.C. Nott and G.R. Gliddon, *Types of Mankind: Or, Ethnological Researches,...*, Philadelphia, 1855.
7. Forrest G. Wood, *Black Scare: The Racist Response to Emancipation and Reconstruction*, Berkeley and Los Angeles, 1970, p. 9.

of the Europeans Lapouge, Ammon, Woltman, Maury and others. This crew penned turgid volumes "proving" the theory of higher and lower human races. But *Count Arthur de Gobineau*, a Frenchman, was the most influential of all. He gained notoriety as the father of modern racist ideology.

Obstinate antipathy to democracy and the conviction that all power had to be in the hands of the mighty — those were Gobineau's guiding lights. He saw the rule of the strong as Nature's unshakeable and supreme law. Gobineau said history was a "mystery" to which only he had discovered the key. The key was race. Race was the material basis of civilization and the "racial question", in his eyes, became the burning question of modern history.

Gobineau devoted his life to proving that there can be no equality between the races of man. Racial inequality determines the world's historical evolution. He denied that natural, geographical and economic agents have any influence on man's cultural development. Of the three races he recognized, White, Black and Yellow, he worshipped the White race as the so-called "purest". He proclaimed it the strongest, most intelligent, and the healthiest, and boasted that it alone had created and enriched human civilization. Not the Hebrews of the Old Testament, but White people were "God's children".

His major work, entitled *Essay on the Inequality of the Human Race*,[8] a poisoned four-volumed diatribe, later to become almost a bible for American and German racists, claimed that Whites were like gods among the other human races, and that within the White race as a whole, the ruling class is the flower of this elite. According to the *Essay*, the White race, the bearer of civilization, can keep alight its luminous qualities and fulfill its brilliant destiny only if it remains pure. Racial purity was the apple of Gobineau's eye. He said the intrinsic value of each person is directly related to the racial purity of his blood. There is an inverse proportion between the degree of racial mingling and the intrinsic worth of the individual offspring. Purity of blood causes noble traits in man. When and if the White race loses its purity of blood, the death of human civilization will inevitably follow, screamed the patriarch of the racists. Without segregation of the races, without prohibition of

8. The first two volumes appeared in Paris in 1853, volumes III and IV three years later. At the time Gobineau was a career diplomat.

intermarriage, organized society would be doomed, and the life of man would revert to its short, nasty and brutish condition.

The "lowest", "vilest" race of all, he alleged, was the Black race. Gobineau said that wherever people of African descent gathered, or wherever mixtures of the Black and Yellow races were to be found, *no history* was possible. History is a natural secretion of contact solely between *White* people. He pictured Black people as dull-minded and "implacably ferocious". Blacks were everything subhuman — lazy, sexually unbridled, cruel, harsh, pitiless. Nothing spiritual, only sensual pleasures are supposed to arouse us. These qualities were said to be unshakeable "racial properties", unchangeable in substance. The Black race is unable to modify itself or its circumstances, or at best only in minor details, announced Gobineau. In major affairs, it is unfit for transformation. Left to our own devices, we are supposed to be incapable of bettering ourselves, we must continue forever on the same path along which a cruel Mother Nature set us.

Most important, Gobineau insisted that Black people are innately hostile to any kind of *morality*. He repeated this lie with the persistence and fury of a lunatic. Why was he so adamant? Well, because the alleged immorality of the "lower orders" is a key justification for the exploitation and oppression of man by man. Morality, rightly understood, is that form of social consciousness which welds the ethical qualities of good, justice and welfare in the mind of the masses. A person's behavior can be said to be moral if it is *objectively* good and just. To be objectively good and just, one must move in accordance with historical development, not against it. Bad or immoral behaviour is action contrary to the long range trend of history. Morality thus involves *evaluation*, and that is why racists, past and present, claim Blacks are immoral or amoral — for Black people are supposed to lack the mental faculties required to evaluate situations.

Spewing such filth, it is no surprise that Gobineau was a precious find for all those then engaged in the practical business of enslaving and exploiting Black labour. His theories served the slaveholding oligarchy in the pre-Bellum South as an ideological weapon in the struggle against the Abolitionist Movement led by Frederick Douglass and John Brown. The chapters in his book which slandered Black people were immediately translated into English by pro-slavery men in the United States.[9] Formalized racist philosophy was thus brought home to America where it has not budged since.

In a capitalist society, the treatment of groups designated as "racial minorities" depends entirely on three sets of circumstances: 1) on the specific content of the relations of the working class with the bourgeoisie; 2) on the overall balance of class forces at any given time; and 3) on the situation at the front of the class war, e.g. whether popular resistance or reactionary repression is prevailing. These relations, in turn, are cradled in the history of the country, and in the degree of advancement of capitalism's general crisis. Furthermore, the "racial minority's" fortunes are sensitive to the variations in the allegiance between the ruling oligarchy and the classes and fractions of classes which move in its slipstream. Present-day discrimination against Blacks is derived from slavery. But it is derived with more immediacy from the bargain northern industrialists — having accomplished their basic economic and political objectives with the defeat of the Confederacy, and beginning to develop monopoly capital — made with cotton planter reaction and budding southern capitalists. The Hayes-Tilden sell-out in 1877 betrayed Blacks after chattel slavery had been overthrown. Though its forms and nuances may have changed through the centuries, racism from the very beginning in America has expressed *class* relations. A clear illustration of this is the development of stylized racist concepts in this country.

Racism in untutored, folkish varieties was the prevailing ideology of the colonialist robbery and extermination of the Native Americans (Indian peoples). Bourgeois-slaveholder ideology guided the planter slaveowning system. Even before it was formalized by pseudo-scientists it was a weapon of reaction and obscurantism.

From the historical point of view, racialism resulted from the slaveowning system as the ideological justification for domination over conquered tribes and over 'low-castes' or classes. In more recent times racialism made rapid headway owing to colonial conquests and the introduction of slavery in the U.S.A.[10]

The fact that western hemisphere capitalism was racist from the

9. Josiah Nott assisted in the translation, and the volume was published in this country in 1856 under the title *The Moral and Intellectual Diversity of Races.*

10. I.R. Grigulevich and S.Y. Kozlov, p. 275.

moment of inception is a distinguishing feature of U.S. historical development. "It is significant of the specifically bourgeois character of these human rights," wrote Engels, "that the American constitution, the first to recognize the rights of man, in the same breath confirms the slavery of the coloured races existing in America: class privileges are proscribed, race privileges sanctioned."[11] Written into law at the birth of the republic two hundred years ago, race, as a *socio-political category*, became a sanctioned folkway of American life. Class relations were transmuted into *"race relations"*. Later on race prejudice survived both the crushing blows thrown at it by the Abolitionists and defeat in the Civil War, and came back stronger than ever under U.S. imperialism. We must be aware of the connection between the betrayal of Black Reconstruction and the rise of segregation on one hand (1877-1896), and the emergence of monopoly capitalism and imperialism (1873-1895) on the other. It is true that America's version of racist ideology is a holdover from chattel slavery. Racism was the philosophy *par excellence* of the 300,000-strong clique of slaveholders. However, once the slaveholders lost their dominant hold on the federal government, racist doctrine was given a thorough overhauling and formalization to meet the needs of the new monopoly capitalists.

Segregation became the norm in the industrializing post-Bellum South. Above and below the Mason-Dixon line, capitalism was propped up by the myths of white racial superiority, European excellence, and "manifest destiny".[12] White working people were sold the idea that they "needed" to define themselves against a non-white "contra-image", and millions bought the idea. Everywhere capitalists were industrializing. To them it meant "civilizing" – profitably of course. "Inferior" peoples who got in the way did so at their own risk. Amerindians were "in the way"; they were exterminated. Hundreds of thousands of landless Black freedmen were available; they were set to work mostly as neo-slave sharecroppers, some as cheap factory hands. The industrialization of the South offered further proof that throughout its history the

11. F. Engels, *Anti-Dühring. Herr Eugen Dühring's Revolution in Science*, 3rd edition, 1894, Moscow, 1969, p. 127.
12. See Joel Kovel, *White Racism: A Psychohistory*, New York, 1971, pp. 23-24 and 29.

American economy has been geared to the extortion of super-profits from the labour of Black workers. Industrial capitalism reinforced segregation.[13] Far from encouraging social integration and equal rights, industrialization of the South initially made apartheid more rigorous in social practice than it had yet been even in the rural communities.

Lynch law and racial oppression heated to fever pitch and racist ideas spread more rapidly with the transition about 1873 to 1895 from competitive capitalism to the reactionary domination of monopoly capital. The rise of U.S. imperialism marked a renaissance of racism. It was then that racist theory was officially adopted as a favourite child by the most aggressive fractions of the big bourgeoisie. In 1896, in the *Plessy v. Ferguson* case, the Supreme Court abrogated the Fourteenth Amendment and sanctioned racial segregation in public facilities. Three years later, in *Cumming v. County Board of Education*, the Court extended segregation of the races to the schools. Imperialism also stoked the fires of racism in the labour movement. From shore to shore rode the impulse of labour in a white skin to brand labour in a Black skin as ignominious, and to ostracize it. After 1890 the AFL insisted on the establishment in certain industrial cities of different locals divided along the "colour line". Class-collaborating labour misleaders made names for themselves cursing "niggers", and demanding their exclusion from "white men's jobs".[14] On the West Coast defamers conjured up a "yellow peril".[15] Pogroms drove Chinese workers and other Asian-Americans together for shelter in closed "Chinatowns" and "Little Tokyos". The western

13. Lawrence J. Friedman, *The White Savage: Racial Fantasies in the Post-bellum South*, Englewood Cliffs, N.J., 1970, pp. 119-125.

14. The literature on racism in the U.S. labour movement continues to grow. It is too large to cite even a substantial part. For a short recent summary see H. Hill, "The Racial Practices of Organized Labor", in B.N. Schwartz and R. Disch, eds., *White Racism: Its History, Pathology and Practices*, New York, 1970, pp. 324-332; still the classical work on the labour movement is Philip Foner, *History of the Labor Movement in the United States*, 4 volumes, New York, 1947-1965; by far the best volume on the relationship between Black workers and the labour movement is Philip Foner, *Organized Labor and the Black Worker, 1619-1973*, New York, 1974.

15. See Stanley Cohen, "The Failure of the Melting Pot", in G.B. Nash and R. Weiss, eds., *The Great Fear: Race in the mind of America*, New York, 1970, pp. 144-164.

rural scene was a living hell for Chicanos and other non-white farm hands.[16] Everywhere Black proletarians were refused protection in wage matters. Lower remuneration for equal or even superior work was the accepted practice for them.

Monopoly capital hired gangs of Social Darwinists and cultural relativists to formalize racist folk wisdom and make it respectable in academic circles. A new generation of racist "scientists" and "scholars" equated the class struggle in human society with the struggle in the animal kingdom. There is a special "racial instinct", they asserted, a "racial xenophobia" that gives rise to enmity and repulsion between the races of man. Around the turn of the century, Herbert Spencer, an Englishman, dreamed up the reactionary theory of Social Darwinism. His *Principles of Ethics* claimed that modern human society is governed by biological laws that are the same as those that operate in the animal kingdom.[17] There is no difference between men and insects, he opined, both are fated to devour one another non-stop. Brute struggle for existence, the survival of the fittest, the extinction of the unfit are supposed to be what social life is all about. The Social Darwinists held that natural selection is crucial in the evolution of modern man, and that a struggle between the races is the basis of the development of mankind. Social Darwinism originated from Spencer's deliberate misapplication of Charles Darwin's legitimate biological discoveries to sociology. Spencer and his followers regarded the struggle for existence and natural selection as the prime movers of social progress. Their real purpose was to convince the world that capitalism was eternal and inviolable, and to justify racism by depicting billionaires as supermen, as heroes who protect civilization by keeping "second-rate" people like workers and "coloured races" from performing "harmful" acts like instituting democracy and people's control over the economy. Social Darwinists preached that the intensified propagation of so-called "inferior races" was the root of all social evil. This was an early version of the theory of "third world overpopulation", and a later version of the misanthropic doctrine of Thomas Malthus. Social Darwinism misused

16. *Ibid*.
17. Spencer's *First Principles* and *System of Synthetic Philosophy* (1862-1896) were laborious applications of mechanistic evolutionism to the analysis of social life in biological terms. His time could have been much better spent.

204

science to explain the injustices of capitalist society saying that people are divided into classes because they are biologically *unequal*. "Empire-builders" Cecil Rhodes and Lord Lugard put these principles in practice in Africa where they slaughtered and pillaged at will.

German fascism (Hitler and his Nazis) was imperialism's most systematic expression of racism in the social life of the 20th century. It was also the most *lethal* outpouring of racist hatred in human history. Nevertheless, *fascist ideology* has never existed in the sense of an established, coherent interpretation of the world. Unlike Marxism, it is not a material force which seizes hold of the masses. In the contemporary world, only Marxism-Leninism does that. Fascist ideas, in comparison, are instrumental. Fascist ideology is opportunistic and basically pragmatic. *Anti-Marxism* is its primary, indispensable feature, *racism* its secondary, though not always present feature (e.g. Italian or Portuguese fascism did not emphasize biological racism). The vagueness of fascist ideology, its indetermination, makes it ready for anything. Without scruple, it tries to be all things to all men — all but those designated as pariahs. Open to all contingencies it is a quadrant, so to speak, passing through the zenith and the nadir. Its adherents advertise it as capable of meeting the most contradictory needs and demands one after another and simultaneously! The result is a total absence of any concrete constructive program. Fascist ideology is *contrary* by character. It is totally *against* something — against communism and sometimes other races — but rarely *for* anything that is not inhuman. Fascist thinkers avoid coming to grips with specific day-to-day problems. In the strict philosophical sense, fascist ideology is anti-historical, and most fascists are objective idealists who regard the essence of things as independent, innate, immutable and absolute. They regard such propositions as race and blood, national destiny, the "warrior instinct" and "Western Christian values" as eternal. Cultural pessimism is a prominent part of fascist thinking: "spiritual regeneration" and "moral rearmament" by means of "reformed life", usually meaning some kind of re-dedication to petty bourgeois values. Anti-bourgeois disputation among bourgeois youth attracted to fascism is usually present in the early stages of fascist movements. Under the banner of preventive counter-revolution we get a wave of irrationalism and revolt by manipulated petty bourgeois intellectuals.

Perhaps the single most striking feature of the fascist doctrine is not its content, but the *technique* by which it is propagated. It borrows the public relations techniques of its parents — monopoly capitalism and imperialism. Commercial publicity, mass advertising, indoctrination (well-financed) through the mass media, by press, radio, films and television are the staples of fascist ideology.

Anti-communist nationalism and militarism are common to all fascist movements. In addition, there are numerous eclectic fragments. For instance, there is the corporative doctrine, taken from social democracy, whose underlying principle is class collaboration and an end to class struggle without ending class exploitation. Further, there is the conception of capitalism according to which *monopoly* capitalism is a degeneration that must be eliminated, while the "true" capitalist economy is that of the early, competitive period. There is a yearning to return to the "good" origins. This is a romantic notion which reveals the futile effort of the petty bourgeoisie to stop historical development, halt the proletarianization of fractions of the petty bourgeoisie, and make a world moving toward socialism turn back. This dream is not shared by the finance capitalists who make fascist ideology the instrument of their class interests. In its most populist, bombastic aspect, fascism promises society a pseudo-revolutionization of the petty bourgeoisie. There is talk of going *beyond* capitalism, abolishing its anarchy through planning techniques borrowed from socialism. Extreme right wing parties or crypto-fascist movements sport "social" preoccupations, style themselves "socialist" or "progressive", and at times even "workers parties" or "working peoples parties" (e.g. American Nazis or NSDAP). This goes hand in hand with a slick mystification of the capitalist exploitation of labour power. There is much phoney glorification of "craftsmanship", "pride in one's work", "rugged individualism", and "decent working people" as opposed to "lazy free-loaders". "Hard work" is writ large, as is "self-sacrifice" on the part of the working people. The aim is to get workers to accept penal servitude through the militarization of the working peoples' values: according to the fascist refrain, the loyal, red-blooded white worker is patriotic, nationalistic and ready, like a soldier, to defend his country's "way of life" at the work bench as well as at the front. He must be ever ready to protect white womanhood from the lechery of "degenerate" coloured races. The pretended concern of the fascists with social problems and with the lot of working people is actually a sign of the growing prestige and authority of world socialism and the power of the worker's movement.

Fascist ideology is thus an instrument which develops organically in such a way as to bind together disparate classes and social strata. It drums up mass support and serves to cement together various factions in the struggle of the most racist elements of finance capital for dictatorship over the working masses. Extreme anti-communism and racism are the main components of fascist ideology because the process of fasczization of the ruling class is the determining factor. In Germany, anti-Semitism coupled with contempt for non-whites and a pseudo-Teutonic paganism, was the barbaric phenomenal form in which this racism expressed itself.

Naturally the Nazi theory of racism divided humanity into races. Some races were regarded as innately inferior, others as inherently superior. The alleged super Aryan race was ascribed the right to dominate and exterminate the inferior races. With his theory that miscegenation kills civilization, Gobineau laid the seed for the worst Hitlerian practices. Anti-Semitism in action was a kind of preliminary schooling in savage contempt for people of other races, and thus served to prepare Germans for total war against other nations.

From 1939 to 1945 Nazism's frantic anti-communism was disguised as racist nationalism. The wartime brand of Nazi racism, it was designed to inculcate in German proletarians and semi-proletarians a *"poor white trash" superiority complex.* By the same token that even the most exploited white North American may learn from the popular racist catechism to feel superior to outstanding and famous Black men, the least of Germans was assured that regardless of his class he was better than any non-Aryan. This ploy worked because the Third Reich was then at war with all of Europe, including the bourgeoisie and aristocracy of the enemy nations. This racist, so-called "soldier's socialism" contributed greatly to instilling in Germans a spirit of blind obedience. It created the determination to "fight to the last man". The anti-communism that had been spewed for so many years prior to Hitler by all the traditional bourgeois parties and by right wing Social Democrats made it exceedingly difficult for the semi-proletarians, peasants, and petty bourgeois ranged on the side of the Nazis to see through this kind of demagogy.

The cultural relativists were slicker than the Nazis, but their intention was just as malicious. Cultural relativism was an anti-evolutionist trend in bourgeois anthropology founded by Melville Herskovits, a liberal U.S. professor.[18] Herskovits' argument was quite subtle, a measure of the progress racist philosophy had made in subordinating the achievements of science and culture to the needs of the colonialists. Attuned to the "liberal" imperialist bourgeoisie, cultural relativism dominated bourgeois anthropology from the onset of the crisis of the imperialist colonial system (ca. 1919) to the collapse of the colonial system in the late 1950s. It co-existed with other forms of racism, including traditional white supremacy and Nazism.

Herskovits insisted that anthropologists should treat every culture as a unique and unrepeatable system. Each culture, he claimed, had immutable and specific traditions, expressed in a unique system of "values". At first sight the cultural relativists appeared to respect all the earth's peoples. But this was merely a subtle way of denying the ideas of progress, evolution, and *ascending development* of mankind, because, they maintained, systems of values created by different peoples are incomparable, and like the thickness of one's lips or the texture of one's hair, are passed on from generation to generation exclusively within closed groups. Herskovits' "values" are not unlike Gobineau's unshakeable "racial properties", both are unchangeable in substance. This variety of racism implied that colonized people of colour are "primitives" condemned forever to backwardness for transmitted cultural reasons — i.e. inherited social traits, not imperialist exploitation, are the cause of underdevelopment.[19] Cultural relativism also implied that humanity is not one single unit which develops as a whole, although unevenly, but rather an assemblage of separate races which share the planet but develop along entirely different lines. There are no general regularities in the history of human society, so it was quite alright for Great Britain and the United States to develop as industrially-advanced capitalist powers, while Africans and Asians floundered in "traditional" poverty and

18. Melville J. Herskovits, *The Myth of the Negro Past* (1941), Boston, 1958.
19. See E. Franklin Frazier's misfounded but strong attack on the Herskovits theory in *The Negro in the United States*, New York, 1949.

ignorance under colonial rule. The alleged "uniqueness" of traditional African cultures was strongly emphasized. The accent on the great difference between these cultures and elite white "Western" civilization rationalized the segregation imposed on colonized peoples in their homelands by the imperialists — ostensibly the restrictions were designed to "protect" native African culture from being "corrupted" by Western customs.[20] The cultural relativists inferred that oppressed peoples' customs and habits were exotic, weird and rather repulsive. They were supposed to share a *pre-logical* way of thinking which had nothing in common with the way whites reason. The implication was that Blacks really do not reason at all, moving rather by instinct and reflex. They can be expected to run faster and jump higher than white men, but the latter are "more cerebral". The cultural relativist anthropologist always saw his own nation as mentally superior to the "primitives" he was studying. The logical outcome of cultural relativism is the belief that each race reasons in a manner peculiar to itself, and that the races of mankind have different conceptions of what is moral and what is immoral.[21] Humanity thus dissolves into separate race-species. The door was opened to the development of a *"psychological" racism.*[22]

20. See Roger Bastide, *African Civilizations in the New World*, New York, 1971, pp. 1-4 and 13-14.

21. The whole cultural relativist concept of "primitive society" and "primitive peoples" is linked to imperialist colonialism. Nevertheless a disguised form of this concept has been picked up by certain confused or ill-intentioned Blacks — the prophets of Negritude and "Africanism" ("Africanité"). Aping the cultural relativists, President L.S. Senghor of Senegal, Carlos Moore and others hawk Black national exclusiveness and nationalistic conceptions, despite the racist assumptions of those conceptions. These cultural nationalists reject the anti-imperialist solidarity of oppressed peoples regardless of skin colour. Senghor claims that Blacks are incurable spiritualists who hold the objective material world in contempt. "Negro-African" cultural nationalism slanders Black people and actually helps to perpetuate racist myths by claiming that the Black race is full of sensuality. This implies that Africans and African-derived people are lacking in intellectual capabilities. They should be reminded that Gobineau, the father of modern racists, also credited Blacks with this quality. He said their sole merit was an artistic capacity expressed largely through the *sensual* art of dance! Objectively, Negritude and other types of cultural nationalism soften our people up for increased exploitation by monopoly capital.

22. See Chapter 4: "Racial Differences and Intellectual Performance" in

Cultural relativism enhanced the ideology of racism and paved the way for the "psychoracism" which is now fashionable. The concept of the incomparability and equivalence of all cultures allowed bourgeois scholars to pretend neutrality in the struggle between the very real values of oppressed peoples and the so-called "values" of colonialists, Nazis, South African agents of apartheid and American racists. Toleration of oppression and genocide was the consequence of the relativist doctrine of ethical neutrality and "objectivity".

*

The pseudo-scientific, phoney-scholarly racism now flooding the U.S. market has several different labels and brands. Nobel Prize-winner Shockley has "discovered" genetic defects in Afro-Americans, and tramps the length and breadth of the land preaching the good news. Educator Jensen bemoans Black people's permanent "dyslexia" — impaired learning ability. Sociologist Banfield offers a racist explanation of crime and urban rot. Student-of-concentration camps Elkins assures us that we internalized infantile traits when we were slaves, and that we have not lost them. Self-styled "Marxian" Genovese credits the slaveholders with honour and benign paternalism, and their "Southern civilization" with morality and says that we "accommodated" enslavement. He and historians Fogel, Engerman and Goldin revive the U.B. Phillips-George Fitzhugh defense of the patriarchal Dixie idyl that was slavery. Psychologists Herrnstein and Eysenck bring back the theory of Aryan superiority. Philosopher Hook claims that discrimination has been "reversed", that now it is the minorities that are favoured over white candidates by quotas in hiring, welfare and education. Harvard pundit Glazer strikes a blow for individualism, and with his back swing pulverizes the affirmative action policy which opposes racism. Sociologist cum diplomat cum Senator Moynihan sells us social action based on "ethnicity" as a substitute for class struggle against racist imperialism.

Below the academic cant and hypocrisy gleems downright Nazism. Once again "reputable scientists" are screaming racist

M.L. Goldschmid, ed., *Black Americans and White Racism: Theory and Research*, New York, 1971, pp. 138-186.

210

epithets and alleging the inferiority of Blacks from university lecterns and conference podiums — only this time it is happening in America, not in Germany. Jensen of the pacesetting University of California graces scientific journals with articles which do their utmost to convince the public that people of African descent suffer intellectual and psychological disabilities as compared with whites. And this doctrine was feverishly acclaimed by the nation's lawmakers at a session of Congress.

The main thrust now in racist ideology is to deny that the whole historical complex of living conditions shaped the emergence, formation, weakening, disappearance, and amalgamation of racial characteristics. Instead, a so-called *"typological hypothesis"* of race is put forward which defines a race as a totality of the individuals belonging to a single *"morphological"* type. This type passes its traits from parents to children in unending succession. Seizing upon minor structural differences between the major races of mankind, the typological hypothesis isolates certain "racial features" and considers them apart from the real function of human beings in social life. These racial features are supposed to be pleiotropic, i.e. dependent on one gene or a group of linked genes located in one chromosome. Thus the tendency is to regard the formation of the races of mankind as the result of the reshuffling of unchanging genes. Racists claim that these genes affect physiological and *psychological* features of men as well as external, morphological features. If the racial (i.e. morphological) type is inherited as a whole and depends on only one gene or a group of linked genes, then, they insist, there is a connection between racial type and the thought, behaviour and historical roles of different peoples.[23]

Contemporary racism thus regards racial features or specifics as being those of a species or even a genus. The implication in extreme cases being that humanity is divided into different kinds of people, or even into groups more distant and dissimilar than different species. Here racial features are the pretext to divide humanity up in different classificatory groups in the same way as lions and house cats and dogs and hyenas are classified differently. Upon this false interpretation it is then fallaciously concluded that observable physical distinctions between the races of mankind are

23. See I.R. Grigulevich and S.Y. Kozlov, pp. 46-49.

paralleled by psychical distinctions. This interpretation is the basis also for the polygenetic theory held by some racists. The polygeneticists distort the origin of man, claiming that the human races had different original ancestors who were not in any way related and who were inimical to one another. These mythical ancestors were the progenitors, some of "rapidly developing, master" races, others of "backward, lower" races, thereby substantiating and defending at once the false idea of the biological inequality of the races, and the right and vocation of some races to lord it over the "inferior" races which are doomed to subordination, slavery and extinction. These pseudo-scientists blame hereditary causes for psycho-historical distinctions, and contend that the study of heredity will enable one to identify groups that are mentally and physically superior and groups that are inferior. Naturally the "inferior race" is a stereotype of all sorts of negative qualities and incapabilities.

The ideologists of capitalism deliberately shut their eyes to exploitation. They refuse to notice the existence of an upper stratum of exploiters in modern bourgeois society. The inequalities that cannot be covered up are ascribed mainly to alleged differences in intelligence and work habits. Mother Nature creates human beings unequal, it is claimed, and from the unequal talents of men spring the ruling classes of society, the elite strata of "chosen" men and women. This theory of the *elite* is the latest refurbishment of the Hitler fascist master-race concept. However, slick liberals have substituted a "psychological" foundation for the discredited Nazi biological "evidence".

A subtle refinement in the fascist doctrine which justifies racist violence against minorities is that which sees aggression as a normal expression of *"human nature"*. This is the focal theory of the ethnologists who, led by Konrad Lorenz, are quite faddish at the moment. Contemporary ethnology studies the behaviour of animals and ... *humans* in their "natural" environment. Human beings are alleged to be like animals capable only of automatic, non-rational behaviour. Men are naturally hostile, cruel and violent with instincts no different from wild beasts. Like the denizens of the wild kingdom, they will "defend territory" and rend one another, if necessary. Aggression is unavoidable, the implication being that we should sit back in Olympian calm and do nothing at the spectacle of racist violence. Carrying this hangman's philosophy to its logical ends, the anti-busing mob which sets out to batter Black school children is blameless — it is merely expressing natural, innate aggression.

There is also a contemporary racist view of *history*. Long ago reactionaries dreamed up a fictitious struggle between the races of man, and ever since they have been trying to substitute it for the *class* struggle, which is the real motive force in the history of class society. This fraud has involved many different hoaxers from many different countries, it is repeated over and over again by writers as different as Banfield, Shockley and Jensen. Nonetheless, it has always been a conscious *falsification* of history.

In fact, the meaning of history is the point at which racists part company with the agnostics and indeterminists who serve the same monopoly bourgeoisie, but who pretend that objective laws of nature and especially of society do not exist, and that mankind cannot really know anything about the universe. Racist philosophers are less modest; unlike their agnostic class-brothers, they accept the principle of ultimate determination and do not claim to be ignorant of the nature of the forces making history. It is true that racist philosophers have insisted that the march of events is governed by an uncontrolled, unalterable force. But they claim to know what this force has wrought in the past and will ordain for the future. Racists are confident they can predict tomorrow's happenings. The time link is inexorable; its relentless element is — *race*. It is useless, according to this view of history, for man to try to influence overpowering genetic traits. Race governs historical events, and the past and the future are not only easily grasped, they are the same, runs the racist refrain. The historical past and future are the reserve of so-called "master races" who must ever hold sway over "inferior races" in order to realize mankind's predestined fate.

If history is interpreted as a struggle between races, or as a series of phoney "accidents" and "coincidences" whereby one race outstrips the others, it follows then that the "superior" white race will dread non-whites as a threat to its existence, or "way of life". The racist view of history denies that aggression in recent history has been the acts of imperialist states or groups of states. Instead, a Black or Yellow or Asian or communist or "third world" *"peril"* for white people and Western civilization has been fabricated for public consumption. A Soviet critic of racist historiography puts it this way:

> The racists maintain that the few 'higher' races have created all culture and civilization, employing the slave labour of the 'lower' races. The 'higher' races, they say, are 'active' and play a leading role in history, while the 'lower' races, being 'inactive', play a subordinate role. The majority of racists are of the opinion that the development of society does not affect racial peculiarities, but, on the contrary, the biological, innate qualities of a race determine the progress or retrogression of human social groups.[24]

Some U.S. imperialist writers now claim that human history is nothing more than a sum of "multilinearly"-developing self-contained systems, thus reiterating cultural relativism's basic line. The false ideas of the polygenetic origin of man, the physical and psychological inequality of races, morphological type and innate racial aggression flow together and are summed up in the racial theory of the historical development of mankind. The racial theories of Gobineau, and of Alfred Rosenberg and other Hitler fascists, claim that working people in general are a lower race counterposed to society's exploiting upper stratum which is an "elite", a pure and chosen master race. Neo-Social Darwinists describe working people as biologically inferior, and for that reason unequal to the struggle for survival. The primary division of mankind is thus into "higher" and "lower" races with the inborn aristocratic nature of the ruling class as the measure of the difference. In order not to efface its genetic superiority, the higher race must maintain its "purity". The means to racial purity as well as the means for propagation, comfort and perfection of the master race are achieved at the cost of exploiting the "inferior" races.

The history of society is thus seen as the history of the replacement of one type of elite by another in a never-ending chain, i.e. there will always be an exploiting minority, and civilization can advance only when the masses are subordinated to the elite. Civilization collapses when the exploited majority rises in revolt against the elite. Mass rebellion represents social regression. Neo-Malthusian ideas of "overpopulation" justify planned oppression, super-exploitation and, where the imperialist bourgeoisie thinks it necessary, mass genocide of oppressed peoples.

24. M. Nesturkh, p. 97.

214

The Red Army's defeat of racist fascism on the battlefields of World War II, combined with the ongoing struggle of oppressed nationalities around the world against racism, has thrown the old-fashioned, red-necked racism into some disrepute. Rude racists are looked down upon in "polite" circles, and often ridiculed, so many educated racists have turned their coats and now pretend to spurn racial prejudice. A special case are the *bourgeois liberals* who condemn racism with their words while practicing it in deeds.

Bourgeois liberalism, especially when voiced by petty bourgeois intellectuals, worries deeply about the moral depravity, demoralization and brutalization of ... oppressors! Both history and the present are assessed in this way. Most typical is the current petty bourgeois intellectual fascination with tales of slaving and slave ships[25] and with the crews and captains of slave vessels, with all those who profited over the centuries from the African slave trade. It is part of the soul-searing liberal "discovery" of Black people and their history which took place in the 1960s.[26] The petty bourgeois liberal is anxious about the emotional states of the *white* folks involved in slave trading and slavery, about their ethics,[27] their gradual degeneration. Picking apart a slaveholder's "soul" is much more captivating and glamorous than examining that of his Black slave; or when the slave is examined somehow he turns out to be dignified, and always accommodating. The same old Rhett Butler-Scarlet O'Hara syndrome in new clothing — it is no accident that *Gone With the Wind* continues to flicker across this nation's movie and television screens year after year, and to draw crowds. Petty bourgeois white historians — ever quick to decry racism in others — show no concern for the moral qualities of slavery's victims, or at best merely as an afterthought. It is no different with current events. It is fashionable to worry about what the act of oppression is doing to the oppressor. American literature and drama are replete with accounts and psychoanalyses

25. See P.D. Curtin, *The Atlantic Slave Trade: A Census.*
26. Still the most notorious example of this cant and hypocrisy is Pulitzer Prize-winner William Styron's *The Confessions of Nat Turner*, New York, 1967.
27. See E.D. Genovese, *The World the Slaveholders Made.*

of the ruling class and their henchmen — sadistic jailers, bigoted, anti-communist "labour aristocrats",[28] brutal, racist cops, degenerate, SS-type army officers, and CIA-FBI spies. But what racist oppression has done and is still doing to its Black and other victims is either ignored or downgraded, or, as with Elkins, Genovese and Co., viewed as instilling "Sambo" traits in the sufferers. White-skinned enemies of humanity, their spokesmen, their sympathizers and descendents, direct or indirect accomplices, their passive or active followers, all who profit from capitalist exploitation, and those who are merely formed by it and share "white skin privilege" — these are the liberal's preferred subjects of concern. How many times have news columnists psychoanalyzed the likes of Nelson Rockefeller and Howard Hughes? Despite the fact that three-quarters of mankind — mostly people of colour — are, or were recently, the victims of imperialist oppression, the liberal mind, groping in its racist fog, never gets beyond the standpoint of the exploiter, it never reaches the standpoint of the victim. It never understands how oppression tempered, hardened and purified the oppressed.

Bourgeois academe has turned out preciously few studies dealing with the internal damage caused to the targets of discrimination. What of the emotional disturbance of an Angela Davis, for instance, when racist police lay hands upon her, weigh her down with chains, fly her by night and in stealth across the country, and deliver her up to reactionary hounds who try to murder her under the cover of the courts? About this the academic pundits have nothing worth hearing to say; in such matters they have no insight at all. What is the academic response to the psychological harm and neuroses of Black, Chicano, Native American and Puerto Rican women who witness their sons, brothers, fathers and husbands shot down by trigger-happy white cops? There is none. Life meaning is given only to exploiters and their hirelings. It is they who must fulfill themselves. They are the ones with whom we must empathize. They alone must "break free" of social conventions. The "greening" of white folks is the matter of sole consequence to the adepts of liberal racism.

28. See Peter Loewenberg, "The Psychology of Racism", in G.B. Nash and R. Weiss, eds., p. 196.

It is an old axiom that everyone who belongs to a ruling class feels that he holds his exalted position by "divine right", or by Nature. Developing this concept and applying it to those social elements which nest under the umbrella of bourgeois ideology, we can say that reactionary petty bourgeois and racist white "labour aristocrats" in the United States aspire to a kind of *ignoble royalty*. In their heart of hearts, they imagine themselves commonplace kings, monarchs of mediocrity. White skin is the mantle of this tawdry royalty. These are the elements which learn racism's litany by rote, simulating robots. But like all divine right monarchs, the two-bit racist imagines himself forever threatened with separation from his "majesty", from his "skin-privilege", and — horror of horrors — even from his head by the revolutionary executioner's sacrilegious blade. And in his nightmare the knife-wielder is ... Black or Brown! The petty bourgeois racist is scared to death of being taken for a common, ordinary person, for one of the "mob". We have all seen how strained and disoriented some very non-descript white folks become when suddenly and unexpectedly surrounded by Black people going about their own business — it happens on city streets every day. Because of racist indoctrination, these anxious "Middle Americans" are haunted by visions of guillotines, by visions of Black people avenging themselves for age-old crimes, by visions of Black youngsters being bused to lily-white schools, by nightmares of manual-labouring and jobless "rabbles" redistributing the wealth. Their anxiety grows with each new crisis of the incurably decrepit capitalist system. Around every corner they fear the ultimate enemy is lurking — an enemy who is "evil" and "godless" because he opposes racism and imperialism in word and deed, an enemy who is from the hungry "third world" and probably communist into the boot!

*

There is an alternative view of race and of the historical role of the races of mankind that is worthy of science and opposes the racist doctrine. It is the *Marxist-Leninist* position on race which is the only correct and scientific understanding of race. It stands in proud contrast to the wrong-headed mythology of "higher" and "lower" races and the distortions of history invented over the centuries by the racists. The unmasking and repudiation of all forms of racism is one of the main activities of Marxist-Leninist scientists, Black and white. Marx, Engels and Lenin bequeathed their followers an incomparable legacy of struggle against racism in ideology and practice.

Passionately devoted to the complete equality of *all* races and nations, Karl Marx characterized the international cooperation of the working class as the *first* condition of its emancipation, and condemned racism as a hindrance to that cooperation, and as sure to cause antagonism between labour in a white skin and labour in a Black skin. Marx, the founder of scientific socialism, regarded Gobineau, the father of modern racism, as a deadly opponent, and he demolished his racist fabrications. He proved scientifically that differences in the cultural levels of people are not connected with racial or national traits but rather with the stages of uneven historical development, and with the exploitation and oppression of a people by the ruling class of another people.

For Marx, Gobineau was an obvious ideological adversary, and he never concealed his contempt and hatred for him and lesser racists. They were the most disgraceful, disreputable contingent of the whole bourgeoisie — the enemy class. Marx exposed them for what they were — a gang with absolutely no redeeming qualities — not even the strength of their convictions. To Marx, Gobineau's main idea was more than unacceptable, it was odious. Marx and Engels (and Lenin after them) were the most consistent enemies of racism in intellectual history. That is why the self-defeating "reverse racism" spouted by Black bourgeois cultural nationalists goes so far out of its way to turn the tables and slander the founders of scientific socialism as so-called "white racists".

Marx was irritated by Gobineau's deep contempt for humanity, democracy and political freedom, and he was worried enough about the effect of his poisonous book to go out of his way to procure it. The Moscow Institute of Marxism-Leninism possesses photocopies of Marx' own copies of Gobineau's first two volumes. Their dog-eared condition shows that they were read carefully, and Marx scrawled remarks in the margins. Very precisely, next to the passage in which Gobineau claimed that the white race was superior to others and had invented history and civilization, Marx penned the word — Ass!

But his brilliant foresight told him that Gobineau's teachings were going to cause grave suffering to untold numbers of human

218

beings. So Marx felt the Frenchman's doctrines had to be refuted before they began their widespread diffusion, particularly the outrageous hypothesis that the mixing of races causes disaster. To Gobineau's contention that intermarriage with Black and Yellow people made India's white Brahmin caste "morally decadent", Marx answered — "Stupid Ox"! He considered anyone who defended any system of castes to be a "knight of barbarism". Marx observed that often those who talk most about racial superiority and "master" races are not themselves the offspring of aristocratic "blue-bloods", but rather the frustrated descendents of pitiful petty bourgeois, "Johnnys-come-lately", social climbers who desperately want to be admitted to the upper circles and thus sick up to and flatter the ruling class. Marx noted that for frustrated little social climbers like Gobineau and other racists who hate Black people, it is a source of satisfaction to have someone who it is safe and fashionable to despise. It is the most despicable people who most need someone to despise. However, Marx never lost sight of the fact that racist propaganda, regardless of its source, always serves the interests of the exploiting capitalist class.

He attacked Gobineau's distortion of history. The spiritual father of modern racism reproached Black Africans with paying tribute to cruelty and monstrosity in their religious ideas, and especially in their material representations of divinities. Marx, on the contrary, realized what the world now admits — that African bronze statues and wood carvings are some of the most sublimely beautiful art ever created by man. Gobineau alleged that Black and Yellow people comprehend only that which is ugly, that they have no eye for beauty, while the white race is said to have always portrayed its gods as noble, free of horrors and absurdities. For these inanities, Marx called Gobineau a "turtle dove", and recalled that the ancient Romans — great representatives of the white race — had numbered a *prostitute* among the goddesses they worshipped.[29]

Lenin was just as anti-racist as Marx, only he reserved his most concentrated fire for U.S. racism. For instance, in February 1913 he wrote a piece entitled "Russians and Negroes"[30] at a juncture

29. V. Daline, *Marx et Gobineau*, Recherches Internationales à la Lumière du Marxisme, Number 74, Paris, 1e trimestre 1973.
30. *Collected Works*, Volume 18, Moscow, 1968, pp. 543-544.

when lynch law and white supremacy were raging in this country. He unmasked the sham freedom of Blacks after the Emancipation Proclamation and the Civil War, explaining that we still bore the marks of slavery because capitalism, by nature, can grant us no more than a ludicrously curtailed legal emancipation. In 1913, fifty years after Emancipation, nearly half of all Afro-Americans (precisely 44.5 percent) could neither read nor write. Illiteracy is a mark of slavery, Lenin noted, and a sign of enforced racism in education. "The position of the Negroes in America *in general* is one unworthy of a civilized country — capitalism *cannot* give either *complete* emancipation or even complete equality."[31] Lenin was so outraged at the racial oppression of Black people he cried, "Shame on America for the plight of the Negroes!"[32] Were he alive today he would repeat his outcry a thousand times over. In 1915 he did a study of *New Data on the Laws Governing the Development of Agriculture*[33] in which he castigated the racism of the American bourgeoisie which he said was no better in this respect than the bourgeoisie of any other country. Having "freed" Blacks, the U.S. bourgeoisie took good care to transform the bulk of them into semi-slave sharecroppers, "under 'free', republican-democratic capitalism."[34] The monopoly capitalists did everything possible to subject Blacks to the "most shameless and despicable oppression."[35]

Lenin regarded relations between racial groups as an aspect of the *national question* involving matters of self-determination and assimilation. Historically the tendency toward racial and national assimilation is a process which begins under capitalism. The victory of socialism, dictatorship of the proletariat strengthens this tendency, as today's growing economic integration of the socialist CMEA countries clearly shows. In his "Theses on the National Question",[36] drawn up in June 1913, Lenin said that socialism will complete the internationalization of economic, political and cultural life which began under capitalism. The "Critical Remarks

31. *Ibid.*, p. 544.
32. *Ibid.*
33. *Ibid.*, Vol. 22, pp. 13-102.
34. *Ibid.*, p. 25.
35. *Ibid.*
36. *Ibid.*, Vol. 19, Moscow, 1968, pp. 243-251.

on the National Question", written later in the same year, suggest a practical remedy for the racial prejudice and hostility which set nationalities and ethnic groups against one another.[37] It is a universal law of mature capitalism for assimilation to occur *naturally* between ethnic and racial groups as the result of "the development and growing frequency of international intercourse in every form, the break-down of national barriers, the creation of the international unity of capital, of economic life in general, of politics, science, etc."[38] Enforced segregation of the races may slow, but can never halt this process. Socio-economic assimilation leads inevitably in the course of history to the intermingling of races, the shedding of national and specifically racial features, and the rise — ultimately — of qualitatively new, racially-composite socialist nations. Contrary to the apartheid dreams of the racists, capitalism's world-historical tendency is to break down some national and racial barriers, obliterate some ethnic distinctions, and assimilate peoples. It is this tendency, said Lenin, which is one of the greatest driving forces transforming capitalism into socialism. In "The Socialist Revolution and the Right of Nations to Self-Determination: Theses", formulated in January-February 1916, he assured us that "the aim of socialism is not only to end the division of mankind into tiny states and the isolation of nations in any form, it is not only to bring the nations closer together but to integrate them."[39] Once the power of the revolutionary proletariat is established over wide regions containing multi-racial groups, and later when it holds sway over the entire globe, it will be in a position to give powerful impulse to the tendency of the masses of working people to gravitate irresistibly towards union and integration in advanced socialist nations.

*

As we can see from its function under imperialism, racism has a class basis, modern racism has its material foundation in imperialism. Racism today still generates and guarantees super-profits. Despite its unscientific character, and because it is reactionary, it

37. *Ibid.*, Vol. 20, Moscow, 1964, p. 27.
38. *Ibid.*
39. *Ibid.*, Vol. 22, p. 146.

fills the social needs of the ruling class. It is a *unifying* political factor which paralyzes and binds the non-monopoly bourgeoisie, the petty bourgeoisie, and the "labour aristocracy" to the reigning monopoly capitalist fraction of the bourgeoisie. It is a *disunifying* political factor which divides the working class along colour lines. Racism still dopes millions of disinherited working class whites who have no other source of information but the monopoly media. And we should recognize that the racism of skin colour that prevails here in North America and over there in southern Africa is the twin of the Nazi racism of blood.

Racism thus runs counter to the achievements of scientific thought and research. Marxism-Leninism has proven conclusively that there is no basis in natural science for racist fabrications about the biological inequality of the races. At certain stages in their historical development all peoples share certain basic features regardless of their racial specifics. Marxism shows that *labour* was the determining factor in the origin of man and society. Its discoveries about the role of production in social development refute racist lies. Regardless of race, man develops in accordance with universal social laws. "In spite of the existence within every nonsocialist nation of antagonistic classes with wide differences between them in culture and everyday life, all social population groups constituting a nation are bound closely together in their economic, social and cultural life."[40] The motivation for the distortion of history and culture has always been to facilitate the exploitation by the ruling class of one nation of the peoples of other nations, or to justify socio-economic and cultural oppression of a group designated as a "racial minority" within the national boundaries. Historical materialism reveals that ever since capitalism arose racial discrimination has been utilized by the European and American bourgeoisie for enslaving Blacks and justifying the colonial oppression of the African, Asian and Latin American peoples. Imperialism utilizes racist ideology to foment chauvinism and misanthropy. It enables the U.S. imperialist bourgeoisie to go on whitewashing neo-colonialism and the annihilation and enslavement of entire peoples and religious and ethnic groups.

An international scientific conference entitled "Racism is the

40. I.R. Grigulevich and S.Y. Kozlov, p. 207.

Ideology of Imperialism and the Enemy of Social Progress" was held in Moscow in December 1971. The conference proved beyond doubt that racism is the ideological secretion of contemporary imperialism, that along with anti-communism, racist doctrine has become imperialism's *authentic* ideology. No matter what the mass media would have us believe,

> the fact of the multi-racial composition of the working class is not the source of racist discrimination and super-exploitation of Black workers. Racism is not a biological characteristic. It is a social phenomenon with a class origin and role. Racism has its source in a ruling class that, in modern times, has added the twin weapon of anti-communism to keep the working class in the U.S. from waging a united class struggle against its monopolist enemy.[41]

Imperialism uses racism as a criterion by which economic and political judgements are reached. In the United States monopoly capital and racism are inseparable. When capitalism is finally overthrown, racism will at the same time receive a mortal blow in its economic aspect, and without a material foundation it must wither away in its ideological aspect. But not before capitalism is overthrown, nor without the overthrow of capitalism. American history bears eloquent testimony to the organic nature of the bond between capitalist social relations and racism.

* * *

41. Henry Winston, *Strategy for a Black Agenda*, New York, 1973, p. 33.

BIBLIOGRAPHY

CLASSICAL WORKS OF MARXISM-LENINISM

Karl Marx, *Capital. A Critical Analysis of Capitalist Production*, Volume I, Moscow, 1959.

Karl Marx, *Capital. A Critique of Political Economy*, Volume II, Moscow, 1957.

Karl Marx, *Capital. A Critique of Political Economy*, Volume III, Moscow, 1959.

Karl Marx, *Grundrisse der Kritik der politischen Ökonomie (Rohentwurf), 1857-1858. Anhang 1850-1859*, Berlin, GDR, 1953.

Karl Marx, *Theories of Surplus-Value (Volume IV of Capital)*, Part I, Moscow, 1969.

Karl Marx, *Theories of Surplus-Value (Volume IV of Capital)*, Part II, Moscow, 1968.

Karl Marx, *Theories of Surplus-Value (Volume IV of Capital)*, Part III, Moscow, 1971.

Karl Marx and Frederick Engels, *The Civil War in the United States*, Third Edition, New York, 1961.

Karl Marx and Frederick Engels, *Collected Works*, Volume 5, *Marx and Engels: 1845-47*, New York, 1976.

Karl Marx and Frederick Engels, *Collected Works*, Volume 6, *Marx and Engels: 1845-48*, New York, 1976.

Karl Marx and Frederick Engels, *Selected Correspondence*, Moscow, n.d.

Karl Marx and Frederick Engels, *Selected Correspondence*, Second edition, revised and supplemented, Moscow, 1965.

Frederick Engels, *Anti-Dühring. Herr Eugen Dühring's Revolution in Science*, Moscow, 1969.

Frederick Engels, *Dialectics of Nature*, New York, 1940.

V.I. Lenin, *Collected Works*, Volume 5, *May 1901 - February 1902*, Moscow, 1961.

V.I. Lenin, *Collected Works*, Volume 9, *June - November 1905*, Moscow, 1965.

V.I. Lenin, *Collected Works*, Volume 18, *April 1912 - March 1913*, Moscow, 1968.

V.I. Lenin, *Collected Works*, Volume 19, *March - December 1913*, Moscow, 1968.

V.I. Lenin, *Collected Works*, Volume 20, *December 1913 - August 1914*, Moscow, 1964.

V.I. Lenin, *Collected Works*, Volume 22, *December 1915 - July 1916*, Moscow, 1964.

Agayev, S. and V. Oganisyan, *Nationalism as an Ideology and Policy*, Moscow, 1975.

Aitken, Hugh G.J., ed., *Did Slavery Pay? Readings in the Economics of Black Slavery in the United States*, Boston, 1971.

Andreyev, I., *The Noncapitalist Way. Soviet Experience and the Liberated Countries*, Moscow, 1977.

Aptheker, Herbert, *American Negro Slave Revolts*, New York, new edition, 1969.

Aptheker, Herbert, *The American Revolution, 1763-1783: A History of the American People: An Interpretation*, New York, 1969.

Aptheker, Herbert, *And Why Not Every Man?: The Story of the Fight Against Slavery Assembled and Edited*, Berlin, GDR, 1961.

Aptheker, Herbert, *The Colonial Era: A History of the American People*, 2nd ed., New York, 1966.

Aptheker, Herbert, ed., *A Documentary History of the Negro People in the United States*, Volume I, *From Colonial Times through the Civil War*, New York, 1951.

Aptheker, Herbert, *Essays in the History of the American Negro*, New York, 1945.

Aptheker, Herbert, *To Be Free: Studies in Negro History*, New York, 1948.

Aptheker, Herbert, *Toward Negro Freedom*, New York, 1956.

Aristotle, *Politics*, London, 1944.

Awdijew, W.I., *Geschichte des Alten Orients*, Berlin, GDR, 1953.

Bastide, Roger, *African Civilizations in the New World*, New York, 1971.

Bénot, Yves, *Idéologies des indépendances africaines*, Paris, 1969.

Blassingame, John W., *The Slave Community: Plantation Life in the Antebellum South*, New York, 1972.

Brutents, K., *A Historical View of Neo-Colonialism*, Moscow, 1972.

C.E.R.M., *Premières Sociétés de Classes et Mode de Production Asiatique*, Paris, 1967.

C.E.R.M., *Sur le "Mode de Production Asiatique"*, Paris, 1969.

C.E.R.M., *Sur les Sociétés Précapitalistes, Textes Choisis de Marx, Engels, Lénine*, Paris, 1970.

C.I.C. Brief, *An Examination of the Multinational Corporations*.

Cox, Oliver C., *Caste, Class and Race*, New York, 1948.

Curtin, Philip D., *The Atlantic Slave Trade: A Census*, Madison, Wis., 1969.

Daline, V., *Marx et Gobineau*, Recherches Internationales à la Lumière du Marxisme, Number 74, Paris, 1e trimestre, 1973.

David, P.A., H.G. Gutman, R. Sutch, and G. Wright, *Reckoning with Slavery: A Critical Study in the Quantitative History of American Negro Slavery*, New York, 1976.

Davidson, Basil., *The African Slave Trade: Precolonial History 1450-1850*, Boston, 1961.

Davidson, Basil, *The Growth of African Civilization: A History of West Africa, 1000-1800*, London, 1967.

Davis, Angela, et al., *If They Come in the Morning. Voices of Resistance*, New York, 1971.

Deborin, Grigory, *Thirty Years of Victory*, Moscow, 1975.

DeGrood, David H., *The New Era*, Special Issue, *Revolutionary World: An International Journal of Philosophy*, Volume 16, Amsterdam, 1976.

Diakonoff, I.M., ed., *Ancient Mesopotamia. Socio-Economic History: A Collection of Studies by Soviet Scholars*, Moscow, 1969.

Diakov, V. and S. Kovalev, eds., *Histoire de l'Antiquité*, Moscow, n.d.

Dieng, Amady Aly, *Classes Sociales et Mode de Production Esclavagiste en Afrique de l'Ouest*, C.E.R.M., Paris, 1974.

Diop, Cheik Anta, *L'Afrique Noire Pré-Coloniale*, Paris, 1960.

Diop, Cheik Anta, *Anteriorité des Civilisations Nègres: Mythe ou Vérité Historique?*, Paris, 1967.

Diop, Cheik Anta, *Nations Nègres et Culture*, Paris, 1955.

Diop, Majhemout, *Histoire des Classes Sociales dans l'Afrique de l'Ouest*, Volume I: *Le Mali*; Volume II: *Sénégal*, Paris, 1971-1972.

Djakow, W.N. and S.I. Kowaljov, eds., *Geschichte des Alten Griechenlands*, Berlin, GDR, 1960.

Dobb, Maurice, *Studies in the Development of Capitalism*, London, 1947.

DuBois, W.E.B., *Black Reconstruction*, New York, 1935.

DuBois, W.E.B., *John Brown*, New York, 1962.

DuBois, W.E.B., *Suppression of the African Slave Trade to the United States of America, 1638-1870*, New York, 1969.

Elkins, Stanley M., *Slavery, A Problem in American Institutional and Intellectual Life*, Chicago, 1959.

Engerman, S.L. and E.D. Genovese, eds., *Race and Slavery in the Western Hemisphere: Quantitative Studies*, Princeton, 1975.

Fage, J.D. and R.A. Oliver, eds., *Papers in African Prehistory*, London, 1970.

Fanon, Frantz, *The Wretched of the Earth*, New York, 1968.

Fogel, R.W. and S.L. Engerman, *Time on the Cross: The Economics of American Negro Slavery*, Boston, 1974.

Fogel, R.W. and S.L. Engerman, *Time on the Cross: Evidence and Methods - A Supplement*, Boston, 1974.

Foner, Philip S., ed., *The Black Panthers Speak*, Philadelphia, 1970.

Foner, Philip, *History of the Labor Movement in the United States*, 4 volumes, New York, 1947-1965.

Foner, Philip, ed., *Life and Writings of Frederick Douglass*, 5 volumes, New York, 1950-1975.

Foner, Philip, *Organized Labour and the Black Worker, 1619-1973*, New

York, 1974.

Foster, William Z., *The Negro People in American History*, New York, 1954.

Franklin, John Hope, *From Slavery to Freedom: A History of American Negroes*, 2nd ed., rev., New York, 1965.

Frazier, E. Franklin, *The Negro in the United States*, New York, 1949.

Frederickson, George M., *The Black Image in the White Mind*, New York, 1971.

Friedman, Lawrence J., *The White Savage: Racial Fantasies in the Postbellum South*, Englewood Cliffs, N.J., 1970.

Gauzner, N., *Social Effects of the Scientific and Technological Revolution Under Capitalism*, Moscow, 1973.

Genovese, Eugene D., *In Red and Black: Marxian Explorations in Southern and Afro-American History*, New York, 1968.

Genovese, Eugene D., *The Political Economy of Slavery: Studies in the Economy and Society of the Slave South*, New York, 1965.

Genovese, Eugene D., *Roll, Jordan, Roll: The World the Slaves Made*, New York, 1974.

Genovese, Eugene D., *The World the Slaveholders Made: Two Essays in Interpretation*, New York, 1969.

Genovese, Eugene D., *Ulrich B. Phillips: The Slave Economy of the Old South*, Baton Rouge, La., 1968.

Gisselbrecht, André, ed., *Le fascisme Hitlérien, Etudes Actuelles*, Paris, 1971-1972.

Gobineau, Joseph Arthur de, *Essai sur l'inégalité des races humaines*, 4 volumes, Paris, 1853-1856.

Goblot, J.J. and A. Pelletier, *Materialisme Historique et Histoire des Civilisations*, Paris, 1969.

Goldin, Claudia D., *Urban Slavery in the American South, 1820-1860. A Quantitative History*, Chicago, 1976.

Goldschmid, M.L., ed., *Black Americans and White Racism: Theory and Research*, New York, 1971.

Grigulevich, I.R. and S.Y. Kozlov, eds., *Races and Peoples: Contemporary Ethnic and Racial Problems*, Moscow, 1974.

Gutman, Herbert G., *Slavery and the Numbers Game: A Critique of Time on the Cross*, Urbana, 1975.

Hall, Gus, *The Crisis of U.S. Capitalism and the Fight-Back: Report to the 21st Convention of the Communist Party U.S.A.*, New York, 1975.

Henry, Frances, *Forgotten Canadians: the Blacks of Nova Scotia*, Don Mills, Ontario, 1973.

Hernton, Calvin C., *Sex and Racism in America*, New York, 1965.

Herskovits, Melville J., *The Myth of the Negro Past*, 2nd ed., Boston, 1958.

Hoffman, John, *Marxism and the Theory of Praxis; a Critique of Some New Versions of Old Fallacies*, New York, 1976.

Hobsbawm, E.J., ed., *Karl Marx: Pre-Capitalist Economic Formations*, London, 1964.

Huggins, N.I., M. Kilson and D.M. Fox, *Key Issues in the Afro-American Experience*, 2 volumes, New York, 1971.

International Monetary Fund, *Balance of Payments Yearbook*, 1970 and 1971.

Iovchuk, Mikhail, *Philosophical Traditions Today*, Moscow, 1973.

Iskenderov, A., *Africa: Politics, Economy, Ideology*, Moscow, 1972.

Ivanov, K., *On the "Rich and Poor" Nations Theory*, Moscow, 1973.

Ivanov, R., *American History and the Black Question*, Moscow, 1976.

Jackson, George, *Blood In My Eye*, New York, 1972.

Jackson, George, *Soledad Brother. The Prison Letters of George Jackson*, New York, 1970.

Jackson, James E., *Revolutionary Tracings*, New York, 1974.

Jalée, Pierre, *Le tiers monde en chiffres, Edition revue, 1974*, Paris, 1974.

James, C.L.R., *The Black Jacobins: Toussaint L'Ouverture and the San Domingo Revolution*, Second edition, revised, New York, 1963.

1972 Joint Economic Report, 92nd Congress of the United States, 2nd session, March 23, 1972.

Jones, Leroi and Larry Neal, eds., *Black Fire: An Anthology of Afro-American Writing*, New York, 1969.

Jordan, Winthrop D., *White Over Black: American Attitudes Towards the Negro, 1550-1812*, Chapel Hill, N.C., 1968, Pelican edition, Baltimore, 1969.

July, Robert W., *A History of the African People*, New York, 1974.

Kapustin, O., *The World Revolutionary Process at the Present Stage*, Moscow, 1972.

King, Martin Luther, Jr., *Why We Can't Wait*, New York, 1964.

Klein, Herbert S., *Slavery in the Americas: A Comparative Study of Virginia and Cuba*, Chicago, 1967.

Kolko, Gabriel, *Wealth and Power in America: An Analysis of Social Class and Income Distribution*, New York, 1962.

Koswen, M.O., *Abriss der Geschichte und Kultur der Urgesellschaft*, Berlin, GDR, 1957.

Koval, Nikolai, *The USSR's First Economic Development Plans (How They Were Compiled and Carried Out)*, Moscow, 1973.

Kovel, Joel, *White Racism: A Psychohistory*, New York, 1971.

Krasnov, L., *Socialist Economic Integration and World Economic Relations*, Moscow, 1975.

Krasin, Y., *The Dialectics of Revolutionary Process: Problems of Methodology*, Moscow, 1972.

Krasin, Yuri, *Sociology of Revolution: A Marxist View*, Moscow, 1972.

Labouret, Henri, *L'Afrique Précoloniale*, Paris, 1959.

229

Leggett, J.C., *Class, Race and Labor: Working-Class Consciousness in Detroit*, New York, 1968.

Leontyev, L., *Fundamentals of Marxist Political Economy*, Moscow, 1970.

Leontyev, L., *Are Socialism and Capitalism Drawing Closer Together? (The Theory of Convergence and What Is Behind It)*, Moscow, 1972.

Lightfoot, Claude M., *Racism and Human Survival, Lessons of Nazi Germany for Today's World*, New York, 1972.

Lockwood, Lee, *Conversation with Eldridge Cleaver. Algiers*, New York, 1970.

Lojkine, Jean, *Pour Une Théorie Marxiste des Idéologies*, C.E.R.M., Paris, 1970.

Luxemburg, Rosa, *The Accumulation of Capital*, London, 1951.

Manfred, A.Z., ed., *A Short History of the World in Two Volumes*, Volume I, Moscow, 1974.

Maquet, Jacques, *Africanité, Traditionelle et Moderne*, Paris, 1967.

Maquet, Jacques, *Les civilisations noires. Histoire, techniques, arts, sociétés*, Paris, 1966.

Markov, Walter, ed., *Studien zur Kolonialgeschichte und Geschichte der nationalen und kolonialen Befreiungsbewegung*, Berlin, GDR, 1961.

Marushkin, Boris, *The American Tradition. What Remains? (From the War for Independence to Neocolonialism)*, Moscow, 1975.

McEwan, P.J.M., ed., *Africa from Early Times to 1800*, London, 1968.

McEwan, P.J.M., ed., *Nineteenth-Century Africa*, London, 1968.

McEwan, P.J.M., ed., *Twentieth-Century Africa*, London, 1968.

Menshikov, S., *The Economic Cycle: Postwar Developments*, Moscow, 1975.

Menshikov, S., *Millionaires and Managers*, Moscow, 1969.

Medvedev, E., *Le Régime Socio-Economique de l'Inde Ancienne*, C.E.R.M., Paris, 1969.

Messner, Gerald, ed., *Another View: To Be Black in America*, New York, 1970.

Mitchell, J. Paul, ed., *Race Riots in Black and White*, Englewood Cliffs, N.J., 1970.

Moody, Anne, *Coming of Age in Mississippi*, New York, 1968.

Morris, Milton D., *The Politics of Black America*, New York, 1975.

Moss, James A., ed., *The Black Man in America*, New York, 1971.

Mshvenieradze, Vladimir, *Anti-Communism Today*, Moscow, 1974.

Mullin, Michael, ed., *American Negro Slavery. A Documentary History*, New York, 1976.

Muschkin, N.A., *Römische Geschichte*, Berlin, GDR, 1953.

Nash, G.B. and R. Weiss, eds., *The Great Fear: Race in the Mind of America*, New York, 1970.

Neelsen, Karl, *Die Akkumulation des Kapitals und die Entwicklung der Arbeiterklasse*, Berlin, GDR, 1973.

The Negro Handbook, Chicago, 1966.

Nesturkh, M., *The Races of Mankind*, Moscow, 1963.

Neznanov, Viktor, *The Logic of History (On the Inevitability of the Transition to Socialism and Basic Features of the Transition Period)*, Moscow, 1975.

Nott, J.C., *Indigenous Races of the Earth: Or, New Chapters on Ethnological Inquiry*, Philadelphia, 1857.

Nott, J.C. and G.R. Gliddon, *Types of Mankind: Or Ethnological Researches, Based upon the Ancient Monuments, Paintings, Sculptures, and Crania of Races, and upon Their Natural, Geographical, Philological and Biblical History*, Philadelphia, 1855.

Oglesby, Carl, ed., *The New Left Reader*, New York, 1969.

Osipov, G., *Sociology: Problems of Theory and Method*, Moscow, 1969.

Osofsky, Gilbert, ed., *Puttin' On Ole Massa: The Slave Narratives of Henry Bibb, William Wells Brown, and Solomon Northrup*, New York, 1969.

Paraf, Pierre, *Le racisme dans le Monde*, 5e édition, Paris, 1972.

Perlo, Victor, *Economics of Racism - Roots of Black Inequality*, New York, 1975.

Perlo, Victor, *The Unstable Economy: Booms and Recessions in the United States since 1945*, New York, 1973.

Pettigrew, Thomas F., ed., *Racial Discrimination in the United States*, New York, 1975.

Phillips, Ulrich B., *American Negro Slavery: A Survey of the Supply, Employment and Control of Negro Labor as Determined by the Plantation Regime*, New York, 1918.

Phillips, Ulrich B., *Life and Labor in the Old South*, Boston, 1929.

Pieck, W., G. Dimitroff, P. Togliatti, *Die Offensive des Faschismus und die Aufgaben der Kommunisten im Kampfe für die Volksfront gegen Krieg und Faschismus, Referate auf dem VII. Kongress der Kommunistischen Internationale, 1935*, Berlin, GDR, 1957.

Pinkney, Alphonso, *Black Americans*, Englewood Cliffs, N.J., 1969.

Piotte, Jean-Marc, *La pensée politique de Gramsci*, Paris, 1970.

Popov, Y., *Marxist Political Economy As Applied to the African Scene*, Moscow, 1973.

Porshnev, B., *Social Psychology and History*, Moscow, 1970.

Poulantzas, Nicos, *Les classes sociales dans le capitalisme aujourd'hui*, Paris, 1971.

Poulantzas, Nicos, *Fascisme et Dictature*, Paris, 1974 édition.

Poulantzas, Nicos, *Pouvoir politique et classes sociales*, 2 volumes, Paris, 1971.

Puel, Hugues, *Chomage et Capitalismes Contemporains*, Paris, 1971.

Quarles, Benjamin, *Black Abolitionists*, London, 1969.

Rawley, James A., *Race and Politics: "Bleeding Kansas" and the Coming of the Civil War,* Philadelphia, 1969.

Resh, Richard, ed., *Black America: Confrontation and Accommodation in the Twentieth Century*, Lexington, Mass., 1969.

Rey, Pierre-Philippe, *Les alliances de classes. "Sur l'articulation des modes de production" suivi de "matérialisme historique et lutte de classes"*, Paris, 1973.

Rey, Pierre-Philippe, *Colonialisme, néo-colonialisme et transition au capitalisme. Exemple de la "Comilog" au Congo-Brazzaville*, Paris, 1971.

Rhodes, Robert I., *Imperialism and Underdevelopment: A Reader*, New York, 1970.

Richel, André, *Contribution à l'étude du développement humain*, Paris, 1969.

Rodney, Walter, *A History of the Upper Guinea Coast, 1545 to 1800*, Oxford, 1970.

Rodney, Walter, *How Europe Underdeveloped Africa*, London and Dar-es-Salaam, 1972.

Rotberg, Robert, *A Political History of Tropical Africa*, New York, 1965.

Rotberg, Robert I., ed., *Rebellion in Black Africa*, London, 1971.

Ryndina, M. and G. Chernikov, eds., *The Political Economy of Capitalism*, Moscow, 1974.

Saifulin, Murad, ed., *The Future of Society: A Critique of Modern Bourgeois Philosophical and Socio-Political Conceptions*, Moscow, 1973.

Scanzoni, John H., *The Black Family in Modern Society*, Boston, 1971.

Schwartz, B.N. and R. Disch, eds., *White Racism: Its History, Pathology and Practices*, New York, 1970.

Shade, William G. and Roy C. Herrenkohl, eds., *Seven on Black: Reflections on the Negro Experience in America*, Philadelphia, 1969.

Shishkov, Yuri, *Two Systems of Economic Integration*, Moscow, 1974.

Shpirt, A., *The Scientific-Technological Revolution and the Third World*, Moscow, 1972.

Sivachyov, N. and E. Yazkov, *History of the USA since World War I*, Moscow, 1976.

Skvortsov, L., *Ideology and Social Progress*, Moscow, 1972.

Smith, Arthur L. and Stephen Robb, eds., *The Voice of Black Rhetoric: Selections*, Boston, 1971.

Smith, Robert S., *Kingdoms of the Yoruba*, London, 1969.

Spencer, Herbert, *System of Synthetic Philosophy*, London, 1862-1896.

Stampp, K.M., *The Peculiar Institution: Slavery in the Ante-Bellum South*, New York, 1956.

Stanis, V.F., G.B. Khromuşhin and V.P. Mozolin, eds., *The Role of the State in Socio-Economic Reforms in Developing Countries*, Moscow, 1976.

Starobin, Robert S., ed., *Blacks in Bondage. Letters of American Slaves*, New York, 1974.

Starobin, Robert S., ed., *Denmark Vesey: The Slave Conspiracy of 1822*,

Englewood Cliffs, N.J., 1970.

Starobin, Robert S., *Industrial Slavery in the Old South*, New York, 1970.

Stavenhagen, Rodolfo, *Social Classes in Agrarian Societies*, New York, 1975.

Streisand, Joachim, ed., *Deutsche Geschichte*, Volume 3, *Von 1917 bis zur Gegenwart*, Berlin, GDR, 1968.

Storing, Herbert J., ed., *What Country Have I?: Political Writings by Black Americans*, New York, 1970.

Styron, William, *The Confessions of Nat Turner*, New York, 1967.

Suret-Canale, Jean, *Afrique Noire Occidentale et Centrale*, Volume I: *Géographie, Civilisations, Histoire*, 2nd ed., Paris, 1961.

Suret-Canale, Jean, *Afrique Noire Occidentale et Centrale*, Volume I: *L'ère coloniale*, Paris, 1964.

Suret-Canale, Jean, *Afrique Noire Occidentale et Centrale. De la Colonisation aux Indépendances (1945-1960)*, Volume I: *Crise du système colonial et capitalisme monopoliste d'Etat*, Paris, 1972.

Tabb, William K., *The Political Economy of the Black Ghetto*, New York, 1970.

Taylor, Clyde, ed., *Vietnam and Black America: An Anthology of Protest and Resistance*, New York, 1973.

Thornbrough, Emma Lou, ed., *Booker T. Washington*, Englewood Cliffs, N.J., 1969.

Togliatti, Palmiro, *Lectures on Fascism*, New York, 1976.

Touré, Ahmed Sekou, *L'Afrique et la Révolution*, Paris, n.d.

Trapeznikov, S., *At the Turning Points of History. Some Lessons of the Struggle Against Revisionism Within the Marxist-Leninist Movement*, Moscow, 1972.

Trelease, Allen W., *White Terror: The Ku Klux Klan Conspiracy and Southern Reconstruction*, New York, 1971.

Twombly, Robert S., ed., *Blacks in White America since 1865: Issues and Interpretations*, New York, 1971.

Ungers, Irwin and David Reimers, eds., *The Slavery Experience in the United States*, New York, 1970.

United Nations, *Survey of Economic Conditions in Africa 1971*, E/CN. 14/560, New York, 1972.

United Nations Secretariat, *Multinational Corporations in World Development*, New York, 1973.

Uya, Okon Edet, ed., *Black Brotherhood: Afro-Americans and Africa*, Lexington, Mass., 1971.

Valyuzhenich, A., *American Liberalism. Myth and Reality*, Book One: *From Free Enterprise to Reformism*, Moscow, 1976.

Weinstein, Allen and F.O. Gatell, eds., *American Negro Slavery. A Modern Reader*, New York, 1968.

Weinstein, Allen and F.O. Gatell, eds., *The Segregation Era 1863-1954. A*

Modern Reader, New York, 1970.

White, John and Ralph Willet, *Slavery in the American South*, New York, 1970.

Williams, Eric, *Capitalism and Slavery*, Chapel Hill, N.C., 1944.

Wilson, Henry S., ed., *Origins of West African Nationalism*, London, 1969.

Winston, Henry, *Class, Race and Black Liberation*, New York, 1977.

Winston, Henry, *Strategy for a Black Agenda*, New York, 1973.

Woddis, Jack, *New Theories of Revolution - A Commentary on the Views of Frantz Fanon, Régis Debray and Herbert Marcuse*, New York, 1972.

Wood, Forrest G., *Black Scare: The Racist Response to Emancipation and Reconstruction*, Berkeley and Los Angeles, 1970.

Woodward, C. Vann, *The Strange Career of Jim Crow*, 2nd rev. ed., New York, 1966.

Yagodovsky, L., *The World Socialist System - Its Role in the World Today*, Moscow, 1975.

Yakovlev, Nikolai, *The Ideas of the American Revolution. Past and Present*, Moscow, 1975.

Yefimov, Anatoly and Alexander Anchishkin, *State Planning: Aims, Ways, Results*, Moscow, n.d.

Yeremin, A., *Economic Advantages of Socialism*, Moscow, 1972.

Yerusalimsky, Arkady, *German Imperialism: Its Past and Present*, Moscow, 1969.

Yetman, Norman R., ed., *Life Under the "Peculiar Institution": Selections from the Slave Narrative Collection*, New York, 1970.

Young, R.P., ed., *Roots of Rebellion: The Evolution of Black Politics and Protest Since World War II*, New York, 1970.

Zagladin, V.V., ed., *The World Communist Movement: Outline of Strategy and Tactics*, Moscow, 1973.

Zagladin, V.V., A.A. Galkin and T.T. Timofeyev, eds., *The Working Class - the Leading Force of the World Revolutionary Process (A Critique of Bourgeois and Reformist Conceptions)*, Moscow, 1976.

Zarodov, Konstantin, *Leninism and Contemporary Problems of the Transition from Capitalism to Socialism*, Moscow, 1972.

Zhilin, Y., *Current Problems of the Communist Movement*, Moscow, 1972.

Zhukov, Y., L. Delyusin, A. Iskenderov and L. Stepanov, *The Third World: Problems and Prospects*, Moscow, 1970.

PERIODICALS

The African Communist, (London).

Asia and Africa Today. Bi-Monthly Scientific and Socio-Political Journal of the Soviet Afro-Asian Solidarity Committee, The Institute of Oriental

Studies and the Institute of Africa Under the USSR Academy of Sciences, (Moscow).

Asien, Afrika, Lateinamerika. Zeitschrift des Zentralen Rates für Asien-, Afrika-, und Lateinamerikawissenschaften in der DDR, (Berlin, GDR).

The Black Scholar, (Sausalito, California).

Daily World, (New York).

Deutsche Zeitschrift für Philosophie, (Berlin, GDR).

Economic Bulletin of Ghana, (Accra).

Einheit. Zeitschrift für Theorie und Praxis des wissenschaftlichen Sozialismus, (Berlin, GDR).

Freedomways. A Quarterly Review of the Freedom Movement, (New York).

International Affairs. A Monthly Journal of Political Analysis, (Moscow).

New Times. A Soviet Weekly of World Affairs, (Moscow).

Political Affairs: Journal of Marxist Thought and Analysis, (New York).

Présence Africaine, (Paris).

Revolutionary World. An International Journal of Philosophy, (Amsterdam).

Tarikh, (London).

World Marxist Review. Problems of Peace and Socialism. Theoretical and Information Journal of Communist and Workers' Parties, (Prague and Toronto).

Zeitschrift für Geschichtswissenschaft, (Berlin, GDR).